The Political Economy of Lula's Brazil

The Political Economy of Lula's Brazil describes the social, political and economic transformations that led to increased interest in the tropical giant at the start of the 21st century. This volume demonstrates that Brazil's rise was the result of the adoption of heterodox economic policies, while also highlighting the obstacles of choosing an egalitarian development path in Latin America.

Adopting an innovative perspective in terms of methodology and interpretation, contributors from Brazil, Latin America and France follow a non-dogmatic critical approach in order to explain the institutional changes that made a new cycle of development possible in Brazil. The authors also argue that the evolution of Brazil, following the implementation of leftist policies, paradoxically gave birth to several economic, political and environmental contradictions. They contend that these contradictions, including the falling rate of profit linked to the full employment of resources; the redistributive process seen as a menace by the conservative middle classes; and the growing intervention of the state in the different markets, eventually led to the end of the early 21st century development cycle.

Providing clues to understanding the contradictory and painful path towards the development of semi-industrialised countries, this book will interest students and academics in the fields of economics, sociology, history and political science. The story it tells may also interest all those searching for independent analysis of the successes and failures of Lula's Brazil.

Pedro Chadarevian is Assistant Professor at Universidade Federal de São Paulo, Brazil, where he teaches economics and public policy. He has been working on several research issues including racial inequalities, affirmative action, economic development and the political economy of the environment and climate change.

Routledge Frontiers of Political Economy

Political Economy as Natural Theology
Smith, Malthus and Their Followers
Paul Oslington

Sharing Economies in Times of Crisis
Practices, Politics and Possibilities
Edited by Anthony Ince and Sarah Marie Hall

Philosophy in the Time of Economic Crisis
Pragmatism and Economy
Edited by Kenneth W. Stikkers and Krzysztof Piotr Skowroński

Public Policy and the Neo-Weberian State
Edited by Stanisław Mazur and Piotr Kopyciński

The Economic Theory of Costs
Foundations and New Directions
Edited by Matthew McCaffrey

The Fascist Nature of Neoliberalism
Andrea Micocci and Flavia Di Mario

The Political Economy of Contemporary Spain
From Miracle to Mirage
Edited by Luis Buendía and Ricardo Molero-Simarro

The Origins of Capitalism as a Social System
The Prevalence of an Aleatory Encounter
John Milios

The Political Economy of Lula's Brazil
Edited by Pedro Chadarevian

For a full list of titles in this series, please visit www.routledge.com/books/series/SE0345

The Political Economy of Lula's Brazil

Edited by Pedro Chadarevian

LONDON AND NEW YORK

First published 2018
by Routledge
2 Park Square, Milton Park, Abingdon, Oxon OX14 4RN

and by Routledge
711 Third Avenue, New York, NY 10017

Routledge is an imprint of the Taylor & Francis Group, an informa business

© 2018 selection and editorial matter, Pedro Chadarevian; individual chapters, the contributors

The right of Pedro Chadarevian to be identified as the author of the editorial material, and of the authors for their individual chapters, has been asserted in accordance with sections 77 and 78 of the Copyright, Designs and Patents Act 1988.

All rights reserved. No part of this book may be reprinted or reproduced or utilised in any form or by any electronic, mechanical, or other means, now known or hereafter invented, including photocopying and recording, or in any information storage or retrieval system, without permission in writing from the publishers.

Trademark notice: Product or corporate names may be trademarks or registered trademarks, and are used only for identification and explanation without intent to infringe.

British Library Cataloguing-in-Publication Data
A catalogue record for this book is available from the British Library

Library of Congress Cataloging-in-Publication Data
Names: Chadarevian, Pedro, 1974– editor.
Title: The political economy of Lula's Brazil / edited by
  Pedro Chadarevian.
Description: New York: Routledge, 2018. | Series: Routledge frontiers of
  political economy | Includes bibliographical references and index.
Identifiers: LCCN 2017061083 (print) | LCCN 2018000704 (ebook) |
  ISBN 9781315168920 (Ebook) | ISBN 9781138050242 (hardback: alk.
  paper)
Subjects: LCSH: Brazil—Economic policy—21st century. | Economic
  development—Brazil. | Saving and investment—Brazil.
Classification: LCC HC165 (ebook) | LCC HC165 .P565 2018 (print) |
  DDC 330.981/065—dc23
LC record available at https://lccn.loc.gov/2017061083

ISBN: 978-1-138-05024-2 (hbk)
ISBN: 978-1-315-16892-0 (ebk)

Typeset in Bembo
by Apex CoVantage, LLC

Contents

List of contributors vii

PART I
The praxis of change 1

1 **Introduction** 3
   PEDRO CHADAREVIAN

2 **Is the change in globalization's rhythm an opportunity for Latin-American emerging economies?** 14
   PIERRE SALAMA

3 **Lula's economic model and post-neoliberalism in Brazil** 33
   PEDRO CHADAREVIAN

PART II
The mechanisms of change 47

4 **Money, politics and the possibility of a mode of regulation based on the internal market** 49
   JAIME MARQUES PEREIRA

5 **Growth, functional income distribution and capital accumulation in Brazil: a prospective analysis of the contemporary period** 82
   MIGUEL BRUNO AND RICARDO CAFFÉ

Contents

6 **Financial markets, public policy and consumer credit growth in Brazil**   114
MARÍA ALEJANDRA CAPORALE MADI

7 **Hits and misses of public investment strategy in Brazil**   131
CRISTINA FRÓES DE BORJA REIS

8 **Sovereign or dependent integration into the world economy? The Brazilian external sector**   162
MARCELO MILAN

PART III
The challenges of change   177

9 Dystonia as domination: how the Brazilian elites have put politics and power out of step   179
FÉLIX RUIZ SÁNCHEZ

10 Rain forests, land rent and the ecological contradictions of development in contemporary Brazil   196
PEDRO CHADAREVIAN

11 Higher education: development of underdevelopment or a tool to overcome it?   209
REGINALDO MORAES

12 The impact of conditional cash transfer programs in Brazil and their limits   218
ROBÉRIO PAULINO

13 **Conclusions**   240
PEDRO CHADAREVIAN

Index   245

Contributors

Miguel Bruno is Professor of Economics at IBGE (The Brazilian Institute of Statistics) and at the State University of Rio de Janeiro (UERJ), Brazil.

Ricardo Caffé is Professor of Economics at the Federal University of Bahia (UFBA), Brazil.

Pedro Chadarevian is Assistant Professor at Universidade Federal de São Paulo, Brazil.

María Alejandra Caporale Madi is Director of The Green Economics Institute, Chair of the World Economic Association Conferences Programme and Assistant Editor of the *International Journal of Pluralism and Economics Education*.

Marcelo Milan is Assistant Professor of Economics at the Federal University of Rio Grande do Sul (UFRGS), Brazil.

Reginaldo Moraes is Professor of Political Science at Campinas University (Unicamp) and a researcher at the Brazilian National Institute of Science and Technology for Studies on United States (INCT-INEU).

Robério Paulino is Professor of Economics at the Department of Public Policies, Federal University of Rio Grande do Norte (UFRN), Brazil.

Jaime Marques Pereira is Professor of Economics at Université de Picardie Jules Verne – Centre de recherché sur l'industrie, les institutions et les systèmes économiques d'Amiens (UPJV/CRIISEA), France.

Cristina Fróes De Borja Reis is Assistant Professor of Economics at the ABC Federal University (UFABC). She is also an International Post-Doc Initiative (IPODI) fellow at the Technische Universitat Berlin, co-funded by Marie Curie/European Union.

Pierre Salama is Emeritus Professor at the Centre d'Économie Paris-Nord-CNRS and Université de Paris, France.

Félix Ruiz Sánchez is a sociologist working in Brazil.

Part I
The praxis of change

1 Introduction

Pedro Chadarevian

The Workers' Party government of the early 21st century: a post-neoliberalism experiment in Brazil

We can divide Brazil into two periods in its contemporary history: before and after the governments of the Workers' Party (Partido dos Trabalhadores/PT). The legacy of the passage of power in its 13 years of command at the beginning of the 21st century is marked by profound economic, social and political transformations. Some of which, paradoxically, would seal the fate of the country tragically, culminating in the coup d'état disguised as impeachment of 2016.

We will pursue here the hypothesis according to which it is possible to identify a change in the Brazilian growth regime in the first decade of the 21st century, marked by an unequivocal evolution in the mediating institutions of the new model inaugurated. These institutions, following the critical tradition of political economy, and in particular the French regulation school,[1] are as follows: money and the country's monetary policy, the state and its fiscal policy, the nature of competition, the capital-wage relation and the external insertion. The articulation between these institutional forms can allow the construction of a reasonably harmonic arrangement, capable of inhibiting distributive conflicts and leading to a regime of lasting growth. Our objective will be to reveal the mechanisms that allowed the construction of this model and to analyze its challenges, internal limitations and its crisis.

In particular, we will ask to what extent the 'Lula years' (2003–2016) represented a pact of innovative social cohesion, a new, post-neoliberal development cycle, supported by qualitative and structural changes.

In this sense, this book is to some extent a history of the present. And what makes it more challenging is the volatile, unstable character of the present that is transformed at every moment. Everyday new measures are taken by congressmen hounded by the threats of the prosecutors – it is estimated that 70% of them are defendants in some investigation. Every night we learn that the illegitimate president in office, following the fall of Dilma Rousseff in 2016, held a meeting outside the agenda with some figure of power. The deconstruction and decay of the country are plotting. There is hurry because on the horizon they see the popular resistance.

The greatest evidence that the country was on the brink of the radical development of its productive forces, raising the social level of its people, lies in the reaction promoted by the regime that assumed the presidency after the seizure of power in 2016. The farce of the impeachment of 2016 was aimed at disrupting a national-popular project initiated by Lula in 2003 and restoring neoliberalism.[2] The dismantling reaches the economic policies of promotion of national capitals by means of the credit expansion in the public banks; reduces public investments and privatizes state-owned energy companies (Petrobras and Eletrobras); cuts resources for social assistance; drastically reduces the science and technology budget; halts funding programs for higher education; freezes public spending for 20 years; reforms the constitution in order to exploit the worker as much as possible, receding decades of labor and social security rights; etc.

In addition to this dramatic dismantling, the reversal in the government's strategy represents the abandonment of a national-popular project, which sought, over 13 years, to pursue a double goal: raising the country's economic potential while promoting the improvement in the living standards of its people. Something unique among the greatest economies of the planet in the period, Brazil managed to achieve economic growth along with a reduction in social inequality. Within a few years, the country reached the sixth largest world economy, shortly after the UK, and advanced several positions on the UN Human Development Index. Its foreign policy became a global highlight; Brazil became an indispensable protagonist in the debate around the main conflicts of the planet. As an example for the countries of the North and South, the iconic social policy of minimum income ('Bolsa Familia') took Brazil off the poverty map for the first time in its long history of misery and deprivation. Thanks to innovative affirmative action policies, the number of blacks in higher education multiplied by three in the period governed by the PT.

The first element that must be kept in mind to understand the troubled Brazilian political moment at the end of the 'Lula years' is the geopolitical dimension of the crisis that has hit the region. Latin America ushered in a new form of coup d'état in the early 21st century. A coup that dispenses arms, but whose violence is present and is not limited to the discourse of hatred against the progressive forces that assume power democratically. Thus, contrary to the military coups of the last century, the reactionary right now uses conservative sectors of the judiciary and parliament as well as the decisive support of mass media corporations. They act under the pretext of combating corruption, administrative impropriety, and state swelling, but their real purpose is to regain full control of the budget machine and economic policies. Their rhetoric is moralistic, but their practice is antisocial and therefore exclusionary and undemocratic. Moralists without morality, because they shout freedom and overlook the truculence of the police against the poor people and torture in the dungeons of the 'operation car wash' (see box 1 below). Their patriotism hides their neglect of public patrimony, the impoverishment of the population and the surrender of national wealth; their anti-corruption struggle is a veil that overshadows their real objective: to deepen the domination of capital over society[3] . . .

Thus, in Honduras, Manuel Zelaya, allied with the progressive axis of Latin American leaders, suffered a conspiracy orchestrated by the Supreme Court and the parliament, which resulted in his forced deposition of the government in 2009. His crime: to try to establish a constituent Assembly. The condemnation of the coup by many of its neighbors and even the Organization of American States did not help; in a short time the situation was normalized and the right could govern without great obstacles.

In 2012 it was Paraguay's turn. Fernando Lugo, another important name of the Latin American left was considered blamed, in a lightning judgment in the parliament, for mismanagement in an agrarian conflict that resulted in 16 dead peasants earlier that year. The conduct of the impeachment process was considered irregular by the Union of South American Nations (Unasur), for not obeying the right of defense. The country was temporarily removed from Mercosur. Soon after Lugo's deposition, the right returned to rule the country.

Just two years later, Dilma Rousseff's re-election was the detonator of a backlash from early putchist forces focused on disrupting the president's term. The opposition, in partnership with the media, tried, without success, two strategies initially. First, to involve Rousseff with scandals of corruption. Then they demanded a ballot recount – PT won the election by a narrow margin in October 2014. Given that these paths proved fruitless, a last round of the alliance between the right and conservative sectors of the media and judiciary began: overthrowing the president through an impeachment process (see box 2 below). The pretext was the ineffective management of public resources, amid a growing sense of economic decay fueled by the press.

Box 1   Operation Car Wash

The operation is a federal investigation that began in March 2014 to determine bribe payments to officials of state-owned Petrobras. The name of the operation is due to a gas station in Brasilia that would serve as a front for the money laundering of the paid fees. The operation was organized from a self-appointed 'task force', which includes public prosecutors and was led by Judge Sergio Moro. The Federal Police were charged with executing the actions of the operation. The investigations, over more than three years, counted on dozens of phases, involving 16 companies and 259 accusations. Moro ran the operation with an iron arm, and does not hesitate to use unorthodox procedures, such as 'coercive conduction' of the accused, pre-trial detention and plea bargains, in exchange for which the accused obtain reductions of sentence or even freedom.

Since then, there have been more than 157 convictions, each accounting for more than 100 years in prison, on average. Sentences disproportionate to the crimes allegedly committed, because in Brazil, a heinous crime receives a maximum penalty of 24 years of imprisonment. Moreover, in many respects the actions of the task force disrespect the Constitution. There are allegations of summary judgment, deliberate exposition of defendants and convicts, non-observance of the Geneva Convention on the law of the prisoners, police violence in unnecessary use of the instrument of coercive conduct (intended for accused persons who pose a real danger to society or refuse to collaborate with justice), disregard of the 'privileged forum' for senators (who should only be tried at the supreme court), selective leaks of tapping for the press. Some members of the task force fed hate speech on the social networks. The prosecutors blame the Workers' Party for the corruption scandal, despite the lack of evidence. Several of its cadres and leaders, including Lula, were targets of the operation. Lula was arrested, momentarily, but released in the middle of the great popular mobilization in March 2016.

Moro defends himself, saying that the ends justify the means. He claimed to be inspired by operation 'clean hands' (mani pulite), which revealed the relations between the Mafia and the political system in Italy in the 1990s. Hence the judge's suggestion that on certain occasions the law becomes an obstacle and its flexibility can be necessary to reveal the legal truth. The prosecutors claim that the superior authorities must be held responsible for the crimes committed by their subordinates – this thesis has been the justification for accusing, convicting and arresting without evidence. Thus, Lula is accused of being the mentor of the Petrobras' corruption scheme merely because he was in charge of the nation, to which the state directors were subordinated.

The objectives of 'car wash' became less palpable as the operation moved away from law enforcement. If the price to be paid to combat corruption is to corrupt the right to liberty, to fair process and to the exemption of justice, the operation seems to have created a bigger problem than the one that sought to be solved initially.

The curse of development

Interestingly, until the beginning of 2014 the scenario was extremely positive in Brazil. Unemployment had reached its lowest level in history, international reserves were at their peak, oil production was high. What could have gone wrong? What led to this radicalization on the political scene? Why so much hatred of a national-popular government?

The PT model clearly pushed the limits of the political system, detonating latent conflicts that surfaced and precipitated the country in its worst crisis in decades. Lula's social pact, based on a broad coalition of groups with antagonistic interests, and which mediated the class struggle in the country for more than a decade, began suddenly to collapse. The hatred of the elites for the Workers' Party was fueled by its regulatory model of the Brazilian economy. By contaminating the middle classes and fractions of the working class, the country became virtually ungovernable after Rousseff's re-election in October 2014.

In 2015, the process of isolation of the President of the Republic, already under intense pressure from the legislative and judiciary, reached its peak with the 'leakage' of a letter from its then Vice-President, Michel Temer, in early December, in which he depicts the reasons for its rupture with the government. The letter, written in an innocent and primary tone, reveals the backstage of a coup in preparation. At the height of the crisis, Rousseff had been pressured by the vice president's party (PMDB, center) to take a right turn. The content of this strategy, rejected by the president, is included in the public document 'A bridge to the future'.[4] It is a plan to return the country to the neoliberal trajectory, withdrawing the participation of the State in the different decision-making spheres, and handing the country over to the private interests of large foreign corporations. It was intended, with this, to rescue the dynamics of growth. Not surprisingly, this economic project proved to be a complete failure. Nevertheless, it had the decisive support of the financial markets, the media, and the ruling classes.

Dilma Rousseff resisted the imposition of this agenda, even though it could cost her dearly. The second Rousseff government (2015–2016) was reduced to a strategy to fight its fall; several concessions were made, especially to the financial markets and multinationals. But the putchists were only content with her head.

The enigma of elites' behavior in Brazil, and in Latin America in general, is easier to understand when one keeps in mind its historical trajectory in the last decades. The bourgeoisie in the region preferred to be subordinated to foreign capital in order to become economically viable, hence the dependent and associated character of the capitalist development in the region.[5] Industrialization initiatives through a sovereign policy, promoted by the State, have always faced resistance from the local ruling classes. This was the case in the first cycle of industrial development induced by the State in Brazil in the post-crisis of 1929. As the force of expansion could not dispense with the internal market, development policy necessarily had a distributional character. Consequently, the return of private investment fell, as well as the previously free space for speculation and action of multinational capital was reduced, because of the greater presence of the State. This is regarded as something unacceptable by rentier elites, who are averse to modernization and the search for an autonomous path of development. The next step is the conspiracy to retake State control. So it was in 1964, and history repeats itself, as the most infamous of farces, in 2016.

In 1964, unlike 2016, the army took to the streets, under the clamor of the elite, to stifle democracy and a popular nationalist development agenda. The pretext was to avoid a communist radicalization, in the midst of an expansion of the ideology in Latin America. Today this threat is nothing more than the delirium of the ruling class. The socialism that survives in Venezuela is not a real force that influences the Brazilian left. What is at stake is access to national wealth, such as oil, commodities, the Amazon. The elites want to reign absolutely over this patrimony, and avoid any popular participation in relation to their destiny. To stop this project, led by the Workers' Party, it was enough to articulate conservative sectors of the judiciary and the legislature, without resorting to the army or United States interference. The stage for a parliamentary coup, aimed at impeaching the president, was armed.

If there was no concrete technical justification for an impeachment, and to date no crime of corruption has been proven against Lula or Dilma, what was the real motivation for the right to rebel against the development model, against the 'way of governing'[6] of the PT? It is an issue that intrigues researchers, but whose answer goes through the understanding that in fact the PT model was particular, consisted of an institutional variation of Brazilian capitalism. An unorthodox approach to political economy, such as the one proposed in this book, will allow us to unveil the nuances of this new model, which some of Lula's supporters have described as 'developmental'. Others still, on the conservative side, would argue that it was a continuation of the previous neoliberal period (which lasted until 2002). From this perspective, the evolution of the country would have been due to the favorable external context, and with its reversal, the economy would have gone bankrupt. An argument that doesn't resist a simple analysis of the available data. . . .

The depletion of the model, and the breaking of the pact with elements that would sponsor the coup, gestate within the model itself, paradoxically. First, one must understand that the coup in Brazil is just another chapter of the neoliberal restoration in Latin America. Neoliberalism, in its long lasting crisis, suffered a retreat from the coming to power of Hugo Chavez in Venezuela in 1999. Then came the victories of popular leaders of different political shades, but always of a progressive nature, such as Lula da Silva himself (2002), Néstor Kirchner in Argentina (2003), Evo Morales in Bolivia (2006). They had in common popular national projects, and the goal of regional integration for the construction of a sphere independent of US influence. Another common aspect is that these regimes, if they have clearly increased popular participation, have also had, to a greater or lesser extent, to reconcile themselves with powerful interest groups and oligarchies to govern. Moreover, the neoliberal decade of the 1990s had left the subcontinent impoverished and indebted to the local and international financial markets. With the advent of the global crisis in 2008, the conflicts within these pacts intensified, and the right wing took advantage of the weakening of the maneuvering margin to regain power and impose its agenda. In Brazil, there are internal and external elements that signal to problems in mediation in the political pact built by Lula. The first is eminently economic, and is linked to a trend of stagnation with full employment in Rousseff's first term (2011–2014). In this period, the average economic growth of GDP was lower than the years governed by Lula (2003–2010), and also below the performance of other emerging countries. The years of the economic boom had lagged behind. The growing reliance on commodity export income, amid the worsening global crisis, has certainly affected the Brazilian economy's plans. The interruption in growth led to a fall in revenue, and the country was pressured to adopt austerity measures to avoid a failure to meet fiscal targets.

In this scenario, the dissatisfaction of the middle classes grows, fueled by reports of corruption involving the Workers' Party in Operation Car Wash; in this sense, it is necessary to analyze the growth of anti-Workers' Party sentiment (*antipetismo*) as a central phenomenon of this Brazilian context, which responds directly to the weariness of the president and her tragic end.

It is a phenomenon in its origin fueled by the opposition and the corporate media, whose evolution is associated with the great demonstrations of June 2013.[7] These demonstrations, a true watershed in the recent political history of the country, began as simple protests against the increase in public transportation fares in large cities, led by students from São Paulo. The movement grew out of control, fueled in part by social media and the demands expanded, asking for improvements in the living conditions in the metropolises, as well as in the public systems of health and education. However, even though these issues are mostly under the responsibility of local governments, the media has begun to convey that the demonstrations were against the national government. At the same time, infiltrated black blocs clashed with the police, and violence became widespread. Seeing the newspaper and television stamped on the narrative that demonstrations were against the PT, the population would quickly reject the government's policies. It was a check against the president. In a few days her popularity would plummet.

It would not be long, and conservative groups would come to take advantage of the situation. Thus, even in June 2013, we would see the first voices rising against PT, preventing the left from participating in the big demonstrations. In 2014, following the re-election of Rousseff, small concentrations are observed in November and December, demanding the departure of the president. At the outset, right-wing leaders are openly flirting with the changing rules of the party political game.[8] Shortly after, on March 15, the first major conservative demonstration, with one million people, mostly upper-middle-class, right-wing voters, dressed in green and yellow, the colors of the motherland, call for an end to corruption, and cry 'get out Dilma'. Extremists became numerous, tolerated by the organizers, and clamored for a military intervention in the country. The police, which harshly repressed acts in support of the government, were solicit to take pictures with reactionary demonstrators. 'Panelaços' (people tapping their pans noisily) sounded at night, not to protest the lack of food, but to silence the president's broadcasts on television. The right had lost the battle at the polls and wanted to impose by means of force its project for the country.

Operation car wash, similar to many others in the Lula and Dilma administrations, which re-equipped the Federal Police to allow a more efficient fight against organized crime, would assume a partisan tone when perceiving the potential of damages to the image of the federal government and the Party of the workers. Judge Sérgio Moro, who leads the task force, attends events promoted by the media, and lets himself be photographed alongside right-wing leaders. The real meaning of the operation, therefore, was to instrumentalize anti-corruption operations to destabilize executive and legislative power, as well as the national productive system itself. With this in mind, it becomes easier to understand the support of the ruling classes to this, which is, above all, a project to seize the power. Although the elements underlying Dilma Rousseff's impeachment have nothing to do with the corruption discovered by the operation car wash, selective leaks, mass media coverage, and the coarse view of the Supreme Court have helped ignite the proto-fascists who took the streets of the country from March 2015.

There is nothing especially new about this phenomenon that brought to power the new right in Brazil in 2016. Neither its authoritarian drift, in a Republic marked for a longer time under dictatorship than democracy, nor in the words of order (and hatred) of the moneyed people who took to the streets. What is absolutely unique is the articulation of this strategy through the mass media instrument, in a way never seen before. The demonstrations, whose supporters marched in the colors of the national flag, invoking a false patriotism, were summoned by virtual movements of right and far-right hitherto unknown. The reinforcement of the mass media, especially Globo Network, was fundamental. There was even a change in the schedule for football games and soap operas to increase adherence to the demonstrations, always marked for Sundays with uninterrupted coverage of television, where 'journalists' did not hesitate to call people to take to the streets.

Box 2 The impeachment process against Rousseff

"It isn't against me. It's against a model of development."

With these words, the president of Brazil, Dilma Rousseff, began the greatest of her battles, since taking office as successor to Luís Inácio Lula da Silva in 2011: the battle of impeachment. The impeachment of presidents of the Republic is foreseen in the constitutional text, but it applies in case of crimes of responsibility.

The process against Rousseff, filed at the National Congress in December 2015, has, however, the contours worthy of a great farce:

- The then president of the Chamber, Eduardo Cunha, later imprisoned for corruption, pressures, without success, the PT to free him of investigation in the Congress. In retaliation, he authorizes an impeachment request for the president, which is analyzed by the congressmen;
- The contents of the impeachment request is a legal piece of fiction. Built to order by the PSDB (center-right), defeated opposition in the

> 2014 election, it contains a number of inconsistencies. The central accusation: administrative impropriety by disrespecting the budgetary law of fiscal responsibility. The alleged maneuvers in the budget, called 'fiscal pedals', had, however, been approved by different legal bodies before being authorized by the president. Nothing is worth this proof, or the defense of more than 12 hours handled in person by Dilma Rousseff in the Congress. She was dismissed by a 2/3 qualified majority of the House and Senate. The infamous speeches of moralist congressmen, against corruption, at the time of voting was a mark of that day. Despite this, the association of the president with deviations or appropriation of public resources is yet to be proven.

The general plan of this work

The book is divided into three parts. The first part, titled 'The praxis of change', will feature two more chapters besides this introduction. Chapter 2, signed by Pierre Salama, gives us the global context to understand the recent transformations in the Latin American economies of the early 21st century. Then, in Chapter 3, we present the central hypothesis of the book, that is, the characterization of the period of the governments of the Workers' Party as a new regime of growth, based on a new institutional arrangement that changes significantly the dynamics of capital accumulation.

In the second part, 'The mechanisms of change', we analyze in detail the mechanisms that enabled the economic evolution of Brazil in the period of the governments of Lula da Silva and Dilma Rousseff. These include: the role of the State and its fiscal, monetary and credit policies, stimuli to the consumer market, changes in the capital-wage relation and the new external insertion of the country. Thus, we have in Chapter 4, a study by Jaime Marques Pereira about the new South American economic model, in a comparison between its two largest economies, Brazil and Argentina, to highlight one of its bases of support: monetary policy. In Chapter 5, Ricardo Caffé and Miguel Bruno show the particularity of the Brazilian wage-capital relation during the Lula years, when the wage share increased alongside the financialization of the economy. In Chapter 6, María Madi points to the role of institutional change in the financial sector to analyze the credit expansion and its effects on GDP growth. Cristina Reis, in Chapter 7, highlights the leap in capital investments led by state-owned enterprises and their impacts on the economy. The text describes the crisis as a conjunction of factors, political-ideological and economic, that ended up undermining investments, sabotaging once again the dream of development. Finally, Marcelo Milan reveals in Chapter 8 that the evident change in the Brazilian economy's external performance in the 'Lula years' was not enough, however, to mitigate the country's financial and technological dependence on the more advanced countries.

Part 3, 'The challenges of change', addresses some of the obstacles that have been imposed on the path of development planned by the PT governments. In Chapter 9, Félix Sánchez analyzes the political obstacles, by showing that the coalition pact with right wing sectors, which allowed the PT to govern the country, started to malfunction in 2014. Like an anomaly, a cancer, it started to ruin the balance of power that once was in place. And eventually it took the power. The political system, and its control by the ruling classes, thus places itself as a huge obstacle to the implementation of a national, autonomous and popular development project in the country. The historical roots of this phenomenon, and its implications, are explored in depth in this chapter. In Chapter 10, we address the environmental obstacles and their fundamental contradiction with the Brazilian development process, which creates a growing dependence on the agrarian elite, a symbol of the country's most backward oligarchic interests. The cultural obstacle is the theme of Chapter 11. In it, Reginaldo Moraes points to a central contradiction that runs counter to any attempt to push the country forward: the peculiar structure of the Brazilian educational model. Although Lula and Dilma had invested billions in the sector, their private, profit oriented nature remained practically untouched. The intellectuality formed there, although more diverse, lacks the critical spirit to embrace a national and popular project that the country needs to overcome its underdevelopment. Finally, in Chapter 12, Robério Paulino discusses persistent inequality in Brazil and recent attempts to combat it with social policies. The author shows how the PT multiplied tenfold the budget of the main social program, the Bolsa Família (family allowances). Despite the negligible spending, around 0.5% of GDP, the policy allowed the eradication of chronic deprivation, and the improvement of the quality of life of the poorest Brazilians, something unheard of in the country in the last 50 years. However, this success caused discomfort in the ruling classes, accustomed to patronage to perpetuate themselves in power. Today, little by little, the program has been deconstructed, which shows an important limit of the Lula years' strategy: the lack of boldness to institute permanent structural changes in Brazilian society. The party, and its policies, has become hostage to the conservative interests that easily work today to erase its legacy. In Chapter 13, we sought to close this reflection with a brief summary of the main results highlighted in the different parts of the book, as well as to present some questions to guide future insights about this which was one of the most important periods in Brazil's recent history.

Acknowledgments

First of all, I thank all the book's collaborators for their serious and passionate dedication to the project.

I thank the Federal University of ABC (UFABC), for the grant of resources that financed part of this project, and the Federal University of Sao Paulo (Unifesp), for the freedom and structure it offered for the development of this research.

I am especially grateful to the Association for Heterodox Economics (AHE) for accepting the reflections, from their most embryonic forms, that would give rise to this book.

I would like to express my gratitude also to the editors at Routledge for trusting the project throughout all the two years of its elaboration.

My thankfulness goes as well to Jonathan Russell, who helped correct much of the manuscript in English.

★ ★ ★

I dedicate this book to Juliana Corrêa, my companion, for her careful reading and reviewing, for understanding the hard moments of work and for the ever rich and inspiring exchange of ideas. And to my daughter, Valentina, who from the height of her six years already sees the contradictory character of our system, and shows the potential of the new generations to radically transform it.

Notes

1 See, for the foundational bases of French regulation theory: Michel Aglietta, *A Theory of Capitalist Regulation: The US Experience*. London: Verso, 2015 [1979]; and Robert Boyer, *The Regulation Theory: A Critical Introduction*. Columbia: Columbia University Press, 1990.
2 For a detailed account of the events leading up to impeachment against president elected Dilma Rousseff, see Perry Anderson, The Brazilian Crisis. *New Left Review*, v. 38, n. 8, 2016.
3 Something realized since the days of Adam Smith, when the Scottish economist pointed out how capital makes an instrument out of justice to ensure its interests prevail against the working class.
4 Partido do Movimento Democrático Brasileiro (PMDB), *Uma ponte para o futuro*, 2015. http://pmdb.org.br/wp-content/uploads/2015/10/RELEASE-TEMER_A4-28.10.15-Online.pdf
5 We owe this definition to the Latin American dependence theory. See, for a review, Matias Vernengo, Technology, Finance and Dependency: Latin American Radical Political Economy in Retospect, *Working Paper No. 2004–06*, University of Utah Dept. of Economics, 2004.
6 Luiz Inácio Lula da Silva, interviwed by José Trajano in July 20, 2017, www.ultrajano.com.br/na-sala-do-ze
7 See Anthony Pahnke, The Brazilian Crisis, *Monthly Review*, v. 68, 2017.
8 Alberto Goldman, Impeachment é golpe?, PSDB official website, January 22, 2015; Fernando H. Cardoso, Chegou a hora, *A Gazeta do Povo*, February 2, 2015.

2 Is the change in globalization's rhythm an opportunity for Latin-American emerging economies?

Pierre Salama

International trade in goods and services increased two to three times faster than global GDP between the 1990s and the 2008 crisis. On average, therefore, all countries are more open than they once were. However, some countries have become more open. Taking the example of Brazil and China, the openness rate[1], measured by exports of goods and services in value terms to gross domestic product, rose in Brazil from 7.2% in 1979 to 13.04% in 2015, with a peak at 16.55% in 2004. In China, it was 5.20% and 22.37% at those same dates with a peak at 35.65% in 2006 according to the World Bank. Between 1960 and 2015, in 55 years, exports of goods and services increased by 85% in Brazil and 415% in China. When comparing Brazil's and China's exports to world exports in the early 1980s, it is roughly equivalent in the two countries at 1%. Thirty years later, Brazilian exports amounted to 1.1% of world exports, while in China they reached 12%. The two countries therefore opened up, but at very different rates.

Since 2008, despite a very slight economic recovery in the advanced countries, globalization seems to be losing momentum. World exports are now growing at a rate close to that of world GDP. Protectionist measures have multiplied since 2012. With Trump's ascension to the US presidency (2017), these could be both more important and widespread. Under these conditions, what are the possibilities for the Latin American countries to face these threats? Could the slowdown in growth in Latin American countries since 2012, or even the deep crisis in Brazil and, to a lesser extent, Argentina, be seen as an opportunity to "positively" integrate region into the international division of labor through exports other than raw materials? This possibility seems to be weak, but it does exist. Relative abandonment of the reprimarization model is a necessary but not sufficient condition for the accumulation of disadvantages to become an opportunity.

A shift in the international division of labor

Relatively closed economies and original industrialization patterns

Growth driven by the emerging domestic market in Latin America

Following the Great Depression of 1929, between 1935 and 1980, some Latin American countries underwent considerable industrialization, known as import substitution, or growth driven by an emerging domestic market. This was characterized by the ability to integrate upstream and downstream activities as much as possible.

In Latin America, in the large countries, industrialization has been relatively incomplete, or even "truncated" according to the expression used by Fajnzylber F. (1980): despite massive state intervention in the heavy sectors, productivity chains could not be fully integrated due to lack of financial, human, and technical capacity. That is why they were called semi-industrialized economies at the time. By the end of the 1970s, difficulties were mounting: industrialization was less dynamic, GDP growth was very volatile, hyperinflation (or very high inflation) was taking root, poverty increased again, and income inequalities were rising even though they were already at a very high level. In the 1990s, price increases were under control, but growth regained remained at a modest level, especially when compared with that of several Asian countries.

Growth driven by exports in Asia under certain conditions

In the 1960s and 1980s, a few Asian countries[2] experienced rapid industrialization through both relocations and large state intervention. Offshoring involved certain segments of the production line of a product for which the unit labor cost (wage rate, productivity and exchange rate combination) was much lower than that of the advanced countries. More precisely, this labor being sent offshore originally concerned few products for which it was possible to use alternative technologies, called *labor using,* using little capital and an abundant and low-paid labor force. The wage gap between these countries of the South and those of the North, the possibility of imposing unimaginable working conditions in advanced countries in view of their legislation, overcompensate the productivity gap so that relocation to the South of certain production segments became more profitable than their production in the North, despite the costs induced by transcontinental transport. As wages increased in these countries, intensified market capitalism followed. As a result, the number of products affected by relocation increased, and the more rapidly the governments of Asian countries, with the notable exception of Hong Kong, favored upstream national integration, made available an increasingly qualified workforce, adopted a consistent industrial policy aimed at integrating positively into the international division of labor, seeking to produce more sophisticated goods demanded in international markets. The growth of this segmented offshoring, sometimes referred to as international subcontracting, concerned two to three players: a firm in the advanced countries, a promoter, one to two enterprises on the periphery, which could be a subsidiary of the advanced countries' firm, but not necessarily as has been the case in South Korea.

In the 1990s and especially in the 2000s, there was a shift in the international division of labor with the development of the Internet, lower transport costs, the possibility that some countries could adapt their offer very quickly to sudden changes in World demand. We went from a relationship between two to three players to a relationship between one actor, the client, and "n" actors located in different countries, especially in the South but also in the North.

The international value chain then broke out, the production line being in "n" countries from design to distribution and all segments. Production techniques have changed, including in assembly. Indeed, the advantage of the low wage cost of low-skilled workers has become insufficient in comparison with gains from the use of more sophisticated, capital intensive production techniques using a more skilled and more expensive labor, but relatively less than in the North. It is in this way that, in addition to the North-South relationship on manufactured goods, South-South relations have become more and more dense, which have sometimes been described as a silent revolution.

Latin American countries have little investment in the international value chain

As Hiratuka and Sarti (2016) point out in the wake of Baldwin (2016), with the international break-up of the value chain in the 2000s, the pursuit of industrialization could have been fostered in Latin America under two conditions: 1) making attractive the possibility of supplying segments of production; 2) to undertake, as it was done in Asia, an industrial policy which would make it possible to partially integrate these offshored segments and replace inputs imported by locally produced segments meeting high-quality international requirements. This was not the case in Latin America, so that the major Latin American economies had relatively little involvement in the process of international value disruption either upstream or downstream[3], including Mexico. Indeed, unlike many Asian countries, Mexico was largely confined to assembly activities, with the exception in part of certain sectors such as the automotive industry where the number of original equipment manufacturers increased. Growing openness has not had a positive effect on growth, as the multiplier effects on GDP are therefore low, which explains why among the major Latin American countries it was the one whose growth was the lowest in the last twenty-five years (Romero Tellaeche, 2014). The complexity of its industrial fabric is also weak and / or apparent and deceptive (Sasses, 1991).

The digital revolution, the fall in transport costs and the labor flexibility have spurred this shift

A revolution. . . .

Once, the so-called periphery countries were specialized in the production of raw materials. Today, some of them, in Asia and Mexico, have become the "workshops of the world"; others, after being industrialized, mainly in Latin America, have returned to a specialization in the production of rent products and thus have been de-industrialized, while others have remained specialized in the production of primary products.

The upheavals observed also concern the advanced countries. Their production lines have become more internationalized, often concentrating on the

Table 2.1 Participation (in %) in the international value chain as a percentage of gross exports in six countries of Latin America and China, 2000 and 2011

Country	Year	Backward participation	Forward participation
Argentine, Brazil, Chile, Colombia, Costa Rica et Mexico	2000	24.8	14.1
Idem	2011	20.1	21
China	2000	32.2	10.8
Idem	2011	32.1	15.6

Source: OECD, Caf et Cepal, 2016, op. cit.

upstream segments, where the research-development coefficient and capital intensity are the highest, and downstream. The other segments have partly relocated to other countries.

With the Internet revolution and digitalization, the boundaries between industry and certain services have become porous. First, because a whole series of activities that were previously part of the industry were outsourced and are now referred to as services, which sometimes makes discussions about de-industrialization irrelevant when comparisons are not made with equivalent patterns. Secondly, because of the so-called dynamic services, the most efficient ones, those whose productivity is not only high but rapidly growing, the methods applied there are those of the industry, the latter spreading to those. The reduction in the cost of transport, the ability to scale up very rapidly, that is, the ability to go to markets that are immediately global, and to mobilize very large financial and human resources to do so (scalability), and finally the increasing flexibility of the workforce, allow rapid adaptability of supply to movements of world demand. This breakdown of the international value chain concerns mainly Asian countries. Trade relations between them have become even denser than they were before, with the final destiny being the markets of the advanced countries.

The trans-nationalization of production in advanced countries is not confined to markets outside the periphery, but also to their internal markets. In China, mainly, rules and modalities differ from those in force for export production. The trans-nationalization of firms in a few peripheral countries, mostly China, is due to other logics: China's massive investments abroad are mainly aimed at ensuring access to raw materials for both production and transportation, to capture the latest technologies produced by companies in advanced countries through their purchase, and secondarily to produce for the domestic markets of both semi-industrialized and advanced countries.

For a variety of products, forms of competition increasingly rely on the control of fixed cost amortization, especially design and investment costs, as Pierre Veltz (2017) points out (p.67). The software industry is an almost perfect example of this, since the costs of reproduction are close to zero (the marginal cost is zero, to quote Jeremy Rifkin's expression). On the other hand, the backward costs are extremely high (the internet infrastructure such as the cloud) and make it very difficult for emerging countries to impose themselves on these very dynamic products. Access to these sectors requires a great deal of research effort and the ability to achieve a considerable scale of production, which is a very strong "barrier to entry". It is only when it is surpassed that the profits arrive.

With the internet revolution, agglomeration economies have gained more strength than in the past. Digitalization has moved farther and closer, which at first sight seems to be a paradox. It moves farther because it allows an international break-up of the value chain. It moves closer because the large cities acquire considerable economic power to the point where they appear to be the "winners" of globalization, to the detriment of medium and small towns, which become the "losers". S. Sassen (1991) had already analyzed the rise of large metropolises in the early 1990s. The economies of agglomeration have grown considerably because the large cities are at the same time basins of demand, and suppliers of skilled workforces. Around large cities there are economic powers which, often establishing networks across national boundaries, are sometimes opposed to the interests defined by national and local governments. Large cities, under certain conditions, are therefore the place where complexity develops, a source of positive insertion into the international division of labor.

Measuring economic complexity

The complexity of an economy depends on the effort made in research and development, the higher it is, the greater the likelihood that the economy can produce complex products. Exports have two characteristics: their ubiquity and their diversification. Ubiquity depends on rarity, which depends either on the natural resources that the country has or does not have, or on the ability to produce sophisticated goods that only a few countries can do. In order to isolate the latter and construct an indicator of complexity, the authors, quoted below, seek to use the diversity of exports to measure the degree of ubiquity and therefore complexity. For example, Pakistan and Singapore have similar GDP and each export 133 large goods, so the diversity of their exports is similar, but Pakistan's exports are also exported by 28 other countries, whose exports are also little diversified. This is not the case in Singapore: only 17 other countries export products similar to their own and their exports are very diversified. The level of complexity of the Singapore economy is therefore higher than that of Pakistan, whose per capita income is much lower. From these two variables: diversity and ubiquity, one can construct an indicator.

> For the analysis of complexity see the work of Hausmann et al. (2004): "Growth Accelerations", mimeo Harvard, Hausmann, Hidalgo and allii (2014), The Atlas of Economic Complexity, Mapping Paths to Perspectives, Harvard University, Harvard Kennedy School, Macro Connections MIT Media Lab, and more recently, using the methodology of Hausman and Hidalgo, see Paulo Gala (2017), Complexidade economica, uma nova perspectiva para entender a antigua questao da riqueza das nacoes, editions: Centro International Celso Furtado et Contraponto, d'où nous avons pris l'exemple du Pakistan et de Singapour (p. 21–26).
>
> The more complex an economy, the more it produces sophisticated goods requiring a high research coefficient and vice versa. This is a tautology. It is these products that have a high income and low elasticity of demand and a low price elasticity one. They are products that allow a positive insertion in the international division of labor because they are a bet on the future.

As a consequence of digitalization, lower transport costs, flexibility and scalability, advanced technologies are immediately available. In other words, the time (from the 1960s to the 1990s) when productive capital could be exported to advanced countries, which can be valued on the periphery, as was the case in the automotive industry, where Ford, Fiat, Renault, Peugeot, Volkswagen, continued to produce old "new" cars (Beetle, Falcon, and others), has come to an end. Today, the level of productivity achieved by multinational firms in emerging countries is close to that of the advanced countries. Given the lower wages and sometimes despite a tendency to appreciate national currencies vis-a-vis the dollar, they are often more competitive than the firms remaining in the advanced countries. The case of the automobile industry in Mexico shows this clearly. The world is no longer composed of Vernon's strata (product cycles), but of networks, it has become an archipelago, as P. Veltz points out.

*Significant consequences for employment and its forms,
and for political representation*

We cannot omit the consequences on work, on employment, on political representation on the pretext that they would appeal to other disciplines than economics. Globalization is both a process of unification and fragmentation in advanced countries. Unification because with increasing openness employment and work are subject to increasingly high external constraints. Employment tends to become more precarious and with the rise of the Internet, the "uberization" of activities is becoming more and more important. It is manifested through a rise in outsourcing. The worker, becoming his own employer, is inserted in constraints imposed on him upstream thanks to the cloud and big data that only master large companies. Fragmentation because not all activities are subject to outsourcing. This recent movement fragmented even more workers than in the past or opposed insiders and outsiders, with the downgrading and above all the disaffiliation that go with it. Work tends to become increasingly flexible in terms of pay (competition from low-wage workers in Asia and the effects of precariousness on wages) and the versatility of tasks without sufficient social mobility opportunities in the case of redundancies. In addition, there is a growing gap in labor compensation between execution and management tasks, coupled with the unequal effects of financial liberalization. Political representation is strongly questioned by this movement at the level of employment - both quantitatively and qualitatively - and wages. They are responsible for the globalization they have promoted and are paying the price today because of their inability to control it and give way to new political configurations whose outlines are difficult to predict.

Latin American economies weakened but that still have opportunities to 'rebound'

A weakened industrial fabric

Large Latin American countries are more protectionist
than Asian countries by their tariffs but less by their exchange rates

We have seen that the main Latin American countries have opened up to world merchandise trade at a more moderate pace than Asian countries (with the notable exception of India until recently). Protectionism is still relatively low in Brazil and Argentina, particularly in comparison with most Asian countries, including capital goods and intermediate products. This is a paradox, since the dominant ideology in foreign trade is rather that of free trade.

Protectionism is more important in Latin America than in the Asian countries, with the exception of a few countries such as Peru, Chile, Colombia and of course Mexico. However, the appreciation of Latin American currencies over a long period of time greatly accentuates or even annihilates the protective effects of customs duties.

This appreciation reduces the price of imports into local currency, which are made cheaper by substituting part of local production for three reasons: the level attained by labor productivity is relatively lower than that of firms exporting the same products[4], labor productivity has increased marginally (see table below), and is much lower than in Asian countries, and finally, in countries with progressive governments, real wage has grown faster than productivity of labor. These three factors, together with the strong appreciation of local currencies vis-à-vis the dollar, inadequate infrastructure and often "less transparent" institutions, undermine the competitiveness of enterprises, reduce the average return on capital employed in the industrial sector.

Table 2.2 Average import prices over the last 20 years

	Mexico	Argentina	Brazil	Peru	Chile	Colombia	South Korea	China	USA
1996 or 1997	14.8	14.5	14.4	13.2	11.0	12.2	9.8	22.0	4.1
2015*	3.0	12.5	13.7	2.8	1.2	5.2	5.2	7.6	2.8

Source: World Bank, statistical annex and Bradesco, * or most recent data

Table 2.3 Average prices on capital goods and intermediate products

Country	Capital goods			Intermediate goods		
	2000	2006	2010	2000	2006	2010
Brazil	16.90	13.20	13.00	13.90	10.70	11.70
China	14.40	8.10	7.70	14.40	7.90	7.40
South Korea	7.20	5.90	6.00	8.00	11.20	11.10
Philippines	4.20	2.80	2.90	5.90	5.00	4.90
India	26.70	14.10	8.40	32.70	17.40	10.00
Indonesia	4.40	3.80	5.50	7.30	6.10	6.00
Malaysia	5.10	4.20	3.60	7.10	6.80	6.60
Mexico	13.10	9.50	3.20	14.80	11.80	6.10
Thailand	10.50	6.40	5.50	14.00	6.00	4.40

Source: *idem*

Table 2.4 Real effective exchange rate in Brazil, from 2000 to 2014, at the eve of the crisis (base 100 in 2000)

September 2001	141	January 2009	110
April 2002	110	July 2011	74
October 2002	177	January 2013	94
October 2003	134	March 2013	87
June 2004	147	April 2013	101
October 2008	85	July 2014	90

Source: Central Bank, and Nassif et alii (2015). In order to facilitate the reading of the table, let us recall that a decreasing curve means an appreciation of the national currency. Exchange rates are expressed in real terms to account for inflation differentials with the United States. Here, we focus on significant dates characterized by either a peak or a trough. One can observe the long period of appreciation of the currency from mid-June 2004 until the beginning of 2013. From mid-2014 onwards, the currency depreciates very strongly.

An early de-industrialization

The appreciation of the national currency, the low level of productivity and its sluggish growth, the rise in real wages in some countries, and indirectly the insufficiency of infrastructure, largely explain the weakness of investment in

Table 2.5 Annual growth rate of labor productivity in industry, several countries

	1970–1979	1980–1989	1990–1999	2000–2007	2010–2014
Argentina	1.7	−1.4	6.9	−0.7	−2.5
Brazil	3.4	−2.8	2.9	0.0	−2.5
Chile	−0.3	−0.5	6.2	0.1	−1.8
Mexico	0.6	−1.7	0.4	0.6	3.7
China	−1.6	4.8	10.4	7.1	6.9
South Korea	3.2	5.0	7.7	5.6	4.3

Source: UNCTAD (2016), Trade and Development Report, p. 69

manufacturing. This precipitates the de-industrialization of these countries in favor of much more lucrative rentier activities (raw materials, finance).

In the end, appreciated exchange rates, the weakness of labor productivity and of its evolution, real wages, which, although low, sometimes rising faster than productivity, open Latin American countries to foreign competition more than relatively higher protectionism prevents it[5].

Early de-industrialization in Brazil

Higher growth is at the expense of industry. Industrial production is stagnating – at the beginning of 2014 when it regained its 2002 level – and collapses with the crisis. For an index of 100 on average in 2002 (seasonally adjusted), it reached a peak of 105.5 in June 2013, then 99 in November 2014, 85 in January 2016 and 83 in February 2016. Despite the further expansion of exports, industry continued to decline. If we ignore the 2015–2016 crisis, in 11 years the processing industry did not grow. After a certain stage of development, it is usual to observe a relative decrease of the share of the industrial sector in the GDP in favor of the services sector, without there being necessarily de-industrialization. The term de-industrialization is generally reserved for an absolute decline in the value added of industry and/or a relative reduction in the weight of domestic industry in the global open economy industry. In Latin America, this phenomenon tends to occur much earlier than in the advanced countries, hence the use of the term 'early' used when the per capita income at the beginning of the process of de-industrialization corresponds to half that of the advanced countries at the time it begins. The share of the Brazilian processing industry in the global (value added) processing industry was 1.8% in 2005 and 1.7% in 2011, after reaching 2.7% in 1980, according to the UNCTAD database of 2013. According to the same source, in China, this share was 9.9%, in 2005 and 16.9% in

2011. It therefore decreases in Brazil while it increases strongly in China. Exports of manufactured goods are falling in relative terms in Brazil, from 53% of the value of exports in 2005 to 35% in 2012, in favor of exports of agricultural and mining raw materials and it is only since February 2016 that it has been rising once again due to the sharp currency devaluation and the fall in commodity prices.

In Brazil, beyond the success of a few industrial sectors such as aeronautics, the automobile to some extent, the oil industry, de-industrialization has been developing since the 1990s and intensified in the 2000s with a relative loss of competitiveness in the processing industry, coupled with inadequate transport infrastructure (railways, port and airport facilities, roads), and insufficient energy capacity.

There is a causal relationship between the appreciation of the national currency and the low average productivity growth. The appreciation makes work expressed in dollars more expensive even though wages would remain stable in national currency. As a result, profitability is affected and the tendency to move towards rent, speculative (real estate) or financial activities, the latter of which may be speculative, strengthens. As a consequence, the relative share of low-productivity services activities takes on a greater relative importance at the expense of those of dynamic processing and service industries, which tends to decelerate labor productivity to a relatively low level. However, this trend hides a relatively high dispersion, and higher than in the past around the mean. Large firms, when they can resist and because they can resist have productivity levels and developments much higher than the average.

Today, with the economic slowdown in China, the price of raw materials is struggling to recover the high prices it had known. De-industrialization in Latin America is losing its momentum, except in Mexico and Central America, where it is not very present, as these countries are not large producers of raw materials[6]. The industry has been weakened but in some countries like Brazil it has not been destroyed as was the case in the past in Venezuela with coffee and then oil. The de-industrialization they are experiencing is both early and relative[7]. It is particularly important, especially in Brazil, as we have just seen. It is relative because often the increase in the deficit in goods of high and medium technology is more the result of a growth of the demand superior to the domestic supply than of an absolute regression of this one.

Recent strong depreciations in their national currencies, large falls in employment and wages to a lesser degree, have shown that exports have rebounded after a rather long period and that their progression has continued despite new reappraisals. However, this situation is fragile, especially since true protectionist measures have not yet been put in place.

Upward or downward recovery?

The hypothesis of this work is that only industry, understood in the broad sense - including so-called dynamic services, whose rise is the consequence of the computer revolution - offers possibilities of exit from the top of the crisis that affects them. It alone can ensure a positive integration in the international division of labor. But to move in this direction is to confront the rentier behaviors, to reverse the rentier logic (de-industrialization and growth of the financial sector) by implementing a tax reform that reduces inequalities (boosting the internal market) and releases resources to finance industrial niches (through non consumerist industrial policy), a consistent policy towards education and research that, while pursuing the one that has been undertaken, develops it.

In this chapter, for lack of space, we will mainly analyze the emblematic case of the Brazilian economy. However, we must be careful not to consider that what is valid for Brazil would be point by point for the other countries. They are more or less different than most of them - with the exception of the Central American countries and Mexico for lack of abundant raw materials. These de-industrialized countries have all experienced an appreciation of their currency against the dollar more or less intensive, interspersed with large depreciations and devaluations, and a more or less important de-industrialization. In Mexico, the latter being limited to industries oriented towards the internal market.

Comparing the changes in manufacturing production according to the technological level with imports and exports is rich in lessons. It provides a more accurate assessment of the industry's sustainable rebound capabilities. We will see that these exist but are reduced if there are no substantial changes in economic policies in order to cope with both the inheritance (loss of competitiveness and the complexity of exports) and protectionism that has been developing since the beginning of the 2010s, and especially with the change of presidency in the United States.

Production and deficit, revealing data

Specifically, manufacturing grew from 2004 to 2008, then fell slightly, recovering slightly and collapsing in 2015 and 2016. These movements are amplified upward and downward for high-tech industries (aerospace, pharmaceuticals, computer equipment, etc.) and those of medium-high tech (electrical machinery and equipment, motor vehicles, chemicals except pharmaceuticals, machinery and mechanical equipment, etc.). This is not the case for other industries, medium-low technology, such as food, beverages, textiles, wood, etc., such as construction, ship repair, rubber and plastics, metal products. The latter has slightly better resisted the crisis in recent years as it has not collapsed. It has decreased less than the average manufacturing sector. Overall, high-tech and, above all, medium-high-tech industries were experiencing a very significant increase in production until the eve of the 2008 crisis. But this increase is

Table 2.6 Production by technological intensity; annual variation, 2004–2017, 1st quarter, changes compared with the previous year's quarter, in percentage, in Brazil

	2004	2005	2006	2007	2008	2009	2010	2011	2012	2013	2014	2015	2016	2017
PI	6.8	3.1	3.9	3.7	6.6	−14.1	17.1	2.7	−5.4	1.3	0.3	−7.8	−11.0	−0.5
HT	17.4	9.3	20.4	0.3	3.9	−4.8	14.1	6.9	−4.9	0.9	16.7	−20.8	−16.0	−3
LT	3.0	3.5	2.1	2.7	1.9	−5.8	8.0	−0.9	−5.3	−1.5	0.6	−3.3	−5.0	−0.2

PI for processing industry, HT for high tech, LT for low tech.

Source: Carta IEDI n°788, 19.05.2017, from IBGE data

Table 2.7 Trade balance of Brazil and trade balance of the manufacturing products according to technological intensity, 1st quarter 2003 to 1st quarter 2017, annualized in variation in millions of dollars FOB

	2003	2004	2005	2006	2007	2008	2009	2010	2011	2012	2102	2013	2014	2015	2016	2017
Manufacturing sector balance	2683	4086	6965	6359	5495	−204	−2668	−7137	−10013	−13290	−16338	−18878	−14671	−2006	−2478
Other sectors (raw materials, etc.)	1129	2077	1482	2969	3233	2961	5656	8018	13155	15707	11156	12739	9115	10393	16896
Trade balance	3822	6162	8348	9328	8728	2757	2988	881	3142	2418	−5182	−6079	−5557	8388	14418
High technology	−1232	−1672	−1601	−2608	−3293	−4550	−3067	−6159	−6804	−7564	−7798	−8336	−6943	−4449	−4764
Mid–high technology	−1326	−1933	−253	−86	−1365	−4843	−5754	−7491	−10991	−12079	−14736	−13863	−12306	−6007	−6301
Mid–low technology	1163	1522	2544	2612	2515	893	563	−1182	−710	−1283	−2930	−4224	−2560	271	−179
Low technology	4082	5269	6177	6436	7648	8296	6400	7695	8491	7637	8525	7603	7139	8579	8756

Source: Development of the IEDI (Instituto de Estudos para o Desenvolvimento Industrial) from the OECD classification, carta IEDI No. 727, April 2016 and No. 784 of 28 April 2017

below that of imports and therefore of domestic demand. On these products, de-industrialization is therefore relative.

1. The trade balance of manufacturing products became negative in 2008. In 2014 it reached its biggest trough (almost $19 billion deficit). It is only in 2016 – following the very sharp depreciation of the national currency and the deepening of the economic crisis leading to a reduction in imports and even as the currency began to re-appreciate – that this deficit was greatly reduced, since it is divided by nine. This deficit is largely offset by the increase in both the price and the volumes traded in raw materials. But this considerable increase is no longer sufficient to compensate for the sharply increasing deficit in the trade balance of manufacturing products as of 2013. From this date, the overall balance of the trade surplus became a deficit and it is only in the first quarter of 2016 that it became a surplus.
2. Only the trade balance of low-technology products remained a surplus throughout the period (2003–2017). The balance of the trade balance of high tech products sees its deficit increase six-fold from 2003 to 2015 and then declined sharply. The balance of the medium-high-tech product balance saw a considerable increase in its deficit multiplied by ten from 2003 to 2015. This deficit then falls by half. Finally, the medium-low-tech products balance shows a deficit from 2010 onwards but tends towards equilibrium from 2016 onwards.

A relatively pessimistic diagnosis

Staying at this level of analysis is, however, insufficient and the conclusions that could be drawn from it may be misleading. Large deficits may hide an increase in production, although demand does not. Balances are only an accounting reflection of the evolution of imports and exports. These are the ones that need to be explained. Exports, classified according to their technological level, may grow less rapidly than imports, or decline. In the first case, local production, although growing, is insufficient for reasons of competitiveness and profitability. It does not export sufficiently and the excess of domestic demand on the net output of exports refers to imports. In the second case, firms are exporting less and less, and imports are partly a substitute for local production that is failing. Finally, it is necessary to refine the analysis within the branches: all production, including that partly destined for export, requires imports, especially since, with the increasing internationalization of production lines, international value chains are more important than yesterday, although it is less consistent than in Asian countries. Thus, from this refinement of the analysis, it can be considered that the industrial fabric for each branch is more efficient if there is the possibility of upgrading and producing both more sophisticated and more complex products.

A priori diagnosis that can be made of the evolution of the whole industrial fabric is relatively negative, but a more refined analysis allows us to retain a certain optimism regarding the rebounding and reintegration in the division of labor seems more favorable than in the recent past if certain preconditions of economic policy are met.

We have seen that the Brazilian trade balance of manufacturing products became negative in 2008. When products are classified according to their degree of technological sophistication, the more sophisticated the product, the more negative the balance becomes. This is a first sign of both loss of competitiveness and inability to produce enough in high-tech industries, with industrial specialization increasingly focused on low-tech products. This is confirmed by the loss in comparative advantages revealed. The curves of the processing industry all decline from the early 2000s in Latin America according to the IMF. This is not the evolution of Asian emerging economies.

When we decompose the complexity of exports into quintiles according to their increasing complexity and compare their evolution, we observe that the Latin American economies and the emerging Asian countries acquire increasing complexity until the end of the 1990s. This is no longer the case. The share of less complex products remains relatively unchanged in Latin America, while they fall sharply in emerging Asia. The other four quintiles, in order of increasing complexity, have a roughly equivalent share in the two country groups in the early 1960s, i.e. 80% and 75% in 1962. At the end of the 1990s, this share rose to 60% in 1998 and 52% in 2012 in Latin America, while it continued to grow in emerging Asia, rising to 70% in 1998 and 80% in 2012.

Among the countries belonging to the BRIC bloc, complexity decreased sharply from the late 1990s in Brazil and Russia, while it increased in China and very slightly in India.

Reasons to hope?

De-industrialization does not mean disappearance. Since 2015, most Latin American economies are depreciating their national currencies against the dollar. In Brazil, this depreciation was very important. At the same time, with the crisis, inflationary surge and rising unemployment, real wages in local currency fell, unit labor costs dropped considerably despite a virtual stagnation in labor productivity. After a few months, the favorable effects of this return to a certain competitiveness favored an increase of exports in Brazil, despite the lethargy of world demand. The share of manufactured exports in total exports increased for the first time, after sharply declining between 2005 (53%) and 2015 (37%). The trade balance of products from manufacturing rose from - $ 19 billion in the first quarter (annualized) in 2014 to - $ 2.5 billion in the first quarter of 2017. Between the same dates, the negative balance of high-tech goods was halved, that of medium-high-tech goods divided by slightly more than two, and that of medium-low technology virtually disappeared.

The industrial fabric thus retains capacity to respond to international demand when competitiveness increases again. However, this capacity is fragile because,

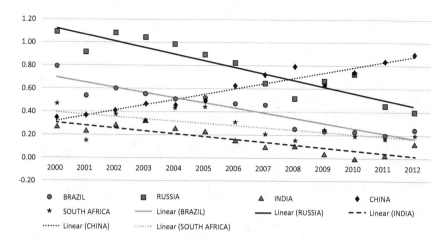

Figure 2.1 BRICS – Economic Complexity Index (ECI)

Sources: Atlas of Economic Complexity, Center for International Development, Harvard University, and Professor Paulo Gala's blog: https://i2.wp.com/www.paulogala.com.br/wp-content/uploads/2015/01/ECI_Brics.png

on the one hand, it is not based on an increase in labor productivity and on the other hand it is the result of both the depreciation of an overvalued currency, and a relative decrease in real wages expressed in local currency. It is therefore not structural, it is conjunctural. The fact that the national currency has been appreciating again since the end of 2016 and that real wages in local currency are not continuing to fall or even begin to recover represent a major risk that the trade deficit will increase again.

That said, if the industrial fabric retains this capacity to rebound, it is because it has not been completely destroyed: complexity has diminished, comparative advantages revealed have deteriorated but Brazil still retains some flags. When comparing data on imports, exports of industrial products according to their technological level and domestic production of these products, it can be seen that high-tech and, above all, medium-high-tech production were experiencing a very significant increase in their production until the eve of the crisis of 2008. We have seen: Growth rates of exports of high-tech products are relatively low but are more resistant to the crisis than others.

Table 2.8 Brazil: imports by technological intensity, annual % change, 1st quarter 2010–1st quarter 2017, percentage, annual change, production (data in brackets)

	2010	2011	2012	2013	2014	2015	2016	2017
High technology	35.2 (14.1)	7.2 (6.9)	9.3 (–4.9)	0.8 (0.9)	–7.1 (16.7)	–12.6 (–20.8)	–25.5 (–16)	3.6 (–3)
Mid-high technology	30.9 (31.9)	33 (4.4)	9.3 (–8.4)	3.8 (4.9)	–2.5 (–2.5)	–16.4 (–11.9)	–29.9 (–19)	9 (3.4)
Mid-low technology	62.1	21.4	18.8	5.8	2.5	–16.4	–41.8	29.6
Low technology	23.7	33.4	18.9	–2.5	3.1	–2.3	–34.2	23.4

Source: Carta IEDI, n ° 784, 28/04/2017 and Carta IEDI n ° 788 op. cit, see below, in gray, years of crisis
Conversely, export growth is high only on medium-high-tech and medium-low-tech products, with Brazil being less and less able to fit into the international division of labor in this sector. However, overall and by sector, there is both a decline in the complexity of exports and comparative advantages in decline, more or less pronounced in different countries.

As a conclusion

Recovery capacities exist, but they are becoming weaker. A sustained recovery in growth is possible. It requires a strengthening of the sectors with a promising future, not weakening them. So the entire economic paradigm has led to both de-industrialization and the decline in the complexity of exports that must be rethought. The resurgence of economies most often leads to irreversible damage to the environment, to the lifestyles and health of the surrounding populations. It naturally produces an appreciation of the national currency, a vector of de-industrialization and increased economic and social vulnerability. This is a necessary but not sufficient condition. Demand must also be more dynamic and competitiveness enhanced so that more sustained demand is not met by imports alone. It seems like an oxymoron. This is the only way to end the crisis and the economic downturn. Reducing inequalities should lead to a reduction in social exclusion, which should make it possible to boost demand. This reduction in inequalities could be achieved through 'progressive' tax reform. Moving from a regressive tax system to a progressive tax system would be a revolution and presupposes that many conflicts are resolved. That is to say the difficulty. To prevent increased demand from increasing imports, it would be necessary both to devalue the currency, to prevent it from being re-evaluated by sterilization mechanisms, and to define an industrial policy that would increase labor productivity. The path is steep, but it is the only one possible.

It has to be said that the Latin American countries have missed the new industrial revolution by adopting a relatively passive attitude towards globalization and the rents that could be derived from them. This path of ease is to be abandoned. The limits of the rentier models have been reached. The time has come for a new way of integrating into the international division of labor. This requires new class alliances, the only ones capable of politically assuming substantial tax reform, a less unequal distribution of incomes, and a less consumeristic industrial policy.

From this point of view, the slowdown in international trade and the rise of protectionism can be an opportunity to opt for another model of development and to achieve sustainable growth that respects citizens and the environment more. History teaches that it advances by rupture. The difficulties faced by most Latin American countries are not economically viable. New class alliances can emerge as in the thirties and allow an economic rebound of these countries. But this is a different story....

Notes

1 This indicator is imperfect: the numerator, the exports in value, is a gross flow. It is not valued as value added and therefore takes into account the imports necessary to produce these exports. Conversely, the denominator, GDP, is measured in value added. There may therefore be a greater or lesser overstatement of the actual openness rate. But it is usually the only available indicator, so we use it cautiously and accompanied by other variables. Moreover, the fluctuations of this indicator depend not only on the value of exports, but also on GDP.

2 Dragons: South Korea, Taiwan, Singapore and Hong Kong, followed by tigers: Malaysia, Thailand, Indonesia, etc.
3 Most Latin American countries are little integrated into international value chains. ECLAC distinguishes two types of integration: backward, which measures for a given country the share of imported intermediate goods incorporated in its exports and forward, which measures the share of intermediate goods exported by a country that are incorporated into exports from other countries. Backward participation was 11.4% in 2000 and 10.7% in 2011 in Brazil instead of 37.2% and 32.1% respectively for China. The decline in the Chinese ratio is indicative of China's effort to integrate its production lines. Forward participation is more important for Brazil (17.1% in 2000 and 24.5% in 2011) than for China (10.8% and 15.6%) because Brazil exports more raw materials to China, which incorporates them into its exports, see: OECD (Organization for Economic Cooperation and Development), CAF (Corporacion Andina de Fomento) and CEPAL (2016), *Latin American Economic Outlook* (2016), *Towards a New Partnership with China*.
4 We must beware of the averages, the dispersion around the average is much higher in Latin American emerging countries than in advanced countries. Large firms, especially subsidiaries of transnational corporations, have productivity levels close to those in advanced countries, while average productivity and growth may be low. When firms are broken down into four groups (large, medium, small and very small), and their average productivity is compared to the corresponding groups in the United States, indexed 100 for each group, the productivity gap is not very large in the large group (it could be added that the productivity of transnational corporations is generally higher than that of national firms, except for special cases). But it increases from the medium group to the small and very small ones (where informal employment is concentrated). Comparable results obtained with respect to labor income show that dispersion is very important. OECD-Cepal (2012), *Perspectives économiques de l'Amérique latine, transformation de l'Etat et développement*.
5 The relative weight of manufacturing is declining at the national level in favor of natural resources and low productivity services. The profitability of capital in the large industrial companies has been falling since the beginning of 2010 in Brazil, that is to say before the decline in the price of raw materials according to the CEMEC studies (see all CEMEC reports at http://ibmec.org.br/cemec/notas-cemec/). This phenomenon can be observed even in countries that have opted for the export of assembled manufactured goods insofar as their domestic market-oriented industry is becoming less and less competitive.
6 However, the *remessas* (monetary remittances of emigrant workers in the United States) play the role of raw materials from which they are relatively deprived. In Mexico, *remessas* amounted to $ 26 billion in 2016 and, combined with foreign direct investment inflows, both "balanced" the trade balance of industrial goods with a slight deficit and the current account deficit, increasing international reserves. Until Trump became President of the United States, they favored an appreciation of their national currencies against the dollar, much like raw materials in Brazil.
7 The de-industrialization of an emerging country is said to be early in relation to the de-industrialization affecting some advanced countries when the per capita income at the beginning of this process corresponds to half that of the advanced countries when their de-industrialization begins. De-industrialization involves not only the relative and absolute decline of industrial jobs, and the destruction of part of the industrial fabric, but also notably the production of low-end products.

References

Baldwin R. (2016), *The Great convergence, Information, Technology end the New globalization*, Harvard University press.

Fajnzylber F. (1980), Industrializacion e internationalizacion de la America Latina, Fondo de Cultura Económica, Mexico.

Hiratuka; Sarti (2016), « Relações econômicas entre Brasil e China: análise dos fluxos de comércio e investimento direto estrangeiro », Revista Tempo do Mundo, Brasil, IPEA, vol 2 n° 1, 2016, pp.83–98.

Nassif A., Feijo, C., and Araujo, E. (2015), Structural change and economic development: Is Brazil catching up or falling behind? *Cambridge Journal of Economics*, vol 39, pp. 1307–1332.

OECD (Organization for Economic Cooperation and Development), CAF (Corporacion Andina de Fomento) and CEPAL (2016), Latin American Economic Outlook (2016), *Towards a New Partnership with China*.

Rifkin J. (2016), *La nouvelle société du coût marginal zéro, L'internet des objets, l'émergence des communaux collaboratifs et l'éclipse du capitalisme*, édition Babel.

Romero Tellaeche J. A. (2014), *Los limites al crescimiento economico de Mexico*, El Colegio de Mexico, Universidad national autonoma de Mexico.

Sassen S. (1991), *The Global City*, New York, London, Tokyo Priceton University Press.

Veltz P. (2017), La société hyper-industrielle, le nouveau capitalisme productif, édition du Seuil.

3 Lula's economic model and post-neoliberalism in Brazil

Pedro Chadarevian

The crisis of the conservative Agenda[1]

Economic liberalism, a broad program of government which proposed the modernization of the productive structure through incentives to private initiative[2], failed to fulfill its main objectives in Brazil. The application, if less strict than in other Latin American countries, of the guidelines recommended by the Washington Consensus – trade liberalization, privatization, financial liberalization, flexible labor market and fiscal discipline in the management of public accounts – resulted in an unprecedented deregulation of the economy, producing strong macroeconomic instabilities that hit the country by the early years of the last decade. The legacy of that model, which succeeded in an extraordinary way in stabilizing inflation, was followed by controversial policies, increasing considerably the external vulnerability of our economy, unemployment and violence, and the denationalization of the industrial sector without the expected improvement in the competitiveness of Brazilian companies abroad.

The growing distrust in the economic efficiency of this conservative agenda fed the desire for a rupture, especially in the wake of the global crises that followed over the years 1990 and 2000. The last of these crises, the Great Recession which started in 2007-2008, reaching the heart of the system, the US, and its key sector, the financial one, ended up legitimizing the trial started in different countries with the adoption of heterodox economic policies. In Latin America, the challenge to neoliberalism and the pressure for a change reached its peak in the early 2000s, given the depth of the economic crisis then registered in the subcontinent, particularly in Venezuela, Ecuador and Argentina, where political instability accelerated the introduction of new economic policies[3]. In Brazil, the adoption of a hard "macroeconomic tripod" after the devaluation of the real beginning of 1999, lead the country to years of stagnation with high unemployment (Bresser Pereira, 2007). The answer to the dissatisfaction of civil society with the model's inability to promote economic growth and social justice is embodied in the election of the leftist leader Luiz Inacio Lula da Silva in 2002[4].

After noting the failure of the conservative agenda, we propose here to describe the transition process then in course for a new development model in Brazil. The research will take place in two dimensions. On the one hand, we will seek to locate in the recent debate of economic ideas the central features of the new model, described especially by those authors who identify themselves with the new-development project. On the other hand, we analyze the nature of the model, specifically in terms of the likely points of break with neoliberalism, relying on instruments of the French school of regulation, given its contribution to the understanding of the transition periods for new forms of capitalism.

After identifying these elements, we will try to compare them to contemporary Brazilian reality, in order to observe breaks from the standard financial-liberal led accumulation regime which has characterized the economy since the early 1990s at least. This will be done through a summary of the main authors linked to the 'new developmentalist' agenda, official statements and government documents containing the description of the recent economic policy, and macroeconomic and financial indicators of the country. This analytical strategy will illustrate the evolution of institutional forms that characterize the regimes of accumulation – monetary regime, wage relation, State, competitive regime and international regime – in order to pinpoint more precisely the moment that characterizes the change from a financial-liberal led accumulation regime for a national-developmental one.

A new regime of accumulation in Brazil?

The French theory of regulation seeks to highlight the political, economic and institutional elements able to characterize the different forms of capitalism that can take place throughout its historical evolution, as well as their different growth and accumulation patterns. Essentially, it highlights five categories of analysis, called institutional forms that guide in understanding the nature of a regime of accumulation. These are: the monetary regime, the form of the state, the type of wage relation, the shape of the competition and the international insertion pattern (Boyer, 2004). Let's see more in detail each of these institutional forms and look at how they can guide us in the interpretation of the Brazilian development path of paradigm shift from 2003 till 2016, as summarized in Table 3.1.

From the view point of the regulation theory, the monetary regime has prominence in configuring a pattern of accumulation (Aglietta, Orléan, 1982). Money is the central institution in the regulation and includes a set of variables, among which stands out variables such as liquidity, credit and interest rates. Given that, until recently, the autonomy of the Brazilian government to change these variables was conditional on the currency stabilization objectives, regulationist authors tended to focus on the characterization of our model as a financial led accumulation regime (Miguel Bruno, 2008; Saludjian, 2007). More recently, the changes implemented in the interest rate policy – whose real base rate for scrolling purposes of public debt has been gradually reduced, and afterwards brought benefits to borrowers in the private sector, especially

Table 3.1 Comparing the most important manifestations of institutional forms in the liberal-rentier and national-development growth regimes in Brazil

Institutional form	Type of accumulation regime	
	Liberal-rentier	*National-developmental*
Monetary regime	• Restrictive monetary policy; • High interest rate regime subjected to inflation targeting; • Market–driven, strict monetary supply submitted to independent Central Bank approval.	• Expansionary monetary policy; • Interest rate unrelated to the regime of inflation targets and linked to other macroeconomic goals; • Monetary supply under government control, and performed by the Central Bank together with the Ministry of Finance.
Wage regime	• "Liberal, Post–Fordist"; • Lack of wage policy; • Concentration of income and wealth stimulated; • Chronic informality; • Flexible labor relations.	• "Interventionist, Post–Fordist"; • Active wage policy, combined with universal mechanisms of social assistance; • Income concentration reduced, war on informality; • Generalization of wage relations; • Incentives for formal labor force and full employment.
State	• Government expenses submitted to fiscal rigor strategy; • Public employment in retreat; • State Investments in retreat; • Increased tax burden to finance spending cuts and rising public debt.	• Countercyclical spending policy to revive the economy; • Redemption of public administration; • Resumption of state investments and major infrastructure projects; • Increased tax collection system efficiency, with stable tax burden and indebtedness.
Competition regime	• Oligopolistic, with incentives for participation of foreign capital; • Nonexistent regulatory apparatus.	• Oligopolistic, with incentives for participation of the national capital; • Strengthening the existing regulatory apparatus.
External insertion	• Submitted to the interests of foreign creditors; • According to the existing comparative advantages; • Free trade; • Absence of stimulus to internationalization.	• Brazil becomes creditor of international funding agencies; • Comparative advantages reinforced by state support; • Protectionism for strategic sectors; • Various stimuli for capital internationalization.

nationals – have led some authors to point to a trend of revision in the monetary regime (Marques-Pereira, 2012), while others remain skeptical of the reach of most recent changes in economic policies (Araújo et al., 2012).

To some extent, therefore, it could be said that changes in the components of the monetary regime (currency, credit, interest rate) at the same time anticipate and shape the economic process, leading it into a new trajectory. In the case of the Brazilian economy, there is a clear sign of easing already at the end of the first term (2003-2006) of the Lula government, when he enhanced the long-term credit channels for the production system, and heavily subsidized interest rates through the BNDES (the national development bank). At the same time, the money supply expanded to facilitate access to the final consumer credit through slight reductions in the prime rate and the pressure exerted by state banks to decrease spreads. Therefore, it is evident in this period, especially the loosening of inflation targeting, inserting, albeit in a veiled way in the first place, other macroeconomic objectives linked to the management of monetary policy[5].

It is known however that currency injections in the production system do not necessarily bring real impacts (which depend on the way it is constituted, and especially distributed) on the purchasing power of households. It is for this reason that the easing of monetary restrictions in a predominantly liberal regime only makes sense if we consider this process in relation to the evolution of the other institutional forms.

The second institutional form that we will discuss, the competition pattern of the accumulation regime, deals with the predominant pattern in the market structure, namely the degree of monopolization of the economy and the level of state intervention to correct any distortions. It seems clear that, in this regard, Brazil was undergoing a major transformation compared with the previous period, which was consecrated by the primacy of the free market and high dependence on foreign capitals. In contrast to this view, the Brazilian government encouraged several mechanisms, the strengthening of national, private and state capital, forming an industrial policy that resulted in an increased share of large domestic conglomerates in the most diverse segments of the Brazilian economy. There are also elements of this transformation in the competition form in the interruption of privatizations and in the resumption of state investment in diverse sectors of infrastructure through policies such as the Growth Acceleration Program (*Programa de Aceleração do Crescimento*, PAC), to the extent that they stimulate the private sector participation in the economy.

Now let us look in more detail to the new credit policy championed by BNDES, as it was a decisive factor in the new configuration of capitalist competition in the country. By that time, the policy of credit concessions observed, in addition to an important change in volume (which quadrupled in the period, reaching R$ 155 billion in 2012), a regionalization trend (towards the marginalized North and Northeast areas) and a revision in the size of the beneficiary firms (for the benefit of micro and small enterprises). From the sectorial point of view, the highlight is the machinery and equipment chain, which enjoyed special lines of funding from 2003, totaling more than R$ 50 billion in 2010[6].

Critics point out, however, that the new industrial policy did not result in the desired effect, in that the impacts on investments stand below what is needed to put the economy on a path of rapid growth. Indeed, gross fixed capital formation, a major aggregate investment indicator pointed in 2014 to a cooling of the boom observed in the mid-2000s. This decline can be attributed to a wide range of factors, all determinants to the level of investment in an economy in transition to developmental accumulation regime, however, not entirely free from the shackles of the finance-led regime. On the one hand, one can cite the long duration of the external crisis, which affects the business expectations, in that it restricts the global demand and alters the relative prices of inputs for the national productive sector. On the other hand, although there was a significant reduction in basic interest rates, speculative allocation still remained attractive[7].

Nevertheless, here again the signs indicate a major transformation, with the configuration of a competition regime tailored to the needs of the new model: the balanced supply of an expanding domestic market and the ability to face increasingly competitive foreign rivals, given that throughout the period the country did not openly question liberalism in international trade relations and regulations established by the WTO. Note, therefore, as in a developmental type of accumulation regime central planning is a very important element of the model, whose configuration shall be reported below.

Although subject to monetary and commercial objectives likewise in any capitalist economy, the state category is a central institution in the debates on regimes of accumulation in regulationist tradition and it can take a variety of forms in different national models around the globe.[8] The composition of classes inside of it as well as its ability to intervene in the economy are some of the variables that emanate from this relationship and to which we turn now in our analysis. In Brazil, one could clearly state that we were facing a new social pact, in which the state became caterer to the demands of sectors previously excluded, such as trade unions, minorities, as well as some fractions of the national bourgeoisie. On the other hand, the minimum state of liberal conception looked definitely outdated at the time in Brazil, especially thanks to the financial recovery, by means of the flexibility of the primary surplus targets and the interruption of the privatization program.[9]

The central variable on which focuses the analytical perspective of regulation concerning the state form is spending or tax policy. In this sense, there were both quantitative and qualitative changes in government revenue and expenditure. From a quantitative point of view, there were clearly expansions in the volume of funds injected by the State in the Brazilian economy, especially in the form of infrastructure projects, as well as direct involvement through state-owned enterprises, re-capitalized over the last three governments. Here equally important was the interruption in the decline trajectory of civil service, thanks to the resumption of a more active role of the state in the period[10]. With respect to qualitative aspects, efficiency in state management and tax collection mechanisms, coupled with the relief in the public accounts caused by reducing the financial burden of public debt, amplified significantly the Union's budget in recent years.

Let us now turn to the evolution of distributive conflict between capital and labor that determines the institutional form of wage relation. The new dynamics of accumulation centered on the domestic market associated with the implementation of distributive mechanisms allowed a reversal in the trend of previous periods clearly unfavorable to workers. A good illustration of the wage relation can be obtained through the inequality indicators, in that they measure how the surplus is being divided among income groups within a country. In the tables below we clearly see two movements in the largest economies in Latin America. First (Table 3.2) we see worsening inequalities as a result of the proliferation of the conservative agenda of the 1990s in the subcontinent. These economies become then extremely vulnerable after a decade of combined debt crisis, in many cases, and hyperinflationary outbreaks. Rapid liberal shift in the management of economic policy resulted in a worsening of the distributive framework in these countries.

In a second phase (Table 3.3) we clearly observe that the largest reductions in inequality following the crisis of neoliberalism in the region is given exactly in countries that have implemented development strategies in response to the accumulation regime inability to promote distributive justice - Venezuela, Argentina and Brazil – which established the most efficient mechanisms of income distribution. It seems clear that a fair allocation of resources does not occur without direct government interference to avoid concentration movements (Montecino, 2011). In the markedly more liberal period, when the surplus widened due to high commodity prices, it did not necessarily benefit equitably between the classes: it was directed primarily to the established economic elites. With the advent of the new developmental regime, wage-capital ratio changes, leading to distributive policies in a context of new correlation of

Table 3.2 Evolution of inequality between 1992 and 2002

Country	1992			2002			Var.
	Upper 20%	Bottom 20%	Inequality	Upper 20%	Bottom 20%	Inequality	
	(a)	(b)	(a)/(b)	(a)	(b)	(a)/(b)	
Colombia	56,7	3,7	15,3	64,1	1,9	33,7	18,4
Argentina	50,7	4,6	11,0	57,5	2,8	20,5	9,5
Venezuela	47,7	5,1	9,4	53,2	3,3	16,1	6,8
Brazil	57,6	2,5	23,0	63,4	2,3	27,6	4,5
Mexico	56,0	4,1	13,7	54,8	4,4	12,5	−1,2

Source: World Bank

forces, a more balanced distribution of the generated surplus was thus allowed. The decline of wages observed in sharp liberalized times – with a profusion of informal forms of subordination of labor to capital – has gone up to a redemption period of wage negotiations, including occupational categories historically marginalized, such as domestic servants in Brazil.

Finally, in regulationist theory, the international insertion system is the institutional form that describes the country's position in the international division of labor, as well as the variables of foreign and trade policy mobilized to promote it. In Brazil, after the subordinate and limited insertion that led to severe external vulnerability in the 1990s, a new international insertion strategy was put in place, with incentives for the internationalization of national capitals, recovery of agro-business and conformation of new blocks of economic integration, as an alternative to existing global and regional organizations, until recently under strong control of North America and Europe. In fact, the capital internationalization strategy is illustrative of the new compounds, the Schumpeterian path, moving the current dynamic accumulation in the country. The search for new markets abroad was perhaps the most emblematic element of the transition phase in the Brazilian economy. Table 3.4 illustrates this process, in which we highlight the recent performance of developing economies, occupying the top rank of countries that have seen the most rapid increase in the number of its companies among the largest in the world.

More recently, in the last act of this conversion on the external insertion strategy, the Brazilian government, in order to avoid the perverse effect of an exchange rate overvaluation of the so-called 'monetary tsunami' caused a mini-devaluation of the currency, which now fluctuates around R$3.00 per dollar[11]. The new level is close to the claims of the industrial lobby supported by academic studies[12]. Maintaining a high purchasing power of the national currency allowed economic benefits that outweighed the costs of an unfavorable balance of services. And that is mainly given for three reasons: firstly it guaranteed access to essential capital goods imported for this new phase of accumulation; secondly it made available to the national bourgeoisie the purchase of assets that promoted the internationalization of Brazilian capital; thirdly, even with relatively overvalued exchange rate, the market control exercised by Brazil of

Table 3.3 Evolution of Gini coefficients at selected countries

Country	Starting point*	End**	Var.
Venezuela	0,500	0,397	−0,103
Argentina	0,578	0,492	−0,086
Brazil	0,634	0,550	−0,084
Colombia	0,601	0,545	−0,056
Mexico	0,514	0,481	−0,033

* Starting point in 2002 for whole countries.
** End in 2011, except Mexico (2010).

Source: ECLAC

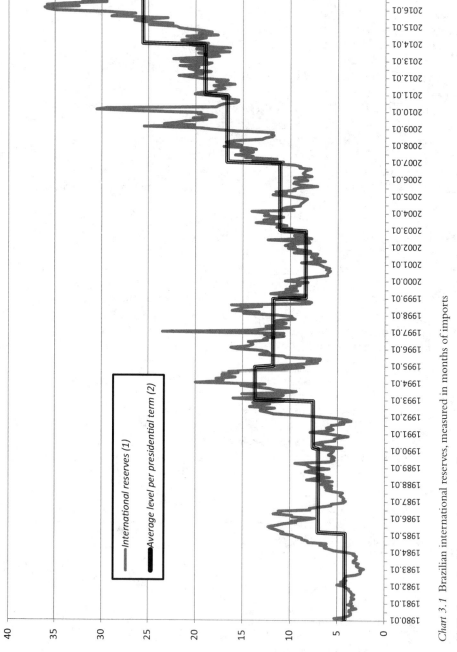

Chart 3.1 Brazilian international reserves, measured in months of imports

(1) Net international reserves, in months of imports.
(2) Average by government mandate.
Source: IPEA

Table 3.4 Number of listed companies among the 1,000 largest in the world, by country

Country	2000	2012	Var. %
India	7	27	285,7%
China	28	68	142,9%
Russia	10	23	130,0%
Hong Kong	16	26	62,5%
Switzerland	17	26	52,9%
Brazil	**10**	**15**	**50,0%**
South Korea	22	30	36,4%
Australia	18	20	11,1%
Mexico	9	10	11,1%
Canada	34	35	2,9%
France	42	43	2,4%
Sweden	16	16	0,0%
Netherlands	16	15	−6,3%
USA	354	292	−17,5%
Taiwan	17	14	−17,6%
Germany	40	31	−22,5%
Great Britain	65	50	−23,1%
Japan	139	99	−28,8%
Spain	20	14	−30,0%
Italy	25	10	−60,0%

Source: Forbes Magazine

exportable commodities (metals and food) generated high balance of trade, offsetting the imbalances.

From the point of view of the balance of payments, the trajectory of the international insertion of the Brazilian economy appeared to be quite sustainable, despite some reservations about its quality, as we will outline in the final section of the chapter. Some indicators support this observation. Not only the absolute level of international reserves is still very high at present, which demonstrates the advantageous position of the country in the international scenario, both in the market for goods and services, as well as in the capital ones. But also in relative terms the reserves have kept pace with the expansion of foreign trade. A key indicator in this respect is given by the number of months of imports that fits the volume of reserves of a country. Note the chart below that in early 2013 this volume amounted to more than 20 months of imports. The black bars on the graph indicate that in the last three governments reserves have been growing to reach record highs. The importance of this analysis is explained by the alert triggered whenever you start a rapid decrease of movement in the indicator because it tends to coincide with phases of large external turbulence or speculative attack on the national currency, causing a drain of resources and a crisis in the balance of payments.

From boom to 'steady state'

Suddenly, the favorable environment, both external and internal, which had allowed Brazil to remain in a cycle of growth with social inclusion, was reversed. Many have emphasized solely the material dimension of the current economic stagnation[13]. Among them is certainly the exhaustion of credit expansion and redistributive policies impacts- income, real and available, no longer increases at the necessary rhythm as to promote high growth rates. Externally, it is also a fact that the decline in commodity prices negatively affected the economic performance, because of accumulated trade deficits. However, it is also important to take into account the political dimension of this process. If these last years the Brazilian economy had been sustained mainly by household consumption and government spending it would not have been for a lack of incentives for private sector investment that originates the current downturn, as we saw earlier. The proximity of the 2014 electoral scenario, which inexorably led to another Workers' Party term in power, caused complex reactions in the right, which makes up an important part of the national bourgeoisie.

On the one hand, industrialists demanded (and obtained) a devaluation of the currency to improve the competitiveness of products manufactured in the country. On the other hand, rentiers demanded (and also obtained!) a change in the loose monetary policy by alleging that loose fiscal surplus targets affect the confidence of private investors.[14]

Paradoxically, the scenario resembled an investment paralysis, with frequent complaints from the business classes regarding the economic and social policy, always readily transmitted in the dominant media outlets[15]. It is still early to assess the economic consequences of this shift in economic policy of the 2nd term of Dilma Rousseff, but some of them could easily be noted.

First, inflation. Due to the increasing economic dependence on imported components, the devaluation tended to endear manufactured products sold in the internal markets. Added to this is the review of government-controlled prices, to contribute to the fiscal effort. Finally, an unprecedented drought in south Brazil raised food prices. In 2015 an 11% inflation was reported, the highest level in many years.

Second, the precariousness of work. Despite all the advances, the current scenario is negative for the working class. The last years represented a setback in both quantitative (increased unemployment) and qualitative terms (laws granting greater flexibility in labor relations have been approved in Congress since 2015).

Concluding remarks

The Brazilian economy is at a crossroads, for both material and political-ideological reasons. The outcome of the struggle between progressive and conservative forces that now divide the country is absolutely unpredictable, but it is what will set the tone of economic policy in the coming years.

Despite this adverse and complex scenario, the decade that opened the new millennium was clearly a period of transition towards a new phase of capitalism, of which Latin America in particular emerged as a laboratory of innovative policy experiences, socially and economically, in response to the legitimacy crisis of neoliberalism.

The theoretical perspective of the French regulation school allowed us to place the recent trajectory of Brazil in an advanced transition period toward a pattern of post-neoliberal type development, given the depth of the changes observed at the time in the group of constituent institutional forms of accumulation regime in recent years.

We identified, however, reminiscences of the rentier-liberal model also strongly intertwined in institutional forms, a proof that the rupture was not totally accomplished by the end of the Workers' Party government in 2016. The allocation of a portion of the surplus in the financial market, the consumption of luxury and land speculation, subtract large sums that could find a more productive application, such as the innovative processes, and public services in general, both aspects essential to productivity developments in the country.

Notes

1 When I finished writing and prepare to submit this manuscript a drastic political scenario took place in Brazil, as the elected president, leftist Dilma Rousseff, has been temporarily suspended from the government by means of a controverted impeachment procedure. The interim government assumed with a radical conservative agenda that seemed banned away just some months ago. Leaked audios and independent journalist investigation reveal a infamous plan involving the judiciary, the opposition parties and the corporate media to insufflate the people against the ruling Workers' Party and put an end to its 13-year long experience in power. That is to say, a coup-d'état – although, not of a classic kind, but a so-called soft, parliamentary one, similar in its mechanics to those that interrupted progressive democratic regimes in Paraguay and Honduras recently. The fact that the putschist government, inaugurated in May 2016, worked hardly since its first moments to dismantle the social, economic and international legacies of their predecessors only reinforces the point we are trying to demonstrate here. Brazil was effectively undergoing a regime chance. The conservative parties, unable to win the 2014 presidential elections, forced the nationalist popular government out of power, in order to restore their elitist open market neoliberal economic strategy.
2 For a description of this program, see the evaluation by one of his main mentors (Franco, 1995).
3 For a chronological overview of the process of political and economic transformations in Latin America in this period, see García Guerrero (2010). For a critical review of the current process of comparative breakdown among the largest Latin American economies, see Salama (2012).
4 While arguing here for the hypothesis of a change in the pattern of accumulation it does not mean that we will not point out the limits and contradictions of this "new" model. We shall however take distances from those who see the new developmental project just as a new guise of speech and liberal economic policy, not being able to promote effective change in the development paradigm. In this regard, see Castelo Branco (2009); and Filgueras et al. (2010).
5 As some authors point out under the new developmental model the regime of inflation targeting becomes subordinated to the economic growth and full employment strategies.

See Oureiro (2012). Which is not to say that the current monetary management allows inflationary acceleration beyond the stipulated limits of fluctuation of the price index, as shown by the Central Bank's operations started in early 2013, when it began raising the benchmark interest rate after a long sequence fall in response to localized increases in consumer prices.
6 Another action aimed to stimulate the national productive sector consisted of a series of tax relief measures to the productive sector, initially as countercyclical strategy, but that would become later the Plano Brasil Maior, during the first Dilma Rousseff mandate.
7 Various indications show the trend of speculative allocation of wealth especially in the financial form by large national private corporations as pointed out, among others, Nakano (2012). Add to this the negative trend, according to Unesco, of the last years of the 2000s in the absorption of researchers by the private sector of the Brazilian economy, considered a central proxy for the innovation capacity and productivity of the national enterprises.
8 See Robert Boyer, 2004b.
9 In this regard, it is worth clarifying that if in fact the complete alienation of state-owned enterprises ceased to occur since the election of Lula, partial divestitures, public-private partnerships and long-term concessions to the private sector were widely adopted. The State, however, remained present in any of these ways, although indirectly, unlike the liberal period, when the general approach was to dispose of state assets.
10 Specifically, between 1998 and 2002 there was a reduction of 8.7 % in total civilian federal active servants; meanwhile, in the period between 2003 and 2012 functionalism expanded 18.9%, according to official data.
11 This move had been anticipated by one of the chief architects of the current economic policy, Nelson Barbosa, in a 2010 paper in which the former Minister for Development together with other government analysts defend the need to situate the exchange rate slightly closer to the equilibrium level (representing the rate that would maximize, according to his model, economic growth) without the devaluation that would undermine the country's inflation targets (Barbosa et al., 2010).
12 An important group of economists defends a exchange rate of R$ 2.70 to the US dollar as a price closer to equilibrium (Araújo, Gala, 2012; Bresser Pereira, 2012).
13 Technically, one cannot talk of economic crisis in 2014, given the situation still close to full employment in the country.
14 Interestingly, the confidence of foreign investors does not seem to have been affected. In 2014, Brazil was the world's fourth largest destination of foreign capital.
15 An impressive result of this effort to mobilize reactionary sectors (parties, associations and the dominant media) was the mass demonstrations organized by the right wing, requesting minimal state and seeking to overthrow the government.

References

Aglietta, Michel, and Orléan, André. *A violência da moeda*. São Paulo: Brasiliense, 1990 [1982].
Barbosa, Nelson. An Unusual Arrangement: The Brazilian Economy During the First Lula Administration. *International Journal of Politics, Culture and Society*, v. 19, n. 3–4, 2008.
Barbosa, Nelson, and de Souza, José Antonio Pereira. A inflexão do governo Lula: política econômica, crescimento e distribuição de renda. In Emir Sader and Marco Aurélio Garcia (orgs.), *Brasil: entre o Passado e o Futuro*. São Paulo: Boitempo, 2010.
Belluzzo, Luiz Gonzaga, and de Almeida, Júlio Gomes. *Depois da Queda: A Economia Brasileira da Crise da Dívida aos Impasses do Real*. Rio de Janeiro: Civilização Brasileira, 2002.
Benjamin, Cesar, et al. *Visões da crise*. Rio de Janeiro: Contraponto, 1998.
Boyer, Robert. *Théorie de la régulation: Les fondamentaux*. Paris: La Découverte, 2004a.

Boyer, Robert. *Une théorie du capitalisme est-elle possible?* Paris: Odile Jacob, 2004b.
Branco, Rodrigo Castelo. O novo-desenvolvimentismo e a decadência ideológica do estruturalismo latino-americano. *Oikos*, v. 8, n. 1, 2009.
Bresser-Pereira, Luiz Carlos. O novo desenvolvimentismo. *Folha de São Paulo*, September 19, 2004a.
Bresser-Pereira, Luiz Carlos. Proposta de desenvolvimento para o Brasil. *Revista de Economia Política*, v. 24, n. 4, 2004b.
Bresser-Pereira, Luiz Carlos. New Developmentalism and Conventional Orthodoxy Compared. Notes for the oral presentation in the panel *Neoliberalism in Latin America: Successes and Failures. XXIV LASA Congress*, Dallas, March 27, 2003.
Bresser-Pereira, Luiz Carlos. *Macroeconomia da estagnação: Crítica da ortodoxia convencional no Brasil pós-1994*. São Paulo: Editora 34, 2007.
Bruno, Miguel. Régulation et Croissance Économique au Brésil après la libéralisation. *Revue de la régulation*, n. 3/4, 2008.
Chadarevian, Pedro C. Contra os dogmas, mas sem apelos radicais. *Valor Econômico*, March 12, 2009.
Chadarevian, Pedro C. Un développement économique et social sans précédent. *Questions Internationales*, n. 55, maio-junho, 2012.
Coutinho, Luciano, and Sarti, Fernando. A política industrial e a retomada do desenvolvimento. In Mariano Laplane, Luciano Coutinho and Célio Hiratuka (orgs.), *Internacionalização e desenvolvimento da indústria no Brasil*. São Paulo: Editora UNESP, 2003.
Coutinho, Luciano, et al. O desafio da construção de uma inserção externa dinamizadora. In *Ciclo de Seminários – Brasil em Desenvolvimento*. Rio de Janeiro: UFRJ, 2003.
de Almeida Magalhães, João Paulo. *Estratégia de longo prazo para o Brasil*. Rio de Janeiro: Papel & Virtual, 2000.
de Almeida Magalhães, João Paulo. *Nova estratégia de desenvolvimento para o Brasil*. Rio de Janeiro: Paz e Terra, 2005.
de Almeida Magalhães, João Paulo. *O que fazer depois da crise*. São Paulo: Contexto, 2009.
da Conceição Tavares, Maria, and Fiori, José Luís. *(Des)ajuste Global e Modernização Conservadora*. São Paulo: Editora Paz e Terra, 1996.
da Conceição Tavares, Maria, de Andrade, Manuel Correia, and Rodrigues Pereira, Rodrigues Pereira. *Seca e poder: entrevista com Celso Furtado*. São Paulo: Perseu Abramo, 1998.
Filgueiras, Luiz. *História do Plano Real*. São Paulo: Boitempo, 2000.
Filgueras, Luiz, Pinheiro, Bruno, Philigret, Celeste, and Balanco, Paulo. Modelo Liberal-Periférico e bloco de poder: política econômica e dinâmica macroeconômica nos governos Lula. In *Os anos Lula: contribuições para um balanço crítico, 2003–2010*. Rio de Janeiro: Garamond, 2010.
Furtado, Celso. Brasil: opções futuras. *Revista de Economia Contemporânea*, v. 3, n. 2, 1999a.
Furtado, Celso. *O longo amanhecer – reflexões sobre a formação do Brasil*. São Paulo: Paz e Terra, 1999b.
Furtado, Celso. *Introdução ao desenvolvimento: enfoque histórico-estrutural*. São Paulo: Paz e Terra, 2000.
Furtado, Celso. Quando o futuro chegar. In Ignacy Sachs (org.), *Brasil: um século de transformações*. São Paulo: Cia. das Letras, 2001.
Furtado, Celso. The Political Factor in the Formation of Brazil. In Alberto Carvalho da Silva et al. (eds.), *Brazil: dilemmas and challenges*. São Paulo: Edusp, 2002.
Furtado, Celso. *Em busca de novo modelo: reflexões sobre a crise contemporânea*. Rio de Janeiro: Paz e Terra, 2002.
Furtado, Celso. *Discurso proferido na entrega do Prêmio Darcy Ribeiro de intelectual do ano*. 2003.

Furtado, Celso. Receita para o crescimento. *Jornal da Unicamp*, September 27, 2004.

Gonçalves, Reinaldo. *Vagão Descarrilado: o Brasil e o Futuro da Economia Global*. Rio de Janeiro: Record, 2002.

Guerrero, Bernardo García. *La nueva izquierda. El poder de la utopía*. Bogotá: Aurora, 2010.

Loyola, Maria A. (org.). *Celso Furtado entrevistado por Aspásia Camargo e Maria A. Loyola*. Rio de Janeiro: EdUERJ, 2002.

Mantega, Guido. O BNDES e o novo ciclo de desenvolvimento. *Revista do BNDES*, 2005.

Marques-Pereira, Jaime. La monnaie, la politique et la possibilité d'un mode de développement à nouveau fondé sur le marché intérieur au Brésil et en Argentine. *Revue de la régulation*, n. 11, 2012.

Nakano, Yoshioki. A grande recessão: oportunidade para o Brasil alcançar os países desenvolvidos. *Revista de Administração de Empresas*, v. 52, n. 2, 2012.

Nakatani, Paulo, and Oliveira, Fabrício A. Política Econômica Brasileira de Collor a Lula: 1990–2007. In Rosa Maria Marques and Mariana Ribeiro J. Ferreira (eds.), *O Brasil sob a nova ordem*. São Paulo: Saraiva, 2010.

Oliveira, Fabrício A., and Nakatani, Paulo. The Brazil Under Lula: A Balance of Contradictions. *Monthly Review*, v. 58, n. 9, 2007.

Paulani, Leda. *Brasil Delivery. Servidão Financeira e Estado de Emergência Econômico*. São Paulo: Boitempo Editorial, 2008.

Pochmann, Marcio. *Desenvolvimento e perspectivas novas para o Brasil*. São Paulo: Cortez, 2010.

Saad-Filho, Alfredo. New Dawn or False Start in Brazil? The Political Economy of Lula's Election. *Historical Materialism*, v. 11, n. 1, 2003.

Sader, Emir, and Gentilli, Pablo (orgs.). *Pós-neoliberalismo: As políticas sociais e o Estado democrático*. São Paulo: Paz e Terra, 1995.

Saludjian, Alexis. Le Régime d'accumulation dans le Cône Sud-Americain depuis les années 1990. Crise de régulation ou crise d'accumulation ? *Revue de la régulation*, n. 1, 2007.

Sicsú, João, de Paula, Luiz Fernando, and Michel, Renault. Por que novo-desenvolvimentismo? *Jornal dos Economistas*. Janeiro: UFRJ, 2005.

Sicsú, João, de Paula, Luiz Fernando, and Michel, Renault. Por que novo-desenvolvimentismo? *Revista de Economia Política*, n. 4, v. 108, 2007.

Sicsú, João, de Paula, Luiz Fernando, and Michel, Renault (orgs.). *Novo-desenvolvimentismo: um projeto nacional de crescimento com eqüidade social*. Rio de Janeiro: Fundação Konrad Adenauer, 2005.

Théret, Bruno, and de Souza Braga, José Carlos. *Regulação econômica e globalização*. Campinas: Unicamp, 1998.

Totti, Paulo. Um Keynesiano pouco ortodoxo. *Valor Econômico*, August 27, 2010.

Part II
The mechanisms of change

4 Money, politics and the possibility of a mode of regulation based on the internal market[1]

Jaime Marques Pereira

In the 2000s, Argentina and Brazil experienced a marked acceleration of growth through a simultaneous increase in domestic and international demand and exports – above all primary goods but also manufactured ones, though to a lesser extent. The dynamism of consumption observable in both countries between 2003 and 2014 contrasts with the two preceding decades when near-stagnation linked to high volatility. This chapter analyses whether these new data may or may not be considered as the beginning of a transition to a new mode of development with the internal market as the driving role of the growth which it had for half a century under the impetus of a policy of industrialization by import substitution.

The realization of such a scenario is far from clear. Its possibility emerges as a result of a political change brought about by the two countries' financial crisis at the turn of the millennium. On the other hand, the surge in demand and material prices has largely counted. By widening the room for maneuvering in the economic situation, it allowed the victory of presidential candidates opposed to the Washington Consensus leading to a revival of consumption and income redistribution. The debate on the sustainability of this policy particularly raises the question of the tendency of currency overvaluation that may be implied by financial liberalization. Considered as an almost unanimous means of competitive disinflation in the 1990s, many economists see this as a factor that aggravates de-industrialization which the opening up of trade has created and of a competitive exchange rate as a pillar of a so-called neo-developmental strategy. This chapter reflects on the conditions for the adoption of such a strategy and its implementation.

In contrast to the Brazilian real, which appreciated strongly due to interest rates, the Argentine peso has practically retained the level at which it was devalued in 2002 after the collapse of its fixed parity. Nevertheless, in one case as in the other, the deterioration of the external accounts is now questioning the possibility of a continuing rise in consumption. The proposed analysis of this common impasse of economic policies, however, ascribes it to their management of distributive conflicts. The comparison of the two countries in this perspective sets out the political challenges of a neo-developmental strategy on understanding the monetary and exchange rate regimes that break with their purely normative conceptualization which dominates the debate. Their macroeconomic effects are considered as governments' intentional result (which may be erratic) of promises of monetary incomes under an institutional and cognitive framework of the formation of expectations determining changes in investment, financial structure and competitiveness.

This proposal implies an original institutional conception of money which connects its economic functionality as a means of payment to its political and symbolic functionality. The active character of money is then approached as a question of monetary sovereignty, defined as the political expression of the nation by announcing with monetary signs the value of different types of income. This means that the exercise of monetary sovereignty raises, in practice, the problem of a social agreement on their unit of account. This hypothesis is based on the schematization proposed by Bruno Théret (2008) of the interaction between these functional properties or forms of money. This application highlights the role of economic theories in governmental action as a cognitive repository of the formation of expectations resulting from macroeconomic dynamics.

The chapter begins by clarifying this grid of analysis with respect to the limits of a normative approach to political economy to account for the centrality of the monetary and exchange rate regime as an impulse for re-industrialization. It is a justified thus a theoretical device characterizing its role as vector of the institutional changes that condition the competitiveness of the economy as a whole, by the inter-sectoral dynamics linked to the distribution. This centrality is then analyzed in the interaction between the three functional forms of money, successively. First, a generic instability of its symbolic form inherent in the persistent difficulty of obtaining a social agreement on a unit of account common to the various types of income. This structural fragility of the account system reflects the tension existing since the beginning of the twentieth century between the two ideas of nation corresponding to a model of development focused on the exploitation of natural resources or also on industry. The next section brings to light the current mark of the history of chronic crisis on the account system that followed. Its national specificity – the continuity of an oscillation between the two models in Argentina and a search for their conciliation in Brazil – explains the use of opposing monetary doctrines to found a government of expectations that make growth possible through redistribution, nevertheless limited to the demand side in both cases. This bounded redefinition of the political functionality of money implies the permanence of the external insertion which has been established with liberalization and accumulation. The last section reports this blockage to the persistence of creditors to format an economic functionality of the currency which increases the public debt to the detriment of the financing of productive capital and thus the competitiveness. We conclude that the interaction between the functional forms of money is established in the arbitrage between levels of public debt and taxation which constrain distributive trade-offs. Since this arbitrage is parameterized by the equilibrium of the trade balance, it has allowed growth to accelerate while becoming simultaneously its Achilles heel. This issue should be seen as the main factor of an uncertainty of government action that reflects in each of the two countries on the mode of development.

Economic policy and strategies of development: the weight of politics in an institutional conception of money

In the previous decade, economic growth reached an average rate of 7.4% in its best years in Argentina, between 2003 and 2008, and 4.8% in Brazil, between 2004 and 2008 (CEPAL, 2010). The optimism of this period initiated by the deterioration of the current account, which accelerated with the strong recovery of 2010 following the brief recession of three quarters at the turn of 2008–2009. The data presented in the following sections shows that the deleterious effects of de-industrialization could be reduced by the dynamism of the consumption of households contributing to a certain recovery in investment which supported the increase in the production of manufactured goods in both Brazil and Argentina. The external environment has encouraged an increase in their exports, but their imports are also increasing and have reduced the trade surplus since 2007, raising the question of an industrial competitiveness gap likely to jeopardize external and budgetary balances.

The debate on de-industrialization is mainly centered on the threat of excessive specialization in the production of commodities, the so-called Dutch disease. To avoid this scenario, the role of economic policy is held to be determinant on the basis of a vision of gains in industrial competitiveness, derived from the paradigm of market failures, now hegemonic. This view can be contrasted with the theory of the relationship between productivity gains and wage gains in a sectoral representation of the economy put forward in the Marxist and post-Keynesian tradition (Pasinetti, 1981). An analysis of the monetary and exchange rate regime as a focal social field on the redefinition of a mode of regulation and therefore of a regime of accumulation completes this second vision which has been characterized as topical in the case of Brazil in the face of competition from China (Bruno, Halévi et Marques Pereira, 2011).

The centrality of monetary and exchange rate policy

The analysis of market failures stresses that the optimality of the allocation of resources according to the comparative advantages acquired is conditioned to the intervention of the State aiming at the reduction of the negative externalities. This paradigm guides two types of analysis depending on whether market failures are considered in the field of innovation and in terms of volatility or exchange rate setting.

The first type of analysis makes the prognosis that the export gains in the primary sector do not lead to the Dutch disease if, on the one hand, the State puts in place incentives for technological innovation, investment in human capital, and, on the other hand, it has the budgetary capacity to reinforce resilience to the volatility of commodity prices by a higher public expenditure when their decline leads to a recession. This type of analysis by international organizations leads to criticism of the pro-cyclical increase in public spending and the weakness of education policies, observable in Brazil and Argentina (Cardoso and Holland, 2009).

This approach seems inadequate to the many economists who emphasize the macroeconomic centrality of the exchange rate. The analysis proposed by Bresser-Pereira (2009) occupies a notable place in the critique of Brazilian economic policy. It advocates a competitive exchange rate as a pillar of a so-called neo-developmental strategy for middle-income countries. In summary, in a country with high exports of natural resources, the Dutch disease is represented by an exchange rate which, if not regulated, tends to be fixed according to the long-term equilibrium of the current account at a level which hampers the price competitiveness of industrial production even if it uses advanced technology. This is a foreign exchange market failure which must be policy aimed at maintaining it at the level of long-term equilibrium of industrial exchanges. The analysis by the author of the Brazilian case (Bresser-Pereira, 2010), however, highlights the practical difficulty of such a competitive exchange rate policy, given the coalition of interests around what he calls 'cambial populism'. This is characterized by the maintenance of a high interest rate pushing the appreciation of the real exchange rate beyond the current account balance, which favors public debt speculators and employees (by the imported component of their consumption).

The much higher growth of Argentina can certainly be associated with the adoption of such a competitive exchange rate policy. The latter is, moreover, theorized as a genuine policy of development through its effects of expected growth in investment in export goods and in the production of goods exposed to foreign competition through lower dollar labor costs and higher employment/product ratios (Rapetti, 2005). However, we can wonder about the limits of the depreciated exchange rate to counter de-industrialization. The shift from the external trade surplus in Brazil, which had prevailed in the 1990s, to a growing deficit since 2003, is a clear indicator given the equivalent growth in both countries of unit labor weighted by the bilateral exchange rate. This deficit suggests that de-industrialization is much more pronounced in Argentina due to wider and earlier liberalization, initiated in the 1970s, which would have eliminated entire sections of the industrial sector (Salama, 2011). This deficit with its main trading partner would then be all the more inevitable with a growth rate almost twice as high.

An understanding of de-industrialization, which takes into account the sectoral structure of the economy, is important in view of the growing commercial relations with China in foreign trade of both Argentina and Brazil. The threat of worsening de-industrialization that represents China must assess beyond the current data[2] when you consider that its manufacturing power cannot be reduced to much lower wages and a competitive exchange rate, but it also involves the use of an interventionist State of the early development of heavy industry to convert it into a sector of production goods which also contributes to reducing the cost of importing *made in China* products. The productivity gains associated with the sectoral structure of the economy are therefore a fundamental dimension of the challenge posed by the asymmetry of trade between Argentina and Brazil with China (Bruno et al., 2011). China's growing demand for raw materials and foodstuffs will have less and less favorable effects as its competitiveness in higher value-added goods increases. Their prices will be even lower than those of local production because their higher costs in direct labor cannot be offset by lower costs of indirect labor due to the increasing import of production goods from developed countries.

The capacity of public policies to induce a re-industrialization arises in relation to this competition. Of course, it concerns a regulation of openness by the exchange rate and an industrial policy. However, it is not only a question of setting up a technical innovation system, but also of macroeconomic dynamics linked to an inter-sectoral complementarity which implies a parallel evolution of productivity gains and wages in a growth regime driven by the internal market.[3] The following analysis of the characteristics of the recent growth of Argentina and Brazil shows that this condition has been introduced without sufficient investment progression and that this is an endogenous factor of the depletion of current growth patterns resulting from the continuing increase in financial gains induced by public debt. Sustainable growth questions the possibility of a link between distribution and competitiveness, which reiterates its former effectiveness of Fordist-type regulations within the framework of the new international division of labor.

The issue of reducing the deficit in industrial competitiveness raises the question of the possible evolution of productive matrices. Beyond its characteristic technical conditions and its international conditions,[4] the societal conditions of new modalities of the functional distribution of incomes, which determine the accumulation regime, are discussed here. This is a matter of institutional change, as the theory of regulation raises. From this perspective, it is sought to detect whether the new political dynamics underlying economic policies aimed at accelerating growth may or may not allow a redefinition of institutionalized social compromises that would lead to a growth regime based on gains of competitiveness beyond the primary sector. The hypothesis of the centrality of money in the conformation of an economic government of collective action, which is explained later, guides the analysis of the obstacles and the possibility of such institutional change.

The need for an original conceptual framework

The method that is mobilized therefore starts from the premise that the action of monetary and foreign exchange policies is primarily cognitive in that it aims to guide the formation of expectations. The resulting private choices confirm the performative character of the development model and thus of its theory to the observable reality of a mode of development. From this premise, one can deduce that the conjunction between a mode of regulation and a regime of accumulation, by which the concept of mode of development is defined in the theory of regulation, is concretized in the formation of the anticipations ordered by the inter-dependence between functional symbolic, political and economic forms of money. The box below shows the characteristic traits of this triple property of money which is taken from Théret's analysis in order to explain its analytical implications in terms of economic governance.

> ### The three functional states and forms of money
>
> Money is a total social fact by its conditions of existence under three simultaneous states, inherent in the contingent functional forms that its properties take. The unit of account is a state of existence of money by which the actor incorporates a numbered symbolization of the values allowing the fixing of prices. The means of payment is a state of the existence of money which objectifies it as a market good. To these commonly recognized properties of money, is added in this scheme that which gives it a state of established existence. The first two are in fact instituted by the authorities fixing the rules for issuing these means of payment and fixing their convertibility, in particular with those of the rest of the world, and hence the exchange rate regime. These properties cover contingent functional forms – symbolic, economic and political – which are their own and interdependent, and explains money as a total social fact. The means of payment have in exchange and financing a functionality properly economical, associated with the state of money which transforms it in commodity. Their value and their issuance are regulated by a monetary authority which thus fulfills a functionality strictly political because its decisions condition the distributive trade-offs which are, as such, constitutive of the monetary and exchange rate regimes. In its existence as signs of value, money covers a specifically symbolic functionality by defining an account and payment system, making the political community also a monetary community; in so far as their adequacy or, more concretely, that between the social values and the values of the means of payment allows the units of account to be incorporated into the practices of exchange in the same way as language can be.

This definition of money leads one to reconsider its active character on macroeconomic policy in view of the role of the unit of account in fixing relative prices. In the two cases studied here, the unit of account was coupled with a plurality of modes of calculation of values during periods of high inflation, that make it possible to see the rate of mark-up margins corresponding to the objectives and various indices or indexing clauses assets, and even wages. This involves a relative price-fixing procedure whereby the unit of account constituted by the national currency multiplies in payments for the various types of income. The high-inflation regimes that prevailed for almost two decades in both countries were an obvious manifestation of the distributive conflict at work in the establishment of the unit of account itself, but this is also detectable, it will be seen, in current schemes through the impact of the ratio price of financial assets (in this case, Treasury bills) on relative prices.

A first analytical consequence of the account system, beyond the specificity of the two cases analyzed,[5] is that it constitutes a central institutional device of economic regulation. By its interdependence with the other functionalities of money, it defines the monetary conditions on the regularity of the growth regime in the articulation of temporal scales of the formation of expectations. The social acceptance of the account system reflects the long-term prediction of a development model. The monetary and exchange rate regime is, by its macroeconomic effects, a guarantee of the medium-term stability of growth. This guarantee implies its influence on the mode of regulation as regards the temporal coherence which it can confer (or not) on the joint effects of all the institutions. The current values of payment flows and the present values of the financial commitments comply with the accumulation regime.

A second consequence of this societal centrality of money is an analysis of the political economy of coalitions of interest groups considering the social manufacture of economic policy choices as a process of ex-post reconciliation by the distribution of incomes, which arises in particular from the units of account used in fixing the relative prices. The national currency is only the number of the account in the calculation of the expected value for those who have a pricing power. This is a complex monetary power that engages the exercise of political sovereignty in monetary matters. The diagram which follows gives a representation of the centrality attributed to money in the effects of economic government on the collective action on which the conformation of a mode of development depends, as analyzed below.

The exercise of monetary power in the determination of relative prices has a history. The analysis of the interdependence of the functional forms of money in the two countries in question makes it possible to discern the mark of a history of distributive trade-offs on their current monetary and exchange rate regimes. It is therefore necessary to relate to this history the obstacles still present in a reorientation of the regime of accumulation which would reconcile the growth of domestic demand with the preservation of external equilibrium. The difference in the choice of monetary policy and exchange rate reflects the difference between the historical permanence of a search for conciliation of the interest groups in Brazil and, on the contrary, that of their frontal opposition in Argentina.

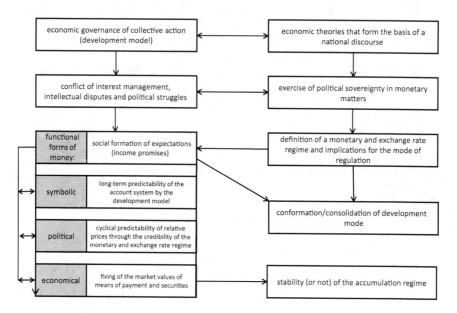

Figure 4.1 Functional forms of money and mode of development

Money at the heart of the tension between development models: uncertainty about symbolic functionality

This tension is rooted in the alternative that elites have faced since the beginning of the twentieth century between two possible modes of development. The enormous expansion of the agro-exporting sector during the second half of the nineteenth century was the source of a substitution of industrial imports which favored a policy of depreciation of the exchange rate raising the exporters' income in national currency. In the first decades of the twentieth century, two representations of the nation were forged. They are expressed in competing discourses which oppose development based solely on the comparative advantages of the primary sector or on the possibility of stimulating it also through industrialization. As a result of the world crisis of 1929, which had halted the demand and prices of exported goods, industrialization by import substitution has become a model of protectionist development. After it was abandoned in the 1990s under the influence of neoliberal criticism of the State, the limits to the accumulation of capital attributable to the excessive concentration of income were reaffirmed in the 2000s with two new parameters defining the current contingency of functional forms of money: a loosening of external constraint and political constraint to a reconfiguration of distributive trade-offs which, as we shall see, remains very partial. At the crossroads of these two new data, the weight of history defines an alternative between a rentier economy model and a development model aimed at reducing the structural deficit in industrial competitiveness and thus making the wage society project viable that had designed the government's industrialization will.

The current symbolic functionality of money is in itself the expression of this story. It holds the redefinition of its political functionality that can be carried out by the governments. They will not be able to solve this inheritance to the point of calling into question the monetary power of the creditors of the State to fix the unit of account of their incomes and hence of all the means of payment defining the economic functionality of money.

The emergence of hyperinflationary crises in the 1990s through the anchoring of exchange and liberalization had not led to any change in the nature of distributive trade-offs, neither in Brazil nor in Argentina. On the contrary, the primacy of financial gains, which had been in place since the 1970s through private external debt and consolidated by public external debt in the 1980s,[6] has been sustained in each of the two countries. On the other hand, the exit from the crises of the exchange anchor will reformulate in both cases the content of the distributive trade-offs by taking advantage of the loosening of external constraint to reconcile a joint progression of wages, transfer incomes, profits and of the financial rent, as set out in the next section. This development reflects a political dynamic common to both countries, but also presents significant differences in the degree of conflict between interest groups. This contrasting mark of long times, it has been said, opposes a recurring oscillation between two conceptions of the nation and of the model of development in Argentina, and the attempt in Brazil, however unfulfilled, to reconcile them. Both countries are characterized by the permanence of what can be called an uncertain symbolic functionality of money involving recurrent crises in the account system that are manifested by public debt crises that call into question the exchange rate regimes. The new distributive compromises did not remove this uncertainty.

Argentina: the recurring conflict between two visions of the nation

The adoption by the government of Carlos Ménem in 1991 of a currency board (fixing the equivalence to the dollar of the national currency and regulating its issuance according to the coverage of the monetary base by foreign exchange reserves) can be assimilated, as most analyzes have done, to an inescapable technical choice to restore the credibility of monetary control and stem a third threat of hyperinflation. The big bang of liberalization made possible by the guarantee of parity reflects a governmental will to redefine social values to the foundation of the national community by adopting a development model that follows the prescriptions of the Washington Consensus (Marques Pereira, 2007). This was a radical ideological reconversion for a government formed by the Justicialist Party bearing the legacy of the wage-society project embodied by the mythical figure of General Perón, who had established in his first presidency (1946–1955) the universality of social rights and inaugurated a policy of growth driven by rising wages.

The redefinition of the nation-state project undertaken by the Ménem government was perceived as a fundamental condition of the possibility of curbing inflation by means of a *currency board*.[7] This was to repeat the liberal wager that the military regime (1976–1983) had already attempted, namely a reversal of the balance of power between interest groups by means of economic restructuring. This first experiment in economic liberalization was based on a relative de-industrialization as a means of destroying the power of trade unions (Schvarzer, 1986). This implicit objective was not achieved but economic policy will give the former agro-export oligarchy the opportunity to extend the diversification of its sources of income between finance, agricultural rent and the profits of joint monopolies with multinational capital in the exploitation of the internal market (Basualdo, 2001). This analysis also showed that all the liberalization measures implemented by the so-called convertibility plan, accompanying the enactment of the law of the same name fixing the nominal parity of the peso to the dollar, enabled the consolidation of the new economic groups which had emerged from the liberalization of the 1970s. Bets on the valuation of assets in privatized public services and on the interests of the public debt were the main lever. Thus, in the author's words, there is a 'business community'. The latter reintegrates with it the external creditors of the public debt and the multinationals which had diverged from it as a result of the degeneration of monetary control in the 1980s.

This patrimonial consolidation was made possible by the neoliberal conversion of the Justicialist Party. What interests us here more particularly is the performative character of a representation of the nation identified with liberalization. Two questions seem to be more significant: the management of poverty and the incomplete pacification of the military character of the distributive conflict. The first point leads us to believe that the Convertibility Plan preserves the historical image of Peronism as the repository of the figure of the people (Tizziani, 2007). This author explains this by the commitment of a new generation of activists who believe that the integration of the excluded is essentially dependent on anti-poverty policies, since the economy functioning in the context of globalization would leave no alternative to their eyes but the choice of liberalism. The second point, complementary to this analysis, emphasizes the symbolic force of the new liberal economic discourse borne by governmental rhetoric (Blaum, 2007). This hypothesis makes the assimilation of the citizen to a mere economic agent an operation of collective repression of the tragic division of the nation, inherited from the 1970s during which the trade union resistance to the economic policy of the military regime led a part of the Peronist militants and left-wing movements to a guerrilla that would be subjected to a bloody repression, experienced as a national trauma.

This liberal re-foundation of the nation will collapse with the loss of credibility of the parity of the peso which begins in 1998 in the wake of the questioning of the anchorages of the exchange in Asia and, especially because of its contagion in Brazil, which accounts for more than a third of exports. The collapse of the currency board regime, which led to a capital flight from the end of 2001, which has increased since 1998, will give rise to a radical reversal of the nation-state project that accompanied its establishment, emphasized by a new governmental rhetoric that opposes the IMF as the result of a desire to follow a 'model of productive development with social inclusion'. The heterodox theorization of the maximization of the employment level by a competitive exchange rate in open economy is the cognitive reference.

This alternation of models is part of a long history that regularly oscillates between these two irreconcilable visions of the nation since the beginning of the twentieth century. The new development project is presented as a direct challenge to the power of interest groups related to the primary export sector. This does not mean, however, as the following section shows, that this project was not beneficial to them. The historical impasse in the political reconciliation of interests that would engender a shared conception of development has been repeated despite the simultaneous expansion of different types of income.

Brazil: reconciliation around the permanence of an industrial development project

To this conflictual structural configuration, one can oppose the permanence of the search for conciliation observable in contemporary Brazilian history. The Brazilian military regime (1964–1984) was already part of this continuity. In the 1970s, the latter abandoned its initial liberal motives and, unlike Argentina, put in place an ambitious development plan aimed at completing industrialization in the sector of production goods at the same time as the modernization of export agriculture, essential to ensure the external balance. The decline in real wages was also programmed. In this context, it is a way of offsetting a higher unit cost of production than in developed countries due to the insufficient internal market size for economies of scale industries, in addition to subsidies for the expansion of production goods and the export of industrial goods. For a time, this strategy succeeded in engendering a virtuous circle of growth that crowned what was then called a Brazilian miracle in view of the growth rates approaching 10% between 1968 and 1972. But, as in Argentina, because of the rise in distributive conflicts, monetary policy becomes far too accommodative. It will degenerate in the 1980s into the threat of uncontrollable hyperinflation due to the vicious circle between rising prices and the explosion of external indebtedness. The solution of a float anchorage regime chosen by the Brazilian government was more flexible than the Argentinian currency board. To this difference, we must add an extent of liberalization, much more limited in Brazil. The conservation of federal public banks and the public monopoly on the management of petroleum exploitation or the maintenance of a system of social protection on a pay-as-you-go basis testify to the permanence within the public administration and the political system of a will defending and updating the old model of state-led development (Sallum, 2001). The anchoring of the exchange was no less constituted as in Argentina the means of a revival of external indebtedness, here also reinforced by the privatizations. The recovered liquidity of the public debt market is also a matter of beliefs but these will be denied by the evolution of the current account. Even new opportunities for gains in public utilities, which are the main focus of foreign direct investment in Argentina, engage conviction in the virtues of competition to increase the competitiveness on which the credibility of the anchor of exchange rate depends. Productivity is progressing significantly, but the reduction in the trade deficit is slow and the repatriation of profits is growing more rapidly than in Argentina.

Neither Brazil's first crisis in 1998 in the aftermath of the Asian and Russian crises, nor its repetition in 2002, triggered by the prospect of left-wing alternation, have degenerated into a crisis of all forms as in the case of Argentina. The 1998 crisis was only an external shock caused by the sudden withdrawal of capital, reflecting the loss of credibility of the currency anchor. The belief in the stability of the exchange rate will be restored once exorcized the risk, at the origin of the crisis of 2002, of a radical political upheaval that the creditors feared. The anticipation of the election of Luiz Ignacio da Silva, said Lula, leader of the Workers' Party, spearheaded the neoliberalism contest, had led to a new capital flight. This was stopped by the solemn commitment to maintain the orthodoxy that the candidate has assumed to guarantee his election. It will be necessary to await the return of confidence of the creditors of public debt so that a political will is realized to make the monetary rigor compatible with a support of the domestic demand. The acceleration of growth through the distributive effects of economic policy redefines the doctrinal compromise between the two competing models that have been confronting each other since the 1990s in the symbolic and political dispute over the nation's vision of the future. The compromise between liberal and neo-developmental models is redefined by the addition of a distributive component.[8] The first resulted in the implementation in 1994 of the Real Plan, the designation of all the liberalization measures by the new denomination of money, associating it here in the same way with a new vision of the nation which guarantees the credibility of the exchange anchor. The second model is the project of an adaptation to a globalized world of the old model of development driven by the State. Its actualization incorporates only the new theories of growth and international trade justifying the necessity of the State in increasing competitiveness. Its main financial and technological support organizations have not been dismantled. To this second model is a willingness to redistribute with the Lula government. It should be added that part of the employers is an actor in the promotion of neo-developmental vision (Diniz and Boschi, 2007). The issue of the exchange rate is the subject of intense controversy.[9]

Account system crises in both Brazil and Argentina

The crises of foreign exchange regimes causing external indebtedness have been perceived as the result of errors in economic policy or its submission to rent-seeking. The theoretical revision which it is the object of these crises is the occasion of a reorientation of the promises of monetary income. This cognitive fact shows that currency crises are crises in account systems that reflect the seizure, or even a crisis, of other functional forms of money.

In high-inflation regimes, the constant change in indexing rules implied an endogenous aggravation of public debt. This is the sign of a breakdown in the payment community reflecting that of the political community. This rupture signals the arrival at its limits of the old mode of development aimed at industrialization backed by the expansion of the internal market. These high-inflation regimes may in fact be characterized by the paradoxical expression of monetary crisis regimes (one might say in a latent crisis)[10] once they anchor expectations to two variables whose interaction is explosive: (1) the price-wage spiral implied by the radicalization of the conflict between wages and 'desired' profits, as it can be characterized in a post-Keynesian conceptualization; and (2) the forecasting of devaluations required to settle the external debt service.[11] The inertial nature of inflation leads to the distributional conflict on the calculation of margin rates and indexes of wages and assets. The distributive conflict is aggravated to the point where it relates to the very definition of the unit of account. The community of means of payment is then divided into three types of units for the calculation of the quantity that can be obtained according to the types of income. Wages have one which is, itself, multiplied by indexing rates that vary according to the localized force of the claims. The profits have another, also variable, depending on the market powers setting the mark up rates that preserve, or even increase, their real value. The financial income unit of account is the required rate of the risk premium underlying the interest rate on the public debt, which increases with inflation and devaluation forecasts. Expectations are limited to the very short term. Monetary policy can only validate this problematic regulation of the account system. Its failure will find a solution in the doctrinal reconversion of governmental action. The expected benefits of industrial planning, which have been eroded for ten years by the State's fiscal crisis, are replacing those of competition and the credibility of monetary policy, which will comfort the creditors of public debt, whose loss of liquidity due to inflation then focuses on the government agenda.

The adoption of fixed or quasi-fixed exchange rate regimes and emission restrictions, together with liberalization, puts an end to inflation. However, the stability of the account system will not be guaranteed over the long term. The processes are similar in both countries. The nominal anchoring of prices is stabilized by the predictability of the exchange rate, but this is a belief, whether it is in Argentina shown by an inscription in the constitutional law of the central bank or that it rests in Brazil only on the (theoretical) perception of the room for maneuvering in economic policy. Nevertheless, the belief remains subject to the (expected) evolving balance of the budget and the external accounts.

The recovery of external indebtedness to cover the foreseeable external trade deficit was apparently assured. It was reinforced by the privatization clauses which ensured the yield prospects in addition to the possibility of partially paying the assets concerned by means of treasury bills at their face value while their market value had collapsed. The theory of imported credibility seemed validated by the foreseeable nominal value of the productive and financial assets. The lowering of customs duties and the appreciation of the real exchange rate were to stimulate the gains in competitiveness, a guarantee of future revenues deemed to be serving external debt, the rise of which was therefore considered temporary. These gains were effectively achieved by the reorganization of labor and the importation of capital goods made cheaper by the appreciation of the real exchange rate. The initial worsening of the trade deficit seemed to be resolvable, but the Asian crisis will challenge the theory of credibility in all emerging markets. The sudden cessation of external financing led to forced devaluation by the markets.

It should also be noted that anchoring the exchange rate had not made the national currency a truly single unit of account. Public debt was either issued in dollars or matched by interest payments at the current rate. Only the units of account relating to profits and wages could be unified because the relative decline of the latter was implemented on the labor market and the organization of production.

The political alternation that the crisis of the anchoring of the exchange rate caused in the two countries[12] reopens the debate on the model of development. It is not decided to this day. The symbolic functionality of money thus remains subject to uncertainty, implying that new monetary and foreign exchange policies (the change is very relative in the case of Brazil) have not been able to solve the structural fragility of the different types of income but only make it capable of accelerating the rate of growth. The liberal redefinition of the modes of regulation in the 1990s will only be called into question at the margins. Accumulation regimes have not been significantly altered. The change was essentially limited to a demand and redistribution policy.

Limited redistributive effects in spite of a new political functionality of the currency

The application of competing economic policies has, it has been said, covered comparable distributive effects: they restore the liquidity and profitability of the public debt, while simultaneously increasing the profits, wages and transfer income. In Argentina, this was not the result of any explicit agreement between interest groups. Measures that conform to this income distribution on the basis of high growth have been unilaterally imposed as an imperative for the restoration of governability, which had as a prior requisite that of the exercise of monetary sovereignty. In Brazil, on the other hand, the redefinition of the distributive compromise, the hope of which was borne by the arrival of a former trade unionist, could not be envisaged without a desire for consensus. The issue of monetary sovereignty could not be put forward in an election that was under pressure from capital flight. The analysis that follows shows that redistribution is similarly limited in both countries by radically different public debt management which limits the redefinition of the political function of money. Also, that of the growth/distribution ratio is restricted to the demand side alone.

Argentina: a distributive compromise by default . . .

The political will to maintain the nominal exchange rate at the level where it has stabilized after the violent devaluation caused by the abandonment of its fixity will have the effect of increasing the price competitiveness of manufacturing production. The peso, initially equivalent to the dollar, collapses to more than 4 to 1 and will quickly reappear around 3 in the exit crisis. The continuation of this appreciation under the effect of the trade surplus could be countered by the central bank until very recently. This was a planned spring of the virtuous circle of high growth allowed by employment and public revenue. The increase in the latter will also be fueled by the introduction of an export tax covering around 15% of tax revenue. The levies increased from 21.5% to 31.6% of GDP between 2000 and 2009 (CEPALSTAT, Marques Pereira, 2010), which will allow from 2003 to 2008 a primary surplus of more than 2% of GDP which covers interest of public debt while allowing for increased public expenditure (CEPAL, 2011). This choice of policy mix will allow a rapid recovery and a maximization of the growth which will make possible the simultaneous progression of the various types of income. Such a strategy takes shape in the resolution of the crisis of the currency board regime choosing the non-negotiated default of the public debt and an equally discretionary reformulation of private contracts. These measures were justified as conditions for the exit of a monetary crisis involving an economic, social and political crisis, the outcome of which seemed unpredictable.[13] They were conceived in frontal opposition to the IMF doctrine. Its stigmatization was the condition of such decisions and it had to be emblematic of a process of neoliberalism as a system of values, held responsible for the shift in poverty of millions of people. The economic policy debate that takes place in this massive impoverishment mobilizes a new representation of the nation.[14] The weight of the history of the political system and the conflict between two ideas of nation that crossed it was decisive. It defined the doctrinal stake.

The exit from the crisis is thus initiated by the restoration of the symbolic function of money. The properties of account and payment of the currency are re-instituted by a 'rape' of the contracts. Against the backdrop of the adoption of the dollar and that of a devalued peso, general acceptance of this second choice proved to be viable by maximizing the growth that it made possible. What was called 'asymmetrical weighing' and the decree suspending the service of a public debt presented as illegitimate were the subject of a vast operation of political communication underlining their character as acts of recovery of monetary sovereignty which had been abandoned to markets with the currency board. The first measure established a conversion of deposits at a rate of 1:1.4 and a 1:1 ratio of liabilities. The declaration of illegitimacy of the public debt will make it possible to propose in 2005, once growth returns, a non-negotiable offer of its conversion into bonds indexed on growth and inflation but whose initial nominal value is reduced on average by 60%.

The macroeconomic analysis of the stimulus sheds light on the way in which an account system forming a payment community is reconstructed through the redefinition of the national community by what has been called the 'productive development model with social inclusion'. This was the basis for the theorization of the relationship between employment rates and the competitive exchange rate.[15] The distributive effects of exchange rate policy and a monetary policy that is initially relatively restrictive but then accommodative will restore the political functionality of the currency, allowing for a revival that will lead to continued strong growth until 2008, in contrast to the bleak forecasts of IMF. The distributive compromise that made this restoration viable had powerful macroeconomic effects. Just a few months after the promulgation of the default, exchange rate flexibility and asymmetric currency conversion, positive short-term expectations are being restored thanks to the virtuous circle of growth that these measures have enabled.[16]

It should be stressed that the unilateral default of the public debt was the first condition: without a restoration of public finances, the adoption of a policy of recovery could not be envisaged. Otherwise, while government liabilities represented 4.1% of GDP on the eve of the devaluation, they would have increased in three years from 9 to 11 points, according to a simulation based on the stabilized exchange rate of 2004 (Damill et al., 2007). The nominal asymmetric conversion of commitments was also decisive. This measure avoided a general insolvency, as banks could be refinanced by the central bank. The devaluation quickly allowed for a revival in production, observable from the third quarter of 2002. This year and 2003 saw a shift to an industrial export balance of more than US $9 billion and US $7 billion respectively, and it is plausible that the devaluation initially generated import substitution opportunities,[17] wage costs are greatly reduced in the absence of indexation to inflation, while the price index was increased by 42.4% between 2001 and 2003 (CEPAL, 2010).

Chart 4.1 shows that the decline in the real average wage, which started in 1998 and collapsed in 2001, would not be erased until 2008. The growth in employment, which enabled the rapid recovery, will gradually push rising wages; all the more so because the agreements of branches that were abolished in the 1990s will be restored. The resumption of production in 2002 reverts to that of employment. The urban open unemployment rate will fall from 19.7% to 7.9% between 2000 and 2008 (CEPAL, 2009). The rapid rise in profits will result in rapid deleveraging of the private sector. The increase in real average profit in 2003 was the strongest since 1990. At the same time, capital flight has

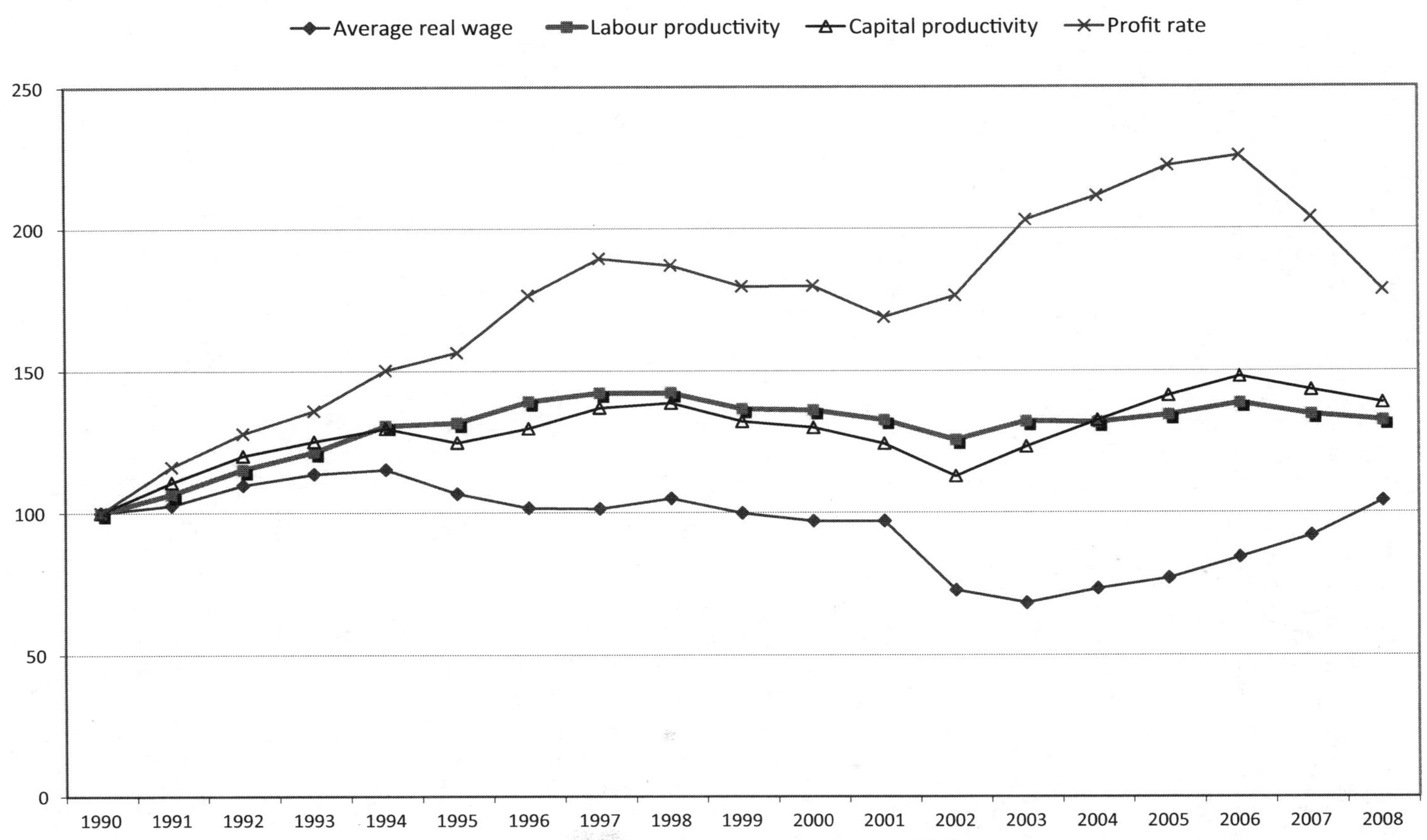

Chart 4.1 Argentina (1990–2008)

Source: CIEPP (2009), INDEC data

been stopped by the obligation to convert the export earnings into national currency at the same time as the central bank resumes issuing securities, initially at very high interest rates. This restrictive aspect of a monetary policy which has also guaranteed the refinancing of the banks initiates the revival of the financial market. Monetary policy becomes accommodative when exchange rate policy begins to counter the pressure to its appreciation due to soaring exports.[18] The sterilization of foreign exchange purchases that allows to support the exchange rate around 3 pesos to 1 dollar until 2008 offered an investment indexed to inflation and growth rate. It thus ensures the consolidation of the public debt market. The financial rent will be able to grow fueled by the increase of its stock. The latter increased from US $137 billion to US $191 billion between 2002 and 2004, decreased to US $128 billion in 2005 as a result of the restructuring of defaulting securities and then increased to US $146 billion in 2008. The external portion of public debt declined over the period from US $88 to US $55 billion (CEPALSTAT). The ratio of total public debt went from 145.9% of GDP in 2002 to 48.5% in 2008 (ECLAC, 2011).

The accommodating monetary policy validates the rise in profits and wages and becomes a sustained policy of demand as evidenced by the accounting share of private consumption in the growth rate. This was 29.9 percentage points as a component of a GDP increase of 46.2% over the period 2003–2008, with investment at 18.8 points and exports at 5.8 (Quenan and Torija Zane, 2011). Profits, wages and labor productivity are growing together but the first widely win the race. Two observations point to the limitations of a distributive trade-off by default and the fragility of the resulting growth regime: labor productivity only receives a slight rise compared to that of the real average wage; the increase in profits and the productivity of capital was reversed in 2006. It can be assumed that the mark-up of prices reflected in the acceleration of inflation from that moment on is augmented by the salary recovery, to the point of making it incompatible with the progression of accumulation because it is essentially dependent on self-financing (Marques Pereira and Lo Vuolo, 2009).

... but a conflictual one over the unit of account

The absence of consensus seeking has not prevented a de facto reconciliation of interests, but this is done on the basis of a relative nominal anchoring of the relative prices which will become problematic from 2007 with the runaway of inflation which underestimates the national official index established by the Institute of Statistics. The manipulation of the inflation index since 2007 highlights the exacerbated level of the dispute over the unit of account, which is reflected in the difference of more than 10 points between the official index and the average of alternative indices established by the provincial statistical offices (Chubut, Neuquén, San Luis and Santa Fé). This average index, after falling as the contagion effect of the global financial crisis lasted, then rose to 30%, which is precisely the floor of nominal rise in wages claimed by the unions in collective bargaining (Barbeito, 2010).

The rise in inflation takes on a number of dimensions that signal the limits of economic policy: (1) it makes clear that the profit target is incompatible with a demand-driven growth regime; (2) it jeopardizes public finances as a source of indexation of debt securities and income from assistance; and (3) it reveals the limit of the competitive exchange rate to compensate for a structural deficit in industrial competitiveness. Torija Zane (2011) clearly points to the convergence between these three manifestations of the fragility of the growth regime. The rise in inflation (measured by the provincial index) in 2010 was faster than the depreciation rate vis-à-vis the dollar or, to a lesser extent, against the foreign exchange basket of currencies, and it accompanies the rise in relative prices of foodstuffs/industrial goods. The author concludes that if the rise in real wages continues to offset that of food prices, it will neutralize the increase in productivity gains and draw a scenario of Dutch disease. A deceleration in industrial output and employment will increase the need for social spending funding while its capacity will decline.

The endogenous factors of a potential crisis in Argentina

In fact, it should be noted that this scenario could not be neutralized by the competitive exchange rate policy and the negative real base interest rate. The monetary and exchange rate regime was able to increase the industrial product by an average of 7.7% over the period 2003–2008 (CEPAL, 2010), but this increase does not permanently reverse the long-term trend towards de-industrialization. The competitive exchange rate allowed a limited import substitution but did not lead to a redefinition of the international integration regime even if the export ratio of the industrial sector could rise from 18.5% to 27.4% between 2001 and 2007.[19] It will not be able to counter the Dutch disease that is responsible for the international integration regime and that exacerbates an increase in export earnings thanks to the growth of China whose counterpart is the increasing competition of its industrial goods. In 2011, the bilateral balance is in deficit. The objective of maintaining the level of the depreciated exchange rate is not sufficient to solve the structural problem of competitiveness which makes inflation cover a supply dimension (Salama, 2011). The latter defines in fact the limit of the monetary and exchange rate regime to support a regime of growth otherwise incompatible with a wage regime signaling since 2006 the possibility of blocking the accumulation once it depends on the profits realized. This is a limitation of the financing structure of the economy that the distributive compromise has not been able to remove and which ultimately constitutes the endogenous factor of a potential crisis in this growth regime through a new crisis of the balance of payments. Its forecast is already profiling the threat in the acceleration of capital outflows while the current account surplus had been decreasing since 2007 and was expected to almost cancel out in 2011.

The fragility of the growth regime is expressed in the market value of the means of payment and of the debts, hence in the time horizon of the economic functionality of money, discussed in the next section. Political change is insufficient; it has in fact only allowed a marginal redefinition of the mode of regulation. The latter has been limited essentially to the monetary and exchange rate regime, to the wage system and to the social protection regime,[20] although these institutional changes have not been able to generate political dynamics capable of sufficiently modifying the fiscal and financial system to stimulate an investment dynamic that would have prevented the foreseeable deterioration of external accounts. The margins of economic policy that had opened up the trade surplus now turn into a dilemma between the need to increase the primary surplus (while declining growth) or a call to foreign capital, which was the Brazilian solution. But the Argentinian government did not have the reputation of rigor of its neighbor.

Brazil: the imperative of redistribution

The exit strategy of the Brazilian exchange rate crisis was symmetrically opposite to that implied by its monetary crisis in Argentina. But it will lead to the establishment of a macro-economy that is partly comparable in terms of the growth/distribution ratio, since the election of Lula also involved a new representation of the nation, which emphasized the imperative of redistribution. However, this change does not occur as a result of a crisis of governability.

The policy of supporting domestic demand has been more limited than in Argentina. There certainly was a political will to shift distributive public intervention and it was not only conceived in terms of social policy, as might be seen from the publicity given to the commitment of rigorous economic policy and the fight against poverty by transference of incomes. The policy mix has indeed been a policy of demand even if the classic new principles prevail in monetary matters. However, their application by a de facto autonomous central bank has left the government room to maneuver in budgetary matters and wage policy.

Since the speculative attacks on the exchange rate anchor in 1998, the restrictive stock follows the theory of inflation targets. This is presented as an alternative nominal anchor, but it is indeed the appreciation of the real exchange rate that is preserved as an implicit target of monetary policy.[21] The interest rate of the central bank (SELIC) remains very high despite its gradual decline from the peak reached during the currency anchor crisis. The real rate falls from its maximum reaching 14.1% in 1999 to 5.3% in 2008 (IMF data). The differential between national and external interest rates has been added to the trade surplus and the current account as a factor in the appreciation of the real exchange rate. The central bank is therefore actively contributing to it, and its interventions are stricted to limiting fluctuations. Maintaining high interest rates will have avoided having to increase the primary budget surplus to more than 2% over the period from 2003–2008 without this ratio covering, as is the case in Argentina, the entire service (which varied between a high of 6.6% of GDP in 2003 and a low of 3.6% in 2008) (CEPAL, 2011). The level of the interest rate attracts investments in Brazilian reals, which resumed the appreciation of the nominal exchange rate.

It should be noted that the stock of total public debt increased from US $202 billion to US $325 between 2002 and 2008 and that its external share declined from US $72 to US $54 billion (CEPALSTAT). The ratio of total federal government debt to GDP, as published in the statistical annex to ECLAC's annual economic survey (2011), can thus show a decline of 37% to 24% of GDP. Since it accounts for the net external debt, which has become an 11% of GDP receivable (thanks to foreign exchange reserves), the internal debt ratio (residents) increased from 24% to 36%. The decline in real interest rates interacts with the rise in the rate of growth. The current commercial rate (called active rate legal personalities) lost 10 points in the period, from 44% to 34%. In addition to the favorable long-term interest rates of the development bank (BNDES), various credit modalities for cheaper credit, consumption and housing meant an increase in credit to the private sector from 32% to 59% of GDP over the period (it increased to 70% in 2010) (CEPAL, 2011). The increase in wages (Chart 4.2 below) and the decline in the open unemployment rate from 12.3% to 7.9% between 2003 and 2008 (CEPAL, 2011) contributed to the increase in growth. Thus, the expansion of household consumption became the main accounting component of the rising growth rate. Its contribution over the period 2003–2008 was 15.8 percentage points, with GDP growth of 22.8%, followed by investment contributing 10.6 percentage points and exports of 8.8 (Quenan and Torija Zane, 2011).[22]

The importance of household consumption in accelerating the rate of growth was also stimulated by a shift in the wage regime without any significant legislative change. The increase in the real minimum wage index 113 in 2003 to 160 in 2008 (ECLAC, 2010), however, is a major political decision. On the one hand, its level indexes transfers income. On the other hand, it constitutes a normative reference which certainly contributed to the increase in the real average wage above the inflation rate and to that of productivity, in addition to the political climate favorable to wage agreements. It should be noted, however, that the decline in the real average wage in the Real Plan period (after its high recovery due to the end of hyperinflation in 1994) was halted only after the downturn in labor and capital productivity, down after 1998. Unlike Argentina, the increase in the real average wage index continues to go hand in hand with that of profit, except for the decline in the latter in the year of recession caused by the 2009 crisis without this being the case for the former.

The decisive role of exchange rate policy

The exchange rate policy was also, as in Argentina, but in a different way, a key condition for the redefinition of the distributive compromise. It has indirectly contributed to the demand policy by allowing an increase in public expenditure and credit, which are complementary to the increase in wages. In the case of Brazil as well, the limit of this compromise of debt management is at the same time the source of crisis for this growth regime. The control mode is only changed at the margin. The only notable but limited changes

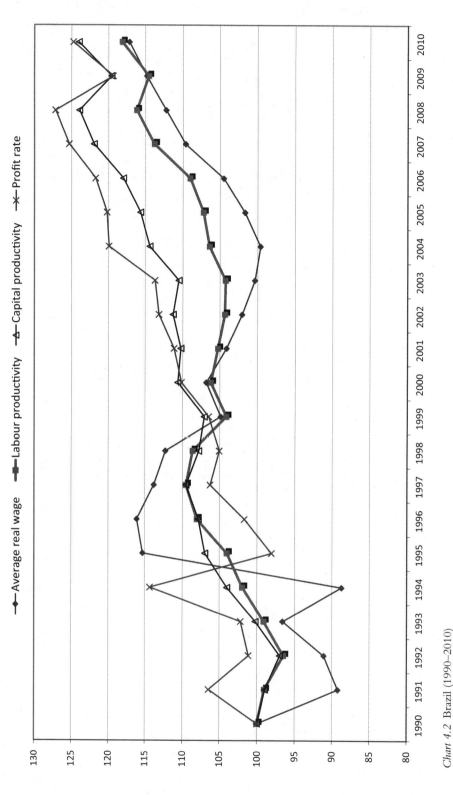

Chart 4.2 Brazil (1990–2010)
Source: IPEADATA

are: (1) as in Argentina, a limited shift in the fiscal-financial regime, which allowed an increase in government revenues, provided that it remains compatible with the maintenance of the rent linked to the public debt; and (2) in the absence of major institutional transformation, the distributional effect of wage and social protection schemes is increased by raising the minimum wage, expanding the beneficiary population of transfers and increasing the indexation on the latter. The international integration regime inherited from liberalization is in no way changed. Unlike Argentina, in addition, the monetary and foreign exchange regime was not in this case redefined. The institutional change that means the changeover to the flexibility of the exchange was only an adaptation made necessary to preserve the possibility of the return to its appreciation that forced the raising of the interest rate. Obviously, the transition to a trade surplus in 2002 made it easier. It helped to reduce the level of the interest rate that guaranteed the appreciation of the exchange rate.

The regulation mode implemented with liberalization could thus have different effects thanks to the relaxation of the external constraint opening redistribution margins of maneuver. The growing trade surplus from 2002 onwards (and the prospects given to it, beyond its downward trend since 2006, the launching of significant new oil fields, or even the export of ethanol) trigger the decline in the interest rate that engages the virtuous circle of rising domestic demand, growth and decline in the ratio of total public debt to GDP. The growing share of domestic debt issued in real terms reflects the critical importance of the exchange rate policy appreciated in credibility. Although the rating of the Brazilian debt was raised, the fact of being kept in the category of speculative investments testifies to the maintenance of a convention of financial defiance in the long term despite the reputation of rigor.

The absence of any change in the international integration regime indicates that there has been no change in the accumulation regime, as in Argentina the worsening of the Dutch disease. Demand-side policy is clearly not sufficient to trigger a change in the productive structure. Manufacturing certainly increased (3.2% yearly average over the period 2002–2008), but the sector deficit forecast for 2010 by the Ministry of Development was to rise to US $30.5 billion (quoted by the newspaper Valor Econômico of 16/11/2010). This deficit widened mainly in the capital goods and chemicals sector, according to the analysis of a center for the study of employers (IEDI, 2008). The result was a growing gap between the increase in imports and exports, which, as highlighted in a report from the research institute of this ministry, was responsible for the shift from a current account surplus of $13.3 billion in 2006 to a deficit of $47.3 billion forecast for 2010 (IPEA, 2010).

Persistent creditor power: public debt more than credit to the economy

The main indicator for welcoming the achievement of macroeconomic stability is the decline in the ratio of public debt to GDP. In terms of volume, it has been observed that this debt has grown, but growth, however, allows a sufficient primary surplus to cover its service or at least to ensure the liquidity of the debt market by reducing its ratio to GDP. Higher growth rates thus reinforced what may be called a liquidity preference in financial form – Treasury bills being acquired as liquid assets with high profitability. Growth is the result of short/medium term bets, but this growing financial liquidity signals the absence of a long-term vision. This temporality of expectations is the main sign of the limit of macroeconomic dynamics, which is reflected in the permanence of an economic functionality of the currency which restricts the financing of the economy (Charts 4.3 and 4.4 *below*). This was alluded to by the decline in the ratio of credit to GDP in Argentina. The share it represents in the total assets of the financial system recovered only slightly, while that of securities increased sharply. The sharp rise in the credit to GDP ratio in Brazil is not enough to increase its share as a source of income given the sharp increase in the share of securities. These are only indicators of the permanence of the financial structure. This is particularly complex with the development of foreign exchange derivatives, which is particularly important in Brazil. What is important for this analysis is that they signal a lack of remission of the monetary power of the debtors that arises between the arbitration between taxation and debt.

In the absence of credit money in the Keynesian sense, and with a stock market still underdeveloped,[23] the investment growth depends on the profits made, and not on those that would be expected to anticipate domestic demand which would be considered sustainable in the long term. The limit to the financing of accumulation plays both on the supply side and on the demand side because of the fundamental importance of public debt in the financial structure, which was overshadowed by the frequent focus of the diagnoses on the decline in its ratio to GDP. Faced with an increasing supply of high-yielding government securities, it may be assumed that the opportunity cost of the investment had not been sufficiently reduced by prospects for expanding domestic demand or that its anticipation does not appear to be in any case reinforced in the long term.

This financial structure is the sign of the ambivalence of the arbitrage between levels of public debt and taxation that has been established. This has certainly been a condition for the possibility of an increase in growth through its distributive inflection, but it also marks its limits. Once the margin of maneuver is curtailed in the current account, maintaining the increase in social spending will then involve an increase in either the tax burden or the public debt burden. Current arbitrage is based on the increase in the budget margins authorized by the exporting boom. The limit to the growth of tax/public debt arbitrage is a function of the trade balance and hence also the integrity of the account system. The plurality of units of account remains beyond the absence of any challenge to the apparently single unit of account represented by the national currency. Although public debt is increasingly internal and issued in national currency, what matters to its creditors is the prospect of high levels of interest

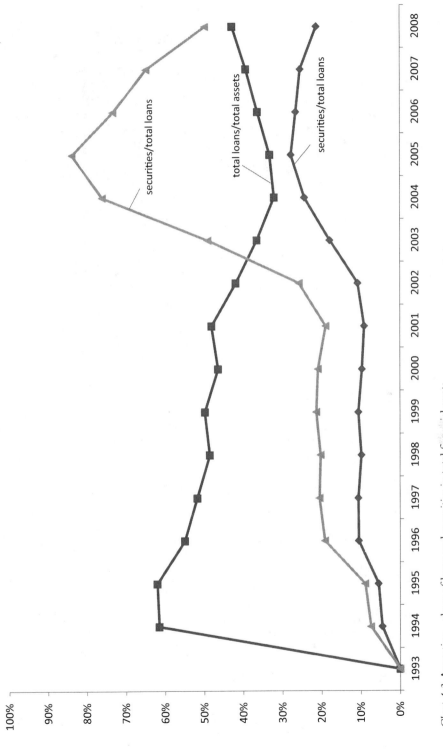

Chart 4.3 Argentina – share of loans and securities in total financial assets

Source: Libro de Entitades Financieras/BCRA (Marques Pereira and Lo Vuolo, 2009)

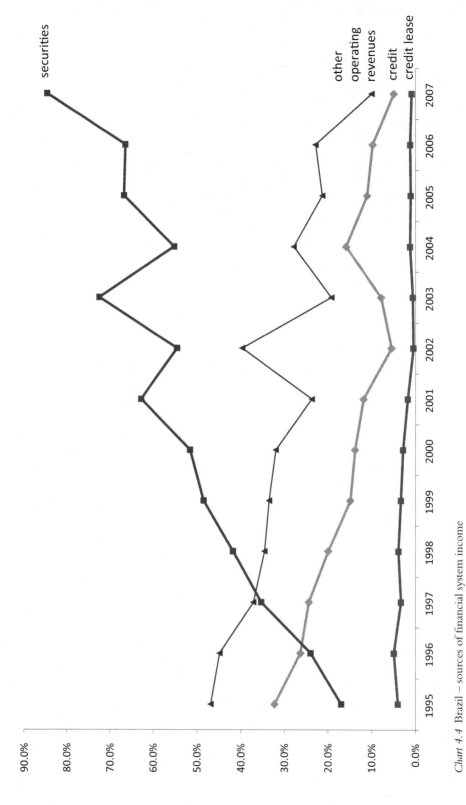

Chart 4.4 Brazil – sources of financial system income

Source: COSIF/BCB (Bruno, 2010)

rates or indexation. Belief has the aura of truth that can be conferred on it by the policy doctrine of inflation targets in Brazil or a more heterodox speech that presents debt service as a growth-compatible remuneration in the case of Argentina. These interest or indexing rates are the unit of calculation of the value of the financial annuities. However, the level of interest payments fixed on the budgetary surplus target allows room for maneuver to increase the rate of growth that allows demand to arise from the level of wages, public spending and credit incentives. The relative value of labor income and productive capital in the domestic sector, as stated by the national unit of account, is thus a function of the interest rate in Brazil and the indexation rate of public debt in Argentina.

Conclusion: tax/public debt arbitrage as an expression of distributive trade-offs

This regulation of the account system is therefore key to the liquidity of the public debt market. However, government legitimacy for employment and wage growth and poverty reduction is a second and equally fundamental condition. The compromise between one and the other is now threatened by the tightening of the external constraint of which it was itself the bearer. The difference of the monetary doctrines which have made it possible to establish it is, to a certain extent, effaced in the light of this common contradiction. It is only a matter of degree of conflict which is still far from being sufficiently attenuated to bring together the institutional conditions for a mode of development based on the internal market.

In Argentina the integrity of the account system and the monetary community it symbolizes is in fact fictitious because there is no political community in the sense of a shared conception of the nation. The conciliation of interests is truly imposed without any social agreement on the unit of account, which allows a political system that concentrates decision-making power in the hands of the presidency (Svampa, 2007). It is thus possible to impose a monetary and budgetary policy without obtaining a consensus on the development model but this is not the case in tax matters, as demonstrated in 2008 by a multi-month strike in urban supply that has succeeded in preventing the adoption of a bill to fix the agricultural export tax on international prices and to limit it for some of them.

The same problem also arises in Brazil. The arbitrage between the level of taxation and the level of indebtedness underlying the nominal price anchoring by the macroeconomic effects of policy and exchange is no more sustainable given the same limits to the financing of the economy which similarly undermine the possibility of an increase in competitiveness that would have avoided the tightening of external constraints; and thus to eliminate the room for maneuver to continue to support domestic demand. It should be noted that the Brazilian political system, which is generally opposed to the Argentine political system by the necessity of electoral alliances (Sallum, 2004), gives the distributive compromise a more consensual dimension, but it is also incapable of calling into question the weight of the public debt that determines the exercise of monetary sovereignty.

The tax/public debt arbitrage thus appears in both cases as the keystone of the interdependence between functional forms of money (see Figure 4.2 below).

Tax/debt arbitrage is the ultimate sign of monetary sovereignty reflecting the nation's conception of the exercise of political sovereignty as an expression of the distributive compromise of a development model. The period that has just been analyzed nevertheless presents a major innovation which must be emphasized in this respect. The latter questions the historicity of the autonomy of the political dynamics vis-à-vis the performance of a government through knowledge. The design and implementation of a policy of increasing growth through domestic demand requires a theory but its adoption was a purely political decision. This choice did not solve the secular tension between two models of capitalism's development and this is expressed in both countries by the permanence until now of the financial form of a chronically unsustainable public debt. A tension manifested when the progress of accumulation eventually butter in the 1970s in Brazil as in Argentina on the political inability to raise wages as a means to trigger a dynamic of inter-sectoral productivity a la Pasinetti. In both cases, one cannot know a priori how irreversible is the weight of history that set limits to institutional change in the 2000s.

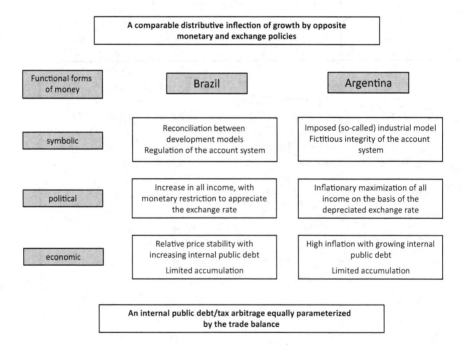

Figure 4.2 A synoptic view of the results of the analysis

The main inertia is the refusal of the elites to accept more taxes. However, the underlying trend has been a rise in taxation since 1980 when tax revenues (including social contributions) amounted to 22.7% of GDP in Brazil and 19.2% in Argentina. Overall revenues increased by 3.9 and 11.1 percentage points respectively between 2000 and 2009, reaching 34.3% and 31.6% respectively, while the rest of Latin America is between 7% and 15% (CEPAL, 2010). The levels of Argentina and Brazil are now similar to those of Japan or the US. These countries have also significantly increased public debt, but have been an instrument of growth or of stimulus. This was not the case in Argentina and Brazil (except in the 1970s), and it was only in the 2000s that growth was compatible with the monetary power of creditors. This difference with the OECD countries refers, as we have seen, to the historical legacy of high levels of income inequality, which also marks another significant difference, the much more regressive nature of taxation.

Notes

1 This chapter was originally published at the *Revue de la Régulation*, in its Spring 2012 edition, volume 11 (http://regulation.revues.org). We thank the editors for having authorized the reproduction of the chapter in this first English version.
2 China is the most expansive export destination in the 2000s for these two countries and other raw material producers in the region. In 2010, it was the second largest external market in Brazil after the EU and the fourth in Argentina after Latin America, the EU and the US. In addition, it is Argentina's third-largest supplier of manufactured goods after Mercosur and the EU and second in Brazil after the EU. (CEPAL, 2011). On the economic place of China in the region and the debates it arouses on both sides, see Arès et al. (2011).
3 China is the counterexample. Maintaining a low cost of direct and indirect labor is the basis for inter-sectoral dynamics that increase competitiveness through the export of manufactured goods by involving the relocation of less competitive producers and capital in China (see Bruno et al., 2011).
4 It should be recalled that the project to supplement the industrial matrix was precisely the explicit objective of several development plans in both countries since the 1950s. Brazil demonstrates, contrary to Argentina, continuity in pursuing this objective until the late 1970s. It should also be noted that Mercosur can be regarded as a territorial extension of such a project with regard to the continuity of a growth dependent on the internal market, as opposed to its bifurcation in Mexico towards the export of manufactured goods, under NAFTA (Pereira and Théret, 2001). The technical and economic viability of an updating of such a project in the context of the present international division of labor and the importance that Mercosur can bring, and its possible extension on a continental scale, on the basis of the new UNASUR (Union of South American Nations), remain open questions. These are beyond the scope of this chapter, but it should be pointed out as important as a horizon for exceeding the limits to growth, essentially based on a demand policy in both countries.
5 The methods of calculating shareholder value and what they imply on wages can be regarded as another manifestation of multiple units of account for payments of various types of income.
6 The external debt inaugurated in the two countries from the 1970s the practice currently called *carry over*. The financial gains then offer an alternative to the loss of profitability of productive capital due to the narrowness of the internal market for new sectors

with economies of scale, which can be seen in an analysis of the accumulation regime as the main factor blocking the mode of self-centered development (Mathías and Salama, 1983). After 1979, the surge in international interest rates as a means of ending inflation in developed countries led to the crisis of this external private debt, which was converted into public debt by the adjustment policies of the 1980s.

7 This fact is deciphered by the very enlightening analysis of an interview with an adviser to the Minister of Finance in a meeting on political communication to accompany the announcement of the promulgation of the currency board (Roig, 2008).

8 Brasilio Sallum, Mesa redonda os desafios da presidente; Um país em transição [Round Table 'Challenges of the Presidency', published in the main Brazilian economic newspaper], *Valor Econômico*, November 5, 2010.

9 The meaning given to the so-called neo-developmental model is modulated by its political appropriation, which can be seen in the dialogue agreed between the central bank and the Minister of Finance. The criticism of exchange rate appreciation is, in a sense, a firewall for neoclassical criticism of the laxness of fiscal policy. What it denounces as a non-cooperative game, forcing the central bank to maintain a high level of interest rates which fuels the appreciation of the exchange rate is the rhetoric of a doctrinal compromise made possible by the appearance of no cooperation.

10 Miguel Bruno (2005) talks about a crisis regime, the paradox being justified by a regime of instability resulting from the collapse of the old institutional compromises without others being able to see the light.

11 The external indebtedness of the 1970s was largely the responsibility of the private sector in both countries. A significant portion of this external private debt was transformed into external public debt in the early 1980s through mechanisms to cover the losses due to the maxi-devaluations. These will be repeated on the basis of the need to ensure the trade surplus required to serve the external debt. The redemption of currencies regulated by treasury bills implies their indexation on inflation and the exchange rate. Public indebtedness becomes unsustainable both because of its runaway service and the so-called Oliveira-Tanzi effect, that is, the devaluation of tax revenues by inflation.

12 In Argentina, the alternation itself is in fact a return of a part of the Justicialist Party to historical Peronism, which in 2003 gives the victory of the presidential election to the one who then makes the leader Nestor Kirchner. This victory is obtained following the withdrawal of Carlos Ménem, the former president, who came second in the first round by campaigning for the adoption of the dollar as a remedy for the crisis.

13 The monetary crisis began with the paralysis of payments following the draconian restrictions imposed on withdrawals from bank deposits. The brutal loss of income in a context already marked by three years of recession triggers a sequence of social explosions. The mass demonstrations by the depositors are accompanied by looting of supermarkets, blockades of roads and urban crossroads by movements of unemployed, all of which fueled the riot which forced the resignation in December 2001 of President Fernando de la Rúa. The latter had won the presidential elections of 1999 against the candidacy of Carlos Ménem. The coming to power of the Radical Party, which has competed with the Justicialist Party since the Perón era, does not call into question the economic policy.

14 It is not anecdotal in this respect that the organization of a large number of economists who promote a widely publicized debate on development strategies capable of somehow restoring the nation from its ashes has been so designated of 'Plan Fenix'. www.econ.uba.ar/planfenix/index2.htm.

15 The economic intervention of the State extends to areas other than macroeconomics, such as the freezing of prices of privatized public services, compensated by the granting of subsidies, and for some, their re-nationalization. High growth was a prerequisite for this, as it allowed for increased spending through revenue, while enabling them to cover debt service.

16 For an analysis of the behavior of the various variables in monthly data, see Heymann (2006).

17 The import coefficient for the industry decreased from 19.7% in 2001 to 10.5% in 2002, returning to its previous value in 2003 and gaining close to 10 points until 2007. The export coefficient increased from 18.5 in 2001 to 28.6 in 2003 and remained at this level until 2007 (Azpiazu and Schorr, 2010).
18 The real interest rate of the central bank (LEBAC) becomes negative. The central bank follows the principle of controlling the monetary aggregate M2 to accommodate supply of liquidity on demand (see Torija Zane, 2011). It should be noted that this interest rate policy does not translate into an increase in domestic credit to the economy, which fell by 23% of GDP in 2000 to 13.6% in 2008 (CEPAL, 2009).
19 Calculation of Azpiazu and Schorr (2010) from the FLACSO and INDEC database. The analysis of these authors explains in detail the industrial trade balance. While it increased substantially in 2002 and 2003 for the sector as a whole only that of the 100 largest industrial enterprises continued to increase thereafter. The total balance is reduced as the deficit of the rest of the industry increases. The export coefficient for this group of companies increased from 28.3% to 41.5% between 2001 and 2007, while the import ratio for the whole industry was 19.7% to 28 1%. They also note that only natural resource processing activities have a positive balance. This study of industrial data from 1976 to 2007 concludes with the consolidation of the regressive restructuring of the sector, initiated under the military dictatorship, and which since then tends to concentrate the accumulation space on the comparative advantages associated with natural resources and low wages.
20 The pension system has been reconverted to the distribution principle and thus 're-nationalized' (see Arza, 2009). It should be noted that the measure was taken as a result of the need to widen sources of public debt financing. In addition to the pension fund, it is also fueled for a growing share by public enterprises and the central bank.
21 The real exchange rate appreciates from the index 100 in 2000 to 135 in 2008. The currency crises had brought it down to 80 in 2003. It is at 166 in June 2011. IIF / Reuters data cited by Torija Zane (2011).
22 However, the share of net exports in GDP growth had been decreasing since 2004 and has remained negative from 2006 until now outside the three quarters of recession caused by the global crisis in late 2008 and early 2009 (National Accounts, IBGE).
23 Market capitalization was 15.6% of GDP in Argentina and 36.6% in Brazil in 2009 (Quenan and Torija Zane, 2011).

References

Arès, M., Deblock, C., and Lin, T-S. La Chine et l'Amérique latine: le grand chambardement? *Revue Tiers Monde*, n. 208, 2011. DOI: 10.3917/rtm.208.0065

Arza, C. Back to the State, Pension Fund Nationalization in Argentina. doc. *CIEPP*, n° 73, 2009.

Azpiazu, D., and Schorr, M. *Hecho en Argentina, Industria y economía, 1976–2007*. Buenos Aires: Siglo XXI, 2010.

Barbeito, A. Re-construcción de índices de precios al consumidor y su incidencia en la medición de algunas variables monetarias reales. *Serie Análisis de Coyuntura n° 24*, CIEPP, 2010.

Basualdo, E. *Estudios de historia económica de Argentina desde mediados del siglo XX a la actualidad*. Buenos Aires: Siglo XXI, 2001.

Blaum, L. Le cas Argentine révisité, de l'utopie libérale au retour de la politique. *Revue Tiers Monde*, n. 189, pp. 135–154, 2007. DOI: 10.3917/rtm.189.0135

Bresser-Pereira, L. C. *Pourquoi certains pays émergents réussissent et d'autres non*. Paris: La Découverte, 2009a.

Bresser-Pereira, L. C. A tendência à sobreapreciação da taxa de câmbio. *Revista Econômica*, n. 11 (1), 2009b.

Bresser-Pereira, L. C. (éd.). *Crise Global e o Brasil.* Rio de Janeiro: Editora FGV, 2010.

Bruno, M. *Crescimento Econômico, Mudanças Estruturais e Distribuição. As Tansformações do Regime de Acumulação no Brasil: uma análise regulacionista.* Paris: Tese de Doutorado em Co-Tutela EHESS and Rio de Janeiro: IE-UFRJ, 2005.

Bruno, M. Poupança, investimento e regime monetario no Brasil. *Relatorio do convênio Institut CDC pour la recherche/UERJ/UPJV – CRIISEA*, Amiens, 2010.

Bruno, M., Halévi, J., and Marques Pereira, J. Les défis de l'influence de la Chine sur le développement du Brésil: avantages comparatifs et conflit distributif. *Revue Tiers Monde*, n. 208, 2011.

Cardoso, E., and Holland, M. *South America for the Chinese? A Trade-Based Analysis.* Paris: OECD, 2009.

CEPAL. *Estudio Económico de América Latina y el Caribe*, Santiago de Chile, 2009, 2010, 2011.

Damill, M., Frenkel, R., and Rapetti, M. La deuda argentina: historia, default y estructuración. In R. Boyer and J. Neffa (eds.), *Salida de crisis y estrategias alternativas de desarrollo.* Buenos Aires: Miña y Dávila, 2007, pp. 353–399. DOI: 10.2307/3655857.

Diniz, E., and Boschi, R. *A difícil rota do desenvolvimentismo, Empresarios e a agenda neoliberal.* São Paulo: Humanitas, 2007.

Heymann, D. Buscando la tendencia: crisis macroeconómica y recuperación en la Argentina. *Serie estudios y perspectivas (Oficina Buenos Aires)*, n° 31, CEPAL, 2006.

IEDI. *O comércio exterior brasileiro no primeiro semestre 2008: evolução, características setoriais e intensidade tecnológica.* 2008. www.iedi.org.br/artigos/top/estudos_comercio/

IPEA. Carta de Conjuntura, n. 10, Junho, 2010

Marques Pereira, J. Monnaie, coordination et risque systémique dans la crise argentine de 2001/2002 et son issue. *Économie et institutions*, n. 10–11, p. 99–153, 2007.

Marques Pereira, J. La politique fiscale en Amérique latine. In C. Quenan and S. Velut (eds.), *Les enjeux du développement en Amérique latine.* Paris: AFD/IdA, 2011, pp. 185–207.

Marques Pereira, J., and Lo Vuolo, R. *La dynamique de l'épargne en Argentine: de l'inertie du cycle macroéconomique au changement structurel?* rapport de synthèse, site UPJV/CRIISEA, 2009.

Marques Pereira, J., and Théret, B. Régimes politiques, médiations sociales de la régulation et dynamiques macro-économiques. Quelques enseignements pour la théorie du développement d'une comparaison des caractères nationaux distinctifs du Brésil et du Mexique à l'époque des régimes d'industrialisation par substitution des importations, avec, Théret, B., *L'année de la régulation*, Presses de Sciences Po, n° 5, 2001.

Mathías, G., and Salama, P. *L'État surdéveloppé. Des métropoles au Tiers Monde.* Paris: La Découverte, 1983.

Pasinetti, L. *Structural Change and Economic Growth: A Theoretical Essay on the Dynamics of the Wealth of Nations.* Cambridge: Cambridge University Press, 1981.

Quenan, C., and Torija Zane, E. Dynamiques économiques, tendances et perspectives. In C. Quenan and S. Velut (eds.), *Les enjeux du développement en Amérique latine.* Paris: AFD/IdA, 2011, pp. 19–82.

Rapetti, M. La macroeconomía argentina durante la post-convertibilidad: evolución, debates y perspectivas. *Policy Paper Economics*, Working Group (EWG) 5, Observatorio Argentino, New School University, Washington, DC, 2005.

Roig, A. La "création" d'une monnaie éternelle, genèse de la convertibilité en Argentine. In F. Lordon (ed.), *Conflits de pouvoirs dans les institutions du capitalisme.* Paris: Sciences Po Les Presses, 2008, pp. 91–137.

Salama, P. Croissance et inflation en Argentine sous les mandatures Kirchner. *Problèmes d'Amérique latine*, n. 82, 2011. DOI: 10.3917/pal.082.0013

Sallum, B. Le libéralisme à la croisée des chemins au Brésil. *Revue Tiers Monde*, n. 167, 2001. DOI: 10.3406/tiers.2001.1522

Sallum, B. (ed.). *Brasil e Argentina hoje, Política e Economia*. São Paulo: Edusc, 2004.

Schvarzer, J. *La política económica de Martínez de Hoz*. Buenos Aires: Sudamericana, 1986.

Svampa, M. Les frontières du gouvernement Kirchner entre aspiration au renouveau et consolidation de l'ancien. *Revue Tiers Monde*, n. 189, 2007.

Théret, B. Les trois états de la monnaie. *Revue économique*, vol. 59, n. 4, 2008. DOI: 10.3917/reco.594.0813

Tizziani, A. Du péronisme au populisme ou la conquête – conceptuelle – du gros animal populaire. *Revue Tiers Monde*, n. 187, pp. 175–194, 2007.

Torija Zane, E. *Dynamique des prix et politique monétaire en Argentine (2003–2011)*, miméo, 2011.

5 Growth, functional income distribution and capital accumulation in Brazil

A prospective analysis of the contemporary period

Miguel Bruno and Ricardo Caffé

Introduction

This chapter investigates the relationship between *wage-labor nexus*, financialization and income distribution in Brazil. Inequality in income distribution is nothing new to the Latin American countries throughout many years. Income distribution has become increasingly unequal in most Latin American economies since the early 1970s. Various scholars and observers have promoted the notion that high and rising levels of poverty and income inequality remained the main problem in the developing countries. Since the 1990s, inequality in wealth distribution is becoming indeed a more pervasive phenomenon. The problems that lead to distributional inequality across countries have undergone major changes.

The application of the concept of *wage-labor nexus* or *rapport salarial*, proposed by regulationnist macro-analysis allows clarify not only the determinants of occupation and their categories. For *régulation* theory the *wage-labor nexus* is defined by the complementarily of the institutions structuring the employment contract and their compatibility with the actual regulation mode. The analysis of the WLN is also able to show, depending on their institutional configuration, how the direct and indirect wages determinants interact with macroeconomic dynamics. In this context, the sustainability of economic growth regime depends not only on public policy stimulus or fiscal and monetary policy. An issue that becomes even more complex when wage relations are subject to the pressures of financial markets and by interests of the rentiers and financial accumulation. Such question becomes even more complex when wage relations are subject to the pressures of financial markets and the interests of the rentier-asset accumulation. In the overall context of changes in the age structure brought by the Brazilian demographic transition, new challenges arise for a consistent analysis of the transformations of the Brazilian labor market. These transformations are not only consequence for the world of labor relations and the 'world of work'. Their impacts can negatively affect the macroeconomic viability of the current accumulation regime in Brazil, blocking the Brazilian socio-economic development process.

This chapter develops a preliminary analysis of contemporary transformations of the Brazilian wage-labor nexus (WLN) under the impact of the finance-dominated accumulation regime currently in effect in that country. This study begins in Section 2 outlining the theoretical and methodological framework used here. Section 3 deals with the main stylized facts of recent economic developments such as the effects of financialization of the economy, just as Brazil is going through its demographic transition. In Section 4, we analyze the distributional impacts of the evolution of the wage share and its main macroeconomic determinants. The income distribution is then analyzed in its structural factors such as productivity and average real wages. Section 5 provides a sectoral perspective, focusing on the evolution of the industry and the services sector in their divergent dynamics.

Theoretical and methodological framework

The regulationnist macro-analysis[1] are characterized by their institutionalist approach and history of contemporary economies. Five major areas of macroeconomic regulation, called institutional forms (IF), are defined by their decisive impact on patterns of economic growth and capital accumulation: the **wage-labor nexus** (WLN) or wage rapport, the form of international insertion, monetary and financial regime, the forms of competition and state-economy relations. Applied globally, the notion of regulation seeks to express the set of institutions and organizational forms able to provide macroeconomic coherence and social cohesion to the economy as a necessary condition of their systemic reproduction.

Throughout history or between different national economies in the same period, the IFs are combined in a certain hierarchy and complementarity determining the particularities of the mode of regulation. Regularities reproduced by mode of regulation so bring out an accumulation regime or growth regime. According to Boyer (1986), the WLN explains the existing settings between the various types of organization of the labor process and the prevailing compensation systems. In determining the workers' way of life, which is more or less closely linked to the acquisition of commodities or the use of collective services outside the market also influences the evolution of aggregate demand and the pace of economic growth.

The present study focuses on WLN by its fundamental place in capitalist economies, which are structured on the basis of wage societies. As well as the productivity/wage relations and the process of formation of direct wages and indirect relationships depend on their institutional characteristics, the WLN is a key element in determining the functional distribution of income. This, in turn, will determine the wage way of life and condition the evolution of aggregate demand and the pace of economic growth.

The WLN as wage relation system

The WLN can be defined as a specific institutionalized configuration of the links between capital and wage labor in its two fundamental dimensions: as primary distribution of income relation (the wage-profit division) and as a production relation (the organizational forms of the labor process). Since the wage labor is the main social relation of production and ownership in capitalist economies, ways of organizing production and remuneration systems associated with them are crucial to explain the direction and technical change speed, as well as the degree of equity in income distribution (Boyer, 2002). The french concept of *wage labour nexus* has a theoretical status, especially, a macroeconomic applicability. Meanwhile, the notion of *relation salariale* (wage relation) is the projection of the WLN in the immediate plans on the involved actors. Therefore, the WLN is a concept synthesis, the macroeconomic result of a combination of wage relations systems operating at sectoral level or firm individually considered. This conceptual distinction is important because each firm or sector has its own wage relations system. But this system is a combination of social and institutional rules that derive from the wage-labor nexus, in which he is inscribed, with rules that are specific to the firm or economic sector. Table 5.1 provides a comparison between the concepts of capital-labor relation, wage-labor nexus and wage relations, making accurate theoretical status and applicability of each.

Five basic components can be selected for an analysis of the WLN, in operationally feasible manner: a) organization of production and labor process include the characteristics of the productive technical bases, the management principles and factors generating productivity gains; b) skilled labor – it is the main factor determining the direct salary and expresses the set of theoretical and practical knowledge skills required by the job; c) rules for the mobilization and wage earners links to firms – including the different forms of contracting, subcontracting, links of intra and inter-firms employment relations and the labor market; d) determinants of the direct and indirect wages – expresses the different forms of direct and indirect compensation (social security and other benefits provided to the labor force), including their indexation mechanisms of wages to productivity gains and the cost of living; and e) workers' life style – standards of consumer goods and public or collective services that are responsible for style and wage-earners living conditions.

The analysis of these five combined dimensions enables a taxonomy of WLN. For example, if it is a competitive or flexible one, or non-competitive or heavily constrained by institutional mechanisms that regulate the capital-labor relationship in accordance with principles of labor law or as a result of union demands and also the basic features of the current accumulation regime.

The polar configurations for WLN on two theoretical models

Depending on the historical period or geographical area, the WLN configurations can be presented as two polar types' variants:

Table 5.1 The capital-labor relation, employment relation and wage-labor nexus: three related links but different theoretical meanings

Concepts	Definition	Application and theoretical status
Capital–Labor Relationship	• Link between capital and wage labor as an essential production and distribution relationship of capitalist economies • It does not specify the institutional components of this relationship	• Can be applied in the field of pure theory or not • In a micro, macro or sectorial level of analysis
Wage Relationship	• Emerges from the intersection of the regularities determined by WLN and those that are specific to firms and sectors of activity	• It's not applicable in the field of pure theory, but in the sectorial and empirical level
Wage–Labor Nexus (*Rapport salarial*)	• Defined by the complementarity of institutions that regulate the links between capital and labor	• It's not applicable in the field of pure theory • Suitable for the application at the macroeconomic level of analysis.

Source: Own elaboration

a) **A competitive WLN** can be observed when consumption of wage-earners is not yet fully inserted into the capitalist production (predominantly in the nineteenth century) or when wage formation occurs primarily by market mechanisms (regions or countries where workers and their associations have weak collective bargaining power and wages reflect the tensions between supply and demand for labor). In such a context, there is no *ex ante* division of productivity gains, but competitive wage determination and the level of institutionalization of contracting or employment relationships tends to be low;

b) **A non-competitive WLN** can be identified when wage formation mechanisms escape, at least partially, the direct influences of the labor market. In this case one can observe a set of rules, conventions and institutions that are responsible for the coding of links between capital and labor, establishing, among other implications, some form of division ex ante of productivity gains and recovery of purchasing power before inflationary losses.

In general, the first type of WLN is characterized by large quantitative and wage flexibility, unlike the second type. However, the non-competitive WLN proves to be better able to reach other levels or internal dimensions of flexibility to the most dynamic and innovative firms (versatility and multi-functionality, flexible remuneration based on the billing, but with stability of employment relationships etc.). Between these two polar theoretical cases, the real economies can generate intermediate configurations according to the degree of informality of labor relations, interdependencies of technical-productive systems with pay systems, patterns of presence and intervention of the state or even factors quantitative that rely on workforce available in view of the accumulation of capital needs.

A simple model for wage formation, given by equation (1) can represent these basic types of wage-labor nexus, against the parameters of data on productivity, indexing to the cost of living and the influences of employment:

$$RW = k \cdot PR + \rho \cdot P + \eta \cdot N \tag{1}$$

where RW is the real average wage; PR is labor productivity; P is the general level of prices; and N is the level of employment. All variables are at varying rates.

- If $k = 0$; $\rho = 0$ and $\eta > 0$, wage formation is predominantly competitive, characterizing the life of a competitive WLN. In this case, the tensions between supply and labor demand are the main factor of wage determination;
- If $k > 0$; $\rho > 0$; and $\eta = 0$ then it is a WLN fundamentally non-competitive because there is indexation of wages related to the evolution of productivity gains and the cost of living. However, the influence of the tensions of the 'labor market' is not statistically significant.

Nonetheless, even if the parameter ρ is statistically greater than zero, in which case there is some degree of indexation of wages subject to changes in the general price index, this is not sufficient to remove the competitive character of the WLN. This is the case of the WLN in the Brazilian economy over the period of high inflation, marked by the generalization of institutional devices indexing wages to changes in the general price index.

The duality of Brazilian WLN

Figure 5.1 seeks schematically to represent two basic axes of the Brazilian WLN, expressing its dual character. The justification to include the segment of self-employed in the informal axis of WLN stems from the existence of macroeconomic and structural interdependencies between these segments.

For example, empirical analysis shows that the reduction in jobs and wages of large and medium enterprises has launched a large mass of workers in the autonomous production of goods and services. According to DIEESE report, the most part of the workers self-employed are inserted in the most precarious economic activities of the country – with low levels of remuneration, qualification, stability and contribution to social security, and in addition, working in

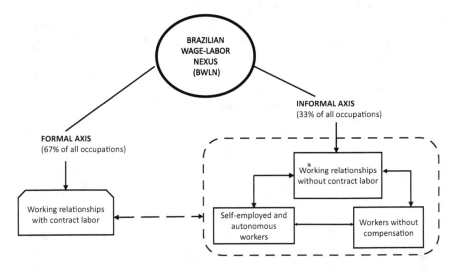

Figure 5.1 The Brazilian *wage-labor nexus* and its axes
Source: Own elaboration

places often without adequate infrastructure. Unlike salaried workers, in general the self-employed are occupied in the less dynamic activities in the country and requiring long working hours to generate a surplus.

Stylized facts of recent developments

Changes in the age structure of the population are among the main consequences of demographic transition. This process has raised quickly the number of people at working age that currently has already reached the mark of 70% of Brazil's total population. At first, the highest percentage of people in total available workforce can be constituted in a 'bonus' or 'dividend' demographic if the economy does its part, generating jobs in quantity and quality sufficient to raise and sustain rising living standards. The fall in dependency ratios of children and older people may then boost socio-economic development to income and population grows at rates compatible with the expansion of the labor supply. However, recent studies (Bruno, 2011, 2014) have shown that the Brazilian economy is subject to a particular process of financialization that does not allow the acceleration of growth on a sustainable basis. In addition, the financialization of the economy promotes the concentration of income and wealth, nullifying significant part of the positive effects of redistributive policies.

The demographic transition impacts the labor market and sets the WLN

The changes in the age structure of the population has direct and indirect effects on the labor market, and other no less significant impacts on the production and distribution of income and wealth structures. However, financialization by its concentrating nature of income and reducing productive investment imposes structural limitations to the continuity of the Brazilian economic and social development, despite the success of anti-poverty policies.

Figure 5.2 shows the evolution of the ratio WAP[2]/Total Population, which expresses the potential supply of labor available to the Brazilian economy between 1950 and 2014. Along with this indicator, the graph plots the general level of employment (N[3]/ Working-age Population-WAP). The level of employment workers includes the self-employed, because the latter holds a structural and macrodinamic relationship with the world of employment.

Between 1950 and 1990, job creation in Brazil followed very closely the expansion of the potential supply of labor force. In this sense, the economy showed no structural problem to absorb the growing numbers of new entrants in the WAP and later in the WF.[4] The ratio N/WAP stood oscillating about the trend growth of reason WAP/Population, but in many sub-periods it has remained above this. The new and disturbing phenomenon will take place from the 1990s, when these two ratios are disconnected abruptly between 1990 and 2001. This was a sub-period when unemployment rates were the highest in the reporting period of the new pattern of international insertion of Brazil. After that, the ratio N/WAP will enter a growth trajectory, parallel to the growth of the WAP, but without ever again intersecting it or even swinging next to this series. From 1997 to 2013, the differences between the two ratios are situated around an average of 10.3%, represented by the bars in Figure 5.2. How to explain these new regularities? Factors arising from the demographic transition, but also from public policies and low rates of economic growth brought about by financialization of the Brazilian economy grant a theoretically and empirically satisfactory explanation. Among these factors, public policies that contribute to the extension of years of study or training/qualification for effective entry into the labor market are considered. In that case, redistributive policies could be applied, which, once articulated with the first, would allow the early entry into the labor market to be postponed.

The fall of the total dependency ratio (children and elderly) has been caused by falling ratio of children, while the elderly continues to grow. However, near the year 2020, the ratio of total dependency will begin to grow, driven by an aging population. Then if the Brazilian economy is not able to reactivate their production and demand structures, a sustained economic growth path, it will lose this demographic opportunity. One of the key factors for this opportunity is the sustained improvement of living conditions of the population. However, this necessarily implies improvement of income distribution in favor of wages, as well as reducing other social inequalities.

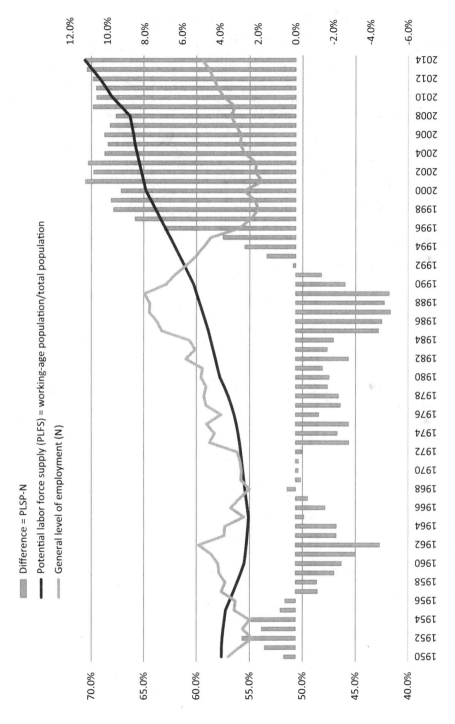

Figure 5.2 Potential labor force supply and employment generation: a long-term perspective (1950–2014)

Source: Own elaboration based on data from IBGE and IPEA

The financialization of the Brazilian economy

The concept of financialization seeks to express the existence of a macroeconomic and structural environment where the revaluation of capital takes place in a predominant and widespread use by financial channels, reducing the directly productive allocation. Figure 5.3 depicts three theoretical economies in accordance with their respective growth and capital accumulation schemes, and examples of countries. The rate of accumulation of productive fixed capital (g) is on the left axis, a key variable for the expansion of employment and income, which drives the dynamics of economic growth. The latter is represented on the right axis (y), while the horizontal axis is the macroeconomic profit rate.

It can be observed that economies showing high rates of accumulation and economic growth are those whose growth regimes are not financialized. In financialized growth regimes, the rate of accumulation is the lowest. Nevertheless, Brazil is in an intermediate situation, due to the demand derived stimuli of distributive policies and the rise in ratio wages/exchange in the period 2004–2008. One might, then, classify the Brazilian case as that of a financialised economy boost from state, in spite of this impulse has been reduced due to the fiscal adjustment that is implemented after 2015. It should also be noted that the financialization in Brazil is based on internal public indebtedness, while in developed countries with low interest rates, it is based on private debt (firms and households).

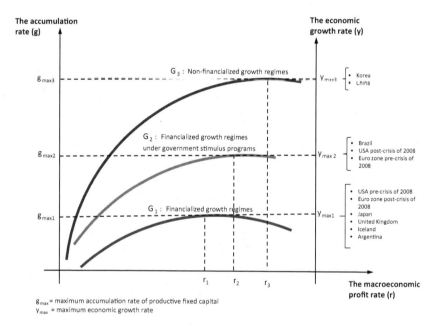

Figure 5.3 Theoretical curve of capital accumulation in financialized and non-financialized economies

Source: Own elaboration

Figure 5.4 shows the macroeconomic financialization rate (total stock of non-monetary financial assets/ productive fixed assets, in a definition similar to that proposed by Aglietta, 2001) along with the rate of accumulation of productive fixed capital. It is clear the contrast between the periods 1971–1991 and 1992–2013. At first, these structural variables remained at levels very close to each other and positive correlation. But in the second period, the disconnection is affirmed with the financialization rate growing exponentially, while the rate of accumulation remains too low for a country still in development with serious structural and social problems.

The distance between the two variables is nothing more than the expression of the degree of financialization of the Brazilian economy and the way in which financial allocations have become more attractive compared with allocations in productive activities. The consequences on employment and income generation are negative because, as studies of financialization acknowledge, this phenomenon reduces the rates of economic growth, increases the concentration of income and wealth and exerts multiple pressures on the WLN in order to make it even more flexible, both in terms of wages and quantitative factors.[5]

A very flexible WLN: the basis for a strong functional concentration of income and weak productivity gains

The WLN is considered central to the definition of the relationship between wages and employment, as each division of labor principle induce a certain type of technical change and then the evolution of productivity (Boyer, 1999, p. 21). This fundamental institutional form arises simultaneously as a production and distribution relation whose institutional framework is highly dependent on socio-technical and organizational factors (technical-productive bases and management practices) and macroeconomic dynamics. It is also conditioned by the fluctuations of short and medium-term labor market and by recurrent conflicts between capital and wage labor on how to share the economic surplus. Therefore one of the forms of evaluate the impacts of the finance-dominated accumulation regime on the reconfiguration of the Brazilian WLN is to analyze the determinants of the wage share as a measure of income distribution.

Determinants of wage share and functional income concentration

The wage share can be decomposed into their determinants both in real terms and at constant prices of a base year, as in nominal terms or current values. The apparent 'relative stability' of the aggregate share of national income that goes to labor over time has acquired the status of a stylized economic growth. One of the exceptions is partly the kaleckian theories, which are more open to variable income shares, since distribution is determined by exogenous factors like the degree of monopoly, or relative economic power of the socio-economic classes, or the current financialization of the economy, highlighted

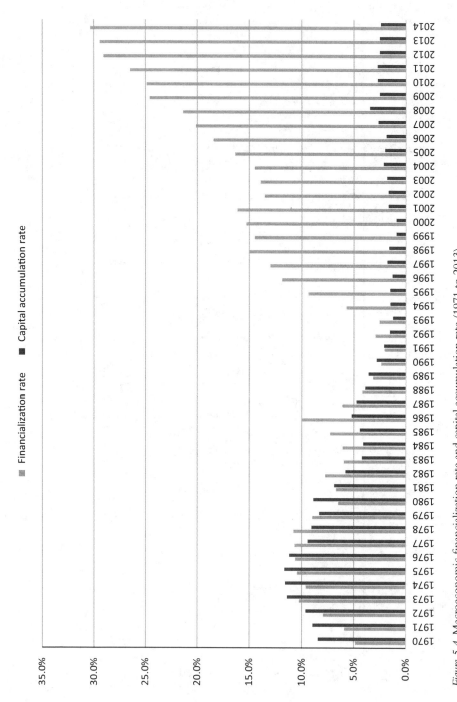

Figure 5.4 Macroeconomic financialization rate and capital accumulation rate (1971 to 2013)

Source: Own elaboration based on data from IBGE and IPEA

in the Stockhammer (2009) analysis. The wage share is a valuable heuristic device of the WLN, since its constant change appears only in the long run and is what allows to define it. In these terms, the variation of functional income distribution in the short and long term is a normal process. It is clear that literal constancy of the wage share cannot be meant. According to Juillard (2002), "The constancy of the wage share is obviously a corollary to the constancy of the profit share, which allows the self-financing of expansion investments, but rationalisation investment too." The link between wage-labor nexus, financialization and functional income distribution emerge as a significant connection of the analysis that comes forward.

Real impact factors

Considering the following symbols for the variables in question:

Real GDP = Y; real wages = W; ws = Wage Share = W/Y; C = general level of employment; RW = real wage or real average wage.

As $W = RW \cdot N$, we can also express ws depending on the general level of employment (N) and of the average real wage.

$$ws = \frac{W}{Y} = RW \cdot \frac{N}{Y}$$

Applying natural logarithms of both sides of equation yields the determinants of the rate of growth of wage share (ws):

$$ws° = RW° + N° - Y°$$

In the above equation, $Y°$ indicates the rate of economic growth. The results of this decomposition of the wage share are shown in Table 5.2, it can be seen that this recovery is due to the increase in the average salary above productivity gains during the 'Lula years'.

Nominal impact factors

We can analyze the evolution of the wage share in the total output of the economy, considering its determinants in nominal terms (Saint-Paul, 2003). Thus,

$$ws = \frac{w \cdot N}{Yn}$$

Table 5.2 Determinants of the wage share: real impact factors (1995–2013)

Ano	Ws=W/Y	dW	drw	dPRn	drw − dPRn
1995	36,38				
1996	37,69	3,59	7,43	3,71	3,72
1997	37,27	−1,09	0,60	1,71	−1,11
1998	38,02	2,00	1,34	−0,65	1,99
1999	36,90	−2,95	−7,11	−4,28	−2,83
2000	36,92	0,05	2,12	2,07	0,05
2001	36,74	−0,47	−1,28	−0,81	−0,47
2002	35,69	−2,86	−3,74	−0,90	−2,84
2003	36,55	2,42	1,94	−0,48	2,41
2004	35,70	−2,34	−0,31	2,08	−2,39
2005	36,68	2,74	4,10	1,32	2,78
2006	38,15	4,01	5,54	1,47	4,07
2007	38,87	1,89	6,26	4,29	1,97
2008	39,81	2,41	4,43	1,98	2,45
2009	41,53	4,34	2,94	−1,34	4,28
2010	41,81	0,66	7,42	6,71	0,71
2011	42,68	2,09	4,12	1,99	2,13
2012	45,28	6,07	5,00	−1,01	6,01
2013	45,14	−0,29	1,28	1,58	−0,30

Note: The "d" letter means the rate of change of the variables.

Source: Own elaboration based on data from IBGE and IPEA

Where w = nominal average wage. Given that RWW/pw, where pw is the IPCA used as a deflator of wages, we can also write the previous expression of ws as:

$$Ws = \frac{\frac{w}{pw} \cdot N}{\frac{Yn}{py}}$$

p_y is the implicit GDP deflator. Applying natural logarithms in both sides of the equation, we arrive at the following expression:

$$Ws° = w° − pw° + N° − (Yn° − py°)$$

But this expression (Yn° − py°) is the same as Y° (real growth rate of GDP). Finally, we arrive at a formula that sets out how the nominal wage, inflation, employment and economic growth impact the evolution of the wage share in the product. The results of this decomposition of the wage share in its evolution nominal or current prices are shown in Table 5.3. The growth of nominal

Table 5.3 Determinants of the wage share: factors of nominal impact (1995–2013)

Ano	Ws=W/Y	dWs	^{dw}nom	dPw	dN	dY
1995	36.38					
1996	37.69	3.59	17.71	9.56	−1.50	2.15
1997	37.27	−1.09	5.85	5.22	1.64	3.38
1998	38.02	2.00	3.01	1.65	0.69	0.04
1999	36.90	−2.95	1.20	8.94	4.73	0.25
2000	36.92	0.05	8.22	5.97	2.19	4.31
2001	36.74	−0.47	6.30	7.67	2.14	1.31
2002	35.69	−2.86	8.32	12.53	3.59	2.66
2003	36.55	2.42	11.42	9.30	1.63	1.15
2004	35.70	−2.34	7.27	7.60	3.56	5.71
2005	36.68	2.74	10.02	5.69	1.82	3.16
2006	38.15	4.01	8.86	3.14	2.45	3.96
2007	38.87	1.89	11.00	4.46	1.73	6.09
2008	39.81	2.41	10.59	5.90	3.13	5.17
2009	41.53	4.34	7.38	4.31	1.02	−0.33
2010	41.81	0.66	13.77	5.91	0.77	7.53
2011	42.68	2.09	10.89	6.50	0.73	2.73
2012	45.28	6.07	11.13	5.84	1.66	0.63
2013	45.14	−0.29	7.26	5.91	0.69	2.28

Note: The 'd' letter means the rate of change of the variables.

Source: Own elaboration based on data from IBGE and IPEA

wages above inflation, together with the expansion of occupancy, accounts for the growth of the wage share, especially from 2005.

$$Ws° = w° - pw° + N° - Y°$$

The results expressed by the two tables are complemented in Figure 5.5. It must be emphasized that as the wage share is mathematically identical to the ratio of average real wages and labor productivity, it is not possible to increase the share of wages in GDP – so necessary to socioeconomic development in Brazil – if they do not grow above productivity gains. This means that the problem that arises in the recent period the Brazilian economy should not be attributed to real wage increases, but the low productivity gains. The next scatter plots reveal still another feature of the Brazilian WLN with their estimates of elasticities concerned.

In Figure 5.6, we can see the strong dependence of job creation relative to activity level. For every 1% of economic growth, employment expands by an average of 0.62%.

In Table 5.4, we can observe the case with the average real income of these segments that compose the Brazilian WLN. The segments of the workers without labor contract and self-employed are very sensitive to economic dynamics. As expected, the greater rigidity is observed in the segment with a

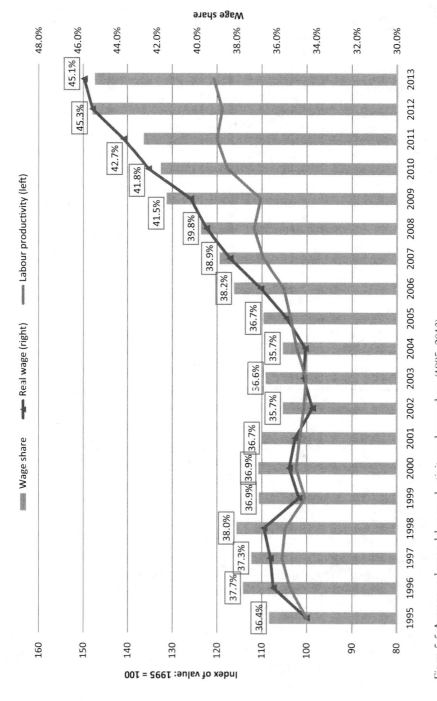

Figure 5.5 Average real wage, labor productivity and wage share (1995–2013)

Source: Own elaboration based on data from IBGE and IPEA

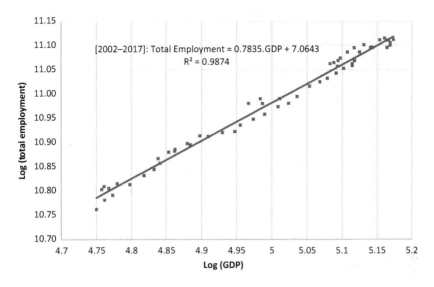

Figure 5.6 The general level of occupation is very dependent of the economic growth (2002–2013)

Source: Own elaboration based on data from IBGE and IPEA

Table 5.4 Elasticity of real average income to economic growth (2002–2013)

Components of Brazilian WLN	Wage-elasticity to the economic growth (2002–2013)
Formal employment (with labor contract)	0.3915
Informal employment (without labor contract)	1.071
Autonomous/sef–employment workers	0.8516

formal contract, since in that case wages are set by contract and do not change significantly with economic growth (GDP elasticity = 0.39).

An econometric estimation of the theoretical relationship for the two polar cases, equation 2 of Section 2, for the period 2002–2015 shows that Brazilian WLN is predominantly competitive and flexible (Table 5.4). The coefficients concerning the indexing to productivity gains (PR) and changes in the cost of living (P) were not statistically significant. Only the coefficient concerning the general level of employment (N), with a value of 0.92, was statistically significant. Real wages are highly sensitive to changes in the labor market, supporting the existence of a competitive wage formation. Econometric tests are in the annex.

Table 5.5 A determination of real wages predominantly competitive

Average real wage (RW)	Labor productivity (PR)	Inflation (P)	General level of employment (N)
Estimated coefficients	n.s.	n.s.	0.918854

Note: n.s. = not statistically significant p value.

Financialization, income and wealth inequality concentration: a structural and perverse link

Among the main effects of the interaction of the competitive setting of the Brazilian WLN, stands out a generation heavily dependent on the services sector compared to the shrinking of industrial production bases. Recent studies show that the Brazilian de-industrialization is premature because the specialization and the subsequent expansion of services has occurred at a level of per capita income of about US $4,000 set in 1990, lower than that of all countries surveyed (Araújo et al., 2012; Carvalho and Kupfer, 2011). In developed countries, the process begins in income levels per capita between US $8,000 to US $16,000. Figure 5.8 shows the evolution of the shares of the economic sectors in the Brazilian GDP. With the rapid decline of industry participation in the total added value, service activities have expanded simultaneously.

Precocious de-industrialization and 'swelling' of the service sector

A strong and early expansion of tertiary activities from the 'lost decade' was rated by Cardoso (1998) as a process of 'swelling' of the service sector, since it did not emerge from a normal growth expected as a usual process when the economy begins to enter the ranks of developed countries. Figure 5.8 is a scatter diagram with linear settings for the sub-periods 1950–1980 and 1981–2013, relating the stock of productive capital assets, weighted by their respective utilization rates, with the overall level of employment. The first sub-period was the strong Brazilian economic growth, with an average rate of 7.5% per year and corresponds to industrial expansion.

The fixed-capital elasticity of long-term employment showed the value of 0.3375, revealing well lower than in the sub-period 1981–2013, to a value of 0.9258. The higher elasticity in the second sub-period can be explained by the strong expansion of service activities that tend to be more labor intensive compared to industrial production units. This higher elasticity expresses the ease of generating jobs in an economy where the service sector has expanded rapidly and early, as seen from the 1980s crisis. During this period, the Brazilian labor market presents a high degree of salary and allocative flexibility, with a high frequency of unemployment, while it registered low rates of duration of

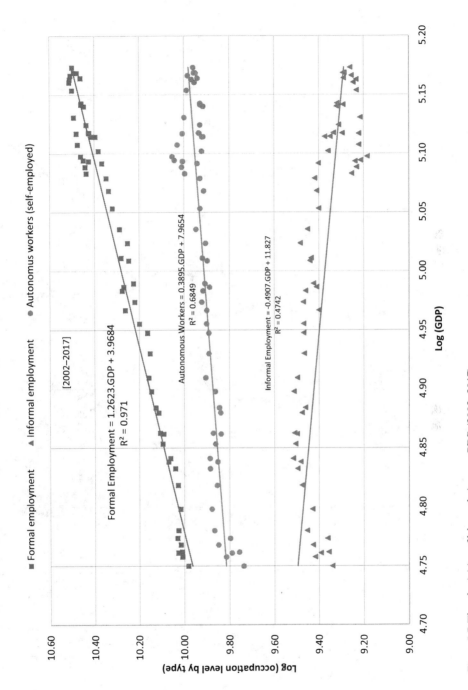

Figure 5.7 The elasticities of labor relations to GDP (2002–2017)
Source: Own elaboration based on data from IBGE and IPEA

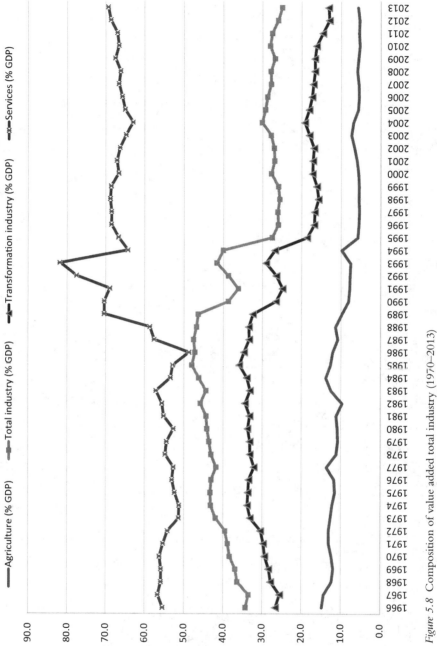

Figure 5.8 Composition of value added total industry (1970–2013)
Source: Own elaboration based on data from IBGE and IPEA

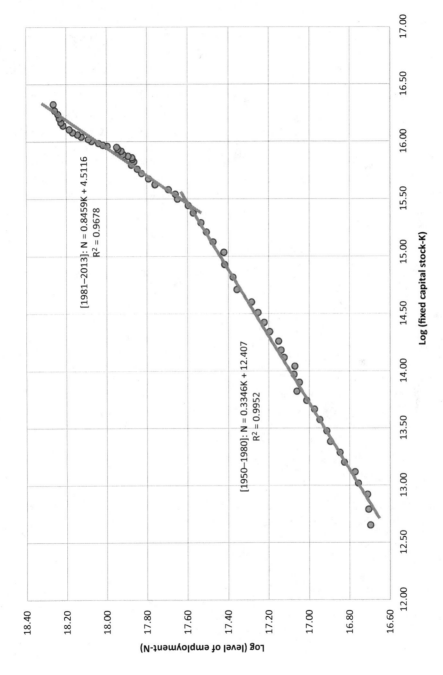

Figure 5.9 Two contrasting periods in the relation between productive FIXED capital and employment (1950–2013)

its occurrence. In that sense, the most regressive forms of flexibility should not be confused, such as the right of unconditional dismissal of workers to recruit cheap labor, forms of part-time work disguised as precarious working relationships and the fixing of a minimum wage for the young workforce, with the recomposition of the WLN that can combine social progress and economic efficiency.

Figure 5.10 show the negative correlation between financialization process of Brazilian economy and the wage share. Figure 5.11 shows a negative correlation between the Gini index and wage share.

Nevertheless, other macroeconomic phenomenon that should be highlighted refers to the behavior of the average real wage (RW) and labor productivity (PR) as shown in Figure 5.12. Until 2011, Figure 5.12 shows a parallel growth of RW with productivity gains (PR). However, from mid-2013, we observe a disconnection between these fundamental variables. Despite the inflexion in the expansion of wages, productivity declines more quickly, which will lead to the fall of the average rate of firm's income, as shown in Figure 5.13. To understand why, just consider that the average rate of profit (r) can be formulated by the following expression:

$$r = PR_k \cdot \left[1 - \frac{RW}{PR_n}\right],$$

where PR_k, RW e PR_n are respectively capital productivity, average real wages and labor productivity.

The growth of the average real wage (RW) without a corresponding increase in the productivity of capital and/or labor, results in a fall in the rate of profit (r). This decrease in the average profitability of fixed productive capital is the explanation for the economic slowdown that occurred in Rousseff's second presidential term, which in turn was aggravated by another adverse trend since then, the decline in the rate of fixed productive capital accumulation. In the same Figure 5.13 one can observe the decline of both. One of these adverse trends is precisely the intensification of pressure on labor, towards the reduction of labor costs, including the rhetoric that the Brazilian economy would already be on their level of full employment, which would explain the increase in inflation.

Low investment rates and economic growth

The low investment rate is another way to express the fact that the capital accumulation rate is still too low for a developing country. The process of financing the Brazilian economy is marked by financialization distinct from that which is based on the typical expansion of fictitious capital (shareholder value). Otherwise, it is focused rather on the mechanisms of interest-bearing

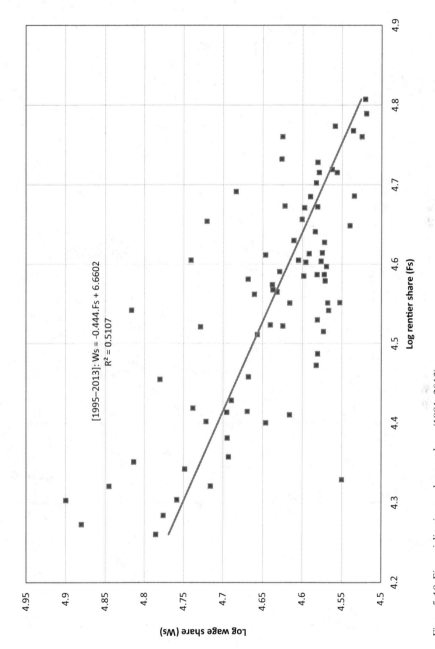

Figure 5.10 Financialization and wage share (1991–2013)

Note: Fs = financial income/GDP in log; Ws = wage share in log.

Source: Own elaboration based on IBGE data base

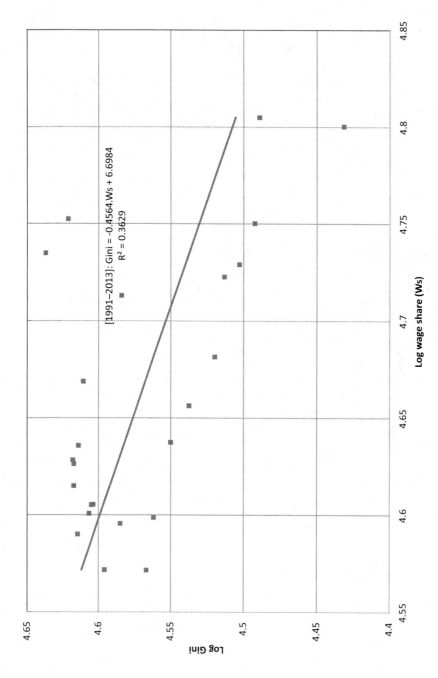

Figure 5.11 Wage share and Gini (1991–2013)
Source: Own elaboration based on IBGE data base

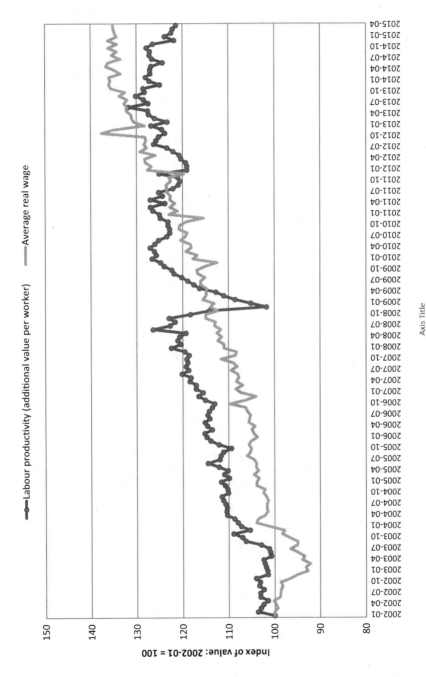

Figure 5.12 Productivity and real wage in manufacturing industry (2002–2015)

Source: Own elaboration based on IBGE data base

capital and, thus, on banks and interest rates as well. This makes a state-driven financialization, based on high interest essentially, constitutes its main form (Becker et al., 2010). The process of funding by interest income that characterizes Brazil, marked by a strong role of interest-bearing capital, directly increases the costs of productive capital allocations, so that the decrease in the corporate profit rate is accompanied by a falling rate of accumulation (Figure 5.13). The exception took place in under 2004–2009 period, when profit rate and accumulation rate grow together. The explanation of this stylized fact leads the analysis to consider the actions of public policy and investment promotion on the domestic front and the 'boom' of commodities internationally. Both factors contributed to raise the average rate of profit and that, consequently, increased the rate of accumulation. The occupation responds quickly since the productive structures are heavily loaded in service activities. As show above, given the high fixed-capital elasticity of employment in this sub-period, especially tertiary, very high rates of economic growth are not required to absorb the supply of labor force. The Brazilian economy rapidly reduced their unemployment rates, despite the growth in real wages and the permanence of low product growth rate until 2014. However, this positive trend will be reversed depending on the downswing that is currently stated. This empirical evidence show that Brazil is **a particular case of financialized growth regime with state push**, whose theoretical representation is in Figure 5.13.

The decline of the wage share in most advanced economies over the past 30 years is evidence that challenges the conventional wisdom. The notion of the relative long-term stability of the wage share is considered a stylized fact or an 'economic law' (Bowley's Law). Krämer (2011) recognizes that the data reveal in fact strong fluctuations of the shares of aggregate income over time, which poses a theoretical and empirical challenge to the major macroeconomic theories of growth and distribution, raised on a highly questionable basis on the real world. Hein (2012) presents a series of indicators that summarize the trends of what has been called a **functional redistribution of income** from the emergence of regimes or finance-dominated capitalisms. The analysis of the income distribution, despite the lack of attention received in the recent past, has had the attention in the study of its determinants, especially for advanced economies, although they also exist for the developing economies. In this sense, the effects of financialization and neoliberalism on income distribution are summarized from a Kaleckian perspective, through which it can be concluded that there is some evidence both contributed to the fall in wage share through three main channels. First, the change in the sectoral composition of the economy favorable to financial corporations from highly profitable financial firms to the detriment of the nonfinancial corporate and the government sectors. A second channel is the rise in overhead costs following the increase in the intra-distributive size of the corporate rentier classes, in particular the high management salaries and the interest payments, as well as the increase of the profit claims imposed on the corporate sector by the shareholders, as indicated

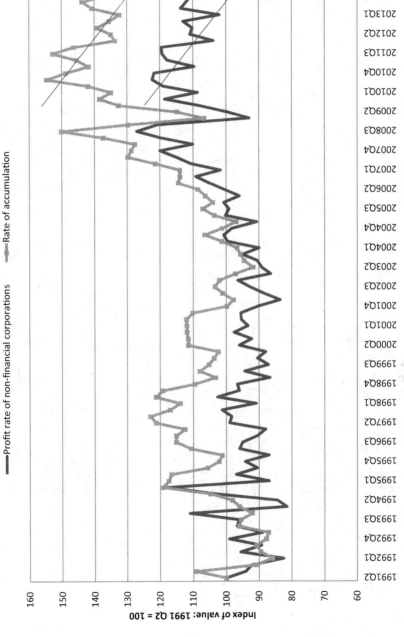

Figure 5.13 Profit rate of enterprises and rate of accumulation (1991–2013)

Source: Own elaboration based on IBGE data base

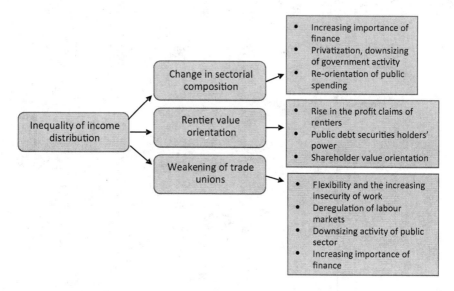

Figure 5.14 The effects of financialization on inequality of functional income distribution (decrease in wage share) – the Brazilian case

Source: Own elaboration based on Barradas and Lagoa (2015)

by Stockhammer (2004). A third transmission channel is the decline in the bargaining power of workers and trade unions triggered by shareholder value orientation and the short-termism of management, increasing the importance of the combination of a financial sector with weak trade unions, the harmful effects of liberalization and globalization of finance and trade, the labour market based on greater flexibility, greater job insecurity and wage moderation, the retrenchment of the government sector and abandoning social policies through a drastic reduction of demand-management policies.

Likewise, Stockhammer (2013) undertake an analytical assessment of the falling wage share of developed economies. In the study of advanced economies where data availability is better, financialization emerges as the most important cause for declining wage share. Reducing the welfare state and globalization has also had negative effects, although the negative effects of technological change have been modest. Figure 5.14 shows the potential determinants of the wage share of income derived from the growing inequality approach arising from the functional distribution of income.

Conclusion: the main results

As was seen with regard to the effects of financialization on the Brazilian functional income distribution, a change in the sectoral composition of the economy has resulted in a growing importance of the financial sector in relation to the non-financial sector in terms of value added, with the consequent loss of government activity. The reduction of direct government activity and the role of public companies promoted by the logic of financialization increased the presence of the market in areas previously under the control of the public sector. On the other hand, the growing importance of the financial sector tends to increase the share of gross profits across the economy because its labor share is proportionately lower than in the non-financial sector.

The rise of a labor share associated with the finance meant a decline in the profitability of the non-financial sector, which in turn implied a contraction of middle-classes, blue-collars and skilled workers wages in the non-financial sector. However, the argument that the Brazilian economy was in full employment in the second Lula term and the first Rousseff term must therefore be relativized. Brazil has a poorly structured labor market, with a high degree of informality and precarious employment relations, and it is unreasonable to consider any kind of occupation as representative of the full utilization, in particular, of the labor factor. An ambiguous policy of sustaining salaried consumption through temporary incomes or precarious jobs, expands a very fragile wage mass. Thus, the prolongation of a period with an intense increase in the labor force occupation rate found a strong reaction among the rentier classes and the *petite bourgeoisie* groups, who feel the decline of their share of the national income. An economy with rentiers, government and foreign trade, a basic conflict of interest between employers and employees will continue to persist with varying degrees of unemployment. When labor costs become an obstacle to increasing rentier profit, two very important things happen: the real wage rises more than productivity and several concomitant factors play a role that can create further tensions within the growth process. The growth rate necessarily begins to decelerate, which leads to a fall, often precipitate, in expectations, in investment, and, finally, in profits. Thereafter, the wage shares and profit shares both fall, but the former less than the latter, so that the share of labour rises whilst the share of profits falls. This is the crux of the crisis.

From the results of our analysis, a policy suggestion for enhanced growth in Brazil will be to pro-labour distributional policies to ensure increased productivity, taking advantage of strong positive effects on labour effort and productivity-enhancing investments. To do so, it should take into account international trade and net exports in assessing the impact of changes in income distribution, which adds a high degree of complexity. Thus, the favorable domestic impact of an increase in wage share can be reversed when we consider the effects on net exports. While the negative impact of a larger wage share on profitability is not very important, one can hypothesize that the economic policy, supposedly heterodox, can persuade the absence of antagonisms between capitalists and workers like in the Brazilian capitalist economy, where inflation target policies controlled by the logic of financialization generate an excess of capacity.[6] In this case, the **classic Kaleckian wage-led growth** is credible under the voluntarist formula that is possible to increase both, real wages and employment, on the one hand, and profits and growth, on the other. However, in an economy open to financialization, where the State itself is the issuer of interest bearing securities that feed the favorable distribution of financial profits, a limit is imposed. The conflict, previously disguised or attenuated, reveals itself in a dilemma between maintaining a favorable redistribution to wages and the support of international competitiveness manifested in the demands of the corporate shareholder value.

In face of what was found, the foregoing is a summary of the main implications. Figure 5.15, in the appendix, seeks to represent the Brazilian WLN under three main forces of transformation. These constraints will affect both the formation of direct wages as well as indirect wages (pensions, welfare, health and education provided by the public sector), through institutional changes in order to further deepen the degree of quantitative and wage flexibility.

As emphasizes Boyer (2004), the feasibility of growth regimes subjected to the financial revaluation depends crucially on the configuration of the WLN. In order for these regimes provide relatively stable trajectories of the product and income growth, WLN cannot be competitive and flexible. Too much competition in the labor market destroys the coherence of the macroeconomic regime of accumulation, because the volatility of the resulting aggregate demand makes labor income extremely volatile and more sensitive to the cycles inherent in such regime. Hence, this is one of the by-products of finance-dominated capitalism (financialization) and rentier asset-accumulation is the increased degree of financial vulnerability of households. In this regime, the rapid reduction of industrial employment raises the degree of deterioration of labor relations and prematurely expands service activities, which does not allow the economy to generate productivity gains needed for a sustained improvement in the living conditions of the population and more specifically for the population subject to the underlying employment relationship.

Notes

1 This refers to the French Regulation Theory.
2 Working-age Population (*WAP*).
3 *N* equal to workers plus self-employed.
4 Workforce.
5 The Law Bill 4.330/2004 provides for the service contract to third parties and is proposed to regulate the so-called outsourcing. Their main legal commentators consider that this bill generalizes and creates a situation conducive to the precariousness of labor relations in Brazil.
6 Blecker (1989).

References

Aglietta, Michel. *Macroéconomie financière. Vol 1 – Finance, croissance et cycles e vol. 2 – Crises financières et régulation monétaire*. La découverte: Repères, 2001.

Araújo, Eliane, Bruno, Miguel, and Pimentel, Débora. Financialization Against Industrialization: A Regulationnist Approach of the Brazilian Paradox. *Révue de la Régulation. 11, 1er semester/spring: Les capitalisms en Amérique Latine. De l'économique au politique*, 2012.

Barradas, R., and Lagoa, S. (2015). *Functional Income Distribution in a Small European Country: The Role of Financialisation and Other Determinants.*

Becker, J., Jäger, J., Leubolt, B., and Weissenbacher, R. Peripheral financialization and vulnerability to crisis: A regulationist perspective. *Competition & Change*, v. 14, n. 3–4, pp. 225–247, 2010.

Blecker, R. A. International Competition, Income Distribution and Economic Growth. *Cambridge Journal of Economics*, v. 13, n. 3, pp. 395–412, 1989.

Boyer, Robert. *La théorie de la régulation: une analyse critique.* Éditions La découverte, Paris, 1986.

Boyer, Robert. Le lien salaire/empli dans l théorie de la régulation. Autant de relations que de configurations institutionnelles. Chiers d'économie politique, n⁰ 34, L' Harmattan, Paris, p.101-161. Boyer, Robert. *Théorie de la Régulation. Les fondamentaux.* La découverte, Repères: Paris, 2004.

Boyer, Robert, and SAILLARD Yves (dir.) Théorie de la régulation. L'état des savoirs, Nouvelle édition completée. Éditions La Découverte & Syros, Paris, 2002

Bruno, Miguel. Financeirização e crescimento econômico: o caso do Brasil. *ComCiência, Maio,* n. 128, pp. 0–0, 2011. ISSN: 1519-7654.

Bruno, Miguel. Desafios do desenvolvimento socioeconômico brasileiro: uma perspectiva institucionalista do período recente. In *Panorama Socioeconômico do Brasil e suas relações com a Economia Social de Mercado,* Fundação Konrad Adenauer, Rio de Janeiro, 2014.

Bruno, Miguel, Diawara, Hawa, Araújo, Eliane, Reis, Anna Carolina, and Rubens, Mário. Finance-Led Growth Regime No Brasil: estatuto teórico, eviências empíricas e consequências macroeconômicas. *Revista de Economia Política,* v. 31, n. 5 (125), pp. 730–750, 2011, edição especial.

Cardoso Jr., José Celso. Crise e desregulação do trabalho. Texto para Discussão -*TD n°814.* Instituto de Pesquisa Econômica Aplicada - IPEA, agosto, Brasília, 2001.

Cardoso Jr., José Celso. Determinantes da recuperação do emprego formal no Brasil: evidências para o período 2001/2005 e hipóteses para uma agenda de pesquisa. *Revista de Economia Política,* v. 29, n. 4 (116), pp. 357–376, 2009, outubro-dezembro.

Carvalho, L., and Kupfer, D. Diversificação ou especialização: uma análise do processo de mudança estrutural da indústria brasileira. *Revista de Economia Política,* n. 4(124), pp. 618–637, 2011.

Checchi, D., and García-Peñalosa, C. Labour Market Institutions and the Personal Distribution of Income in the OECD. *Economica,* v. 77, n. 307, pp. 413–450, 2010.

Colletis, Gabriel. Evolution du rapport salarial, financiarisation et mondialisation. *Association Recherche & Régulation. RR Working n° 2005–6 série C.*

De Aguiar Medeiros, C. A influencia do Salário Mínimo sobre a Taxa de Salários no Brasil na última Década. *Economia e Sociedade,* v. 24, n. 2, 2017.

Dünhaupt, Petra. *Determinants of Functional Income Distribution – Theory and Empirical Evidence.* Global Labour University, International Lbour Organization, 2013.

Dutt, A. K. *Growth and Personal Versus Functional Income Distribution: Issues and Heterodox Models,* mimeo, UC Berkeley, April 2014.

Freeman, Richard. It's financialisation! *International Labor Review,* v. 149, n. 2, 2010.

Giovannoni, Olivier. Functional Distribution of Income, Inequality of Poverty: Stylized Facts and the Role of Macroeconomic Policy. *UTIP Working Paper n. 58,* 2010.

Gomme, P., and Rupert, P. Measuring Labor's Share of Income. *Policy Discussion Paper no. 7,* Federal Reserve Bank of Cleveland, 2004.

Harrison, A. *Has Globalization Eroded Labor's Share? Some Cross-Country.* 2002.

Hein, Eckhard. *The Macroeconomics of Finance-Dominated Capitalism and Its Crisis.* Northampton, MA: Edward Elgar Publishing, 2012.

Hein, Eckhard. *Finance-Dominated Capitalism and Redistribution of Income: A Kaleckian Perspective*. 2013.
Juillard, M. Accumulation Regimes. In R. Boyer and Y. Saillard (eds.), *Régulation Theory: The State of the Art*. London: Routledge, 2002.
Köhler, K., Guschanski, A., and Stockhammer, E. How Does Financialisation Affect Functional Income Distribution? A Theoretical Clarification and Empirial Assessment. *PKSG, Working Paper 1507*, July 2015.
Krämer, H. M. Bowley's Law: The Diffusion of an Empirical Supposition Into Economic Theory. *Cahiers d'économie politique/Papers in Political Economy*, n. 2, pp. 19–49, 2011.
Kristal, T. Good Times, Bad Times: Postwar Labor's Share of National Income in Capitalist Democracies. *American Sociological Review*, v. 75, n. 5, pp. 729–763, 2010.
Liew, K. S. Which Lag Length Selection Criteria Should We Employ? *Economics Bulletin*, v. 3, n. 33, pp. 1–9, 2004.
Marquetti, A. *Nota metodológica sobre as informações estatísticas utilizadas na análise do padrão de progresso técnico na economia brasileira, 1950–1998*. Instituto de Economia/ PUC-RS, 2003.
Palley, Thomas. Financialisation: What It Is and Why It Matters. *Working Papers n° 525*. The Levy Economics Institute of Bard College, 2007.
Paulani, Leda. A crise do regime de acumulação com dominância da valorização financeira e a situação do Brasil. *Estudos Avançados*, v. 23, n. 66, 2009.
Pesaran, M. H., and Shin, Y. An Autoregressive Distributed-Lag Modelling Approach to Cointegration Analysis. *Econometric Society Monographs*, v. 31, pp. 371–413, 1998.
Pesaran, M. H., Shin, Y., and Smith, R. J. Bounds Testing Approaches to the Analysis of Level Relationships. *Journal of Applied Econometrics*, v. 16, n. 3, pp. 289–326, 2001.
Pichler, W. A. Tendências da sindicalização no Brasil: 1992–2009. *Indicadores Econômicos FEE*, v. 38, n. 3, 2011.
Rebérioux, Antoine. *La financiarisation du rapport salarial: étude économetrique sur reponse, 1998*. Paris: Fórum de la Régulation, 2003.
Saint-Paul, Gilles. Interpreter correctement l'evolution de la part salariale. Université de Toulouse I et Ministère de l'Ecologie www.oocities.org/gspaul_8047/soft/comm1.pdf. 2003.
Stockhammer, E. Financialisation and the Slowdown of Accumulation. *Cambridge Journal of Economics*, v. 28, n. 5, pp. 719–741, 2004.
Stockhammer, E. *Determinants of Functional Income Distribution in OECD Countries* (No. 5/2009). IMK Study, 2009.
Stockhammer, E. Why Have Wage Shares Fallen? An Analysis of the Determinants of Functional Income Distribution. In *Wage-Led Growth* (pp. 40–70). London: Palgrave Macmillan UK, 2013.

Appendix

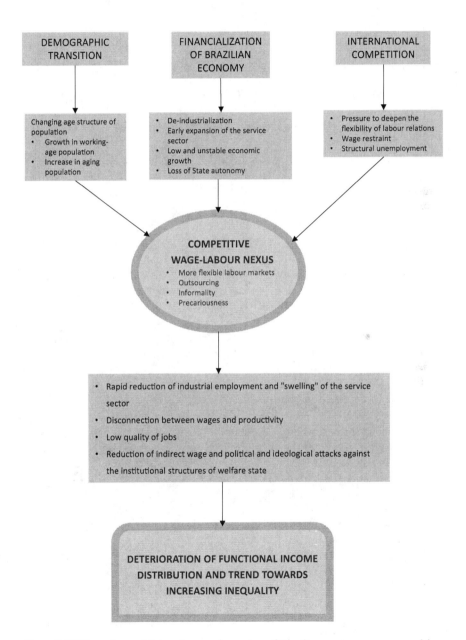

Figure 5.15 Three forces driving the transformation of Brazilian contemporary wage-labor nexus

6 Financial markets, public policy and consumer credit growth in Brazil

María Alejandra Caporale Madi

Introduction

Throughout the last decades, different growth models have overwhelmed the global scenario: while some countries have presented a consumption-driven growth model fueled by credit, generally followed by current account deficits, other countries have shown an export-driven growth model, mainly characterized by modest consumption growth and large current account surpluses (Stockhammer, 2008; Stockhammer and Wildauer, 2016). Despite differences in the models of growth, the finance-led accumulation regime fostered the deregulation of financial markets and promoted the enlargement of access to credit and other financial services to people that have been historically excluded from formal financial markets, both in developed and developing countries (World Bank, 2004). Indeed, since neoliberalism has had decisive impacts on labor markets, new forms of credit access conditions have been considered by global governance guidelines to shape the conditions of social reproduction (Gonçalves and Madi, 2005).

Since the early 2000s, the Brazilian government favoured new institutional mechanisms to increase the process of financial inclusion (Secretaria de Política Econômica, Brasil, 2002). Thus, the deregulation of the consumer credit market was a result of the redefinition of federal government intervention strategies aimed at promoting economic growth and social inclusion in the context of global economic integration. In fact, the intervention strategies of the federal Government underscored the importance of the credit system to shape the conditions of economic growth.

According to FEBRABAN (Brazilian Federation of Banks), the volume of total credit reached 58.9% of gross domestic product (GDP) in 2014 – while it reached only 26% in 2003. The access to financial services was encouraged by multiple delivery channels, mainly bank correspondents that consolidated their national physical presence, besides automatic teller machines, internet and mobile banking. In this setting, the number of people with an active relationship with a financial institution increased to almost 84% of Brazil's adult population above 15 years old (BACEN, 2012a). It is in this context that the national strategy of financial education and the supervision of conduct were introduced as new issues in the arena of public policy (Madi, 2017).

Considering this background, this chapter aims to analyze the evolution of the consumer credit market in Brazil in the period between 2003 and 2015. This chapter addresses that the enlargement of credit access was the result of the federal government's policy interventions oriented to promote financial inclusion as a driver of economic growth. As a result, the consumer credit market expanded and this expansion is referred to personal loans that mainly include: a) consigned loans,[1] b) overdrafts of bank accounts, c) consumer loans made against housing, vehicles or durable goods and d) credit cards.

Section 1 shows how these interventions favoured new institutional mechanisms in the financial sector that turned out to shape the enlargement of credit access to all the Brazilian population. Section 2 presents an overview of the changes in the consumer credit market after the global financial crisis of 2007–2008. Section 3 considers the evolution of the consumer credit market between 2014 and 2015, in a context of recessive trends. Finally, the conclusions.

Institutional changes and credit access, 2003–2007

In the period between 2003 and 2008 a striking feature of the Brazilian economy has been the speed of growth of the consumer credit market (Gonçalves and Madi, 2013b). The private banks led this movement – with a market share of 64% of total credit at the end of 2008 (Paim, 2013). During the same period, the total credit as a proportion of GDP rose from 25.7% to 40.7%. The expansion of personal loans turned out to happen after the removal of historical obstacles associated with the lack of access to formal credit markets, mainly by low income people (Madi and Gonçalves, 2007). In fact, since the early 2000s, the federal government strategies favored new institutional mechanisms to promote financial inclusion- the so-called bancarization, in order to increase the level of access to and the degree of use of formal financial services. As a result, the indicators of bancarization mainly refer to the percentage of population that access and use the banking services. The main features of the new legal and institutional setup are shown in Table 6.1.

Among the measures oriented to microfinance and the supply of financial services to low-income populations, the federal government privileged:

- The creation of simplified bank accounts that could be opened without income certification and handled primarily by means of magnetic cards;
- The expansion of bank correspondents;
- The regulation of the consigned loans to waged workers and retired people of the public pension system;
- The reduction of the bank's credit risk by new legal physical guarantees in credit contracts associated with durable goods (mainly vehicles);
- The creation of institutions that could promote the credit expansion to low income population besides the retail banking channels, such as the Popular Bank of Brazil, micro-credit institutions, cooperative banks and credit cooperatives;

Table 6.1 Financial inclusion: legal and institutional set up, 2003–2005

Year	Institutional issue	Legal framework
2003	Bank representatives	CMN Resolution No 3153
	Popular Bank of Brazil (Banco Popular do Brasil)	Law No 10738
	Microcredit societies	CMN Resolution No 3182
2004	Simplified accounts	CMN Resolution No 3211
	Consigned loans	Law No 10820/2003
	Cooperative banks	CMN Resolution No 3188
	Credit cooperatives	Law No 10865
	Micro–credit Program oriented to production	Decree No 5288, Law No 11110/2005
2005	Credit risks and Guarantees	CMN Resolution No 3258

Note: CMN: National Monetary Council
Source: Madi and Gonçalves (2007)

- The creation of a micro-credit program oriented to productive activities;
- The definition of new funding based on bank deposits to expand micro-credit loans;
- The reduction of costs related to fees and taxes in simplified accounts and micro-finance operations.

(Madi and Gonçalves, 2007)

As a result of these changes, from 2003 to 2006, the number of bank current accounts evolved from 87 million to 102.6 million, while the number of savings accounts totaled 75 million as of 2006. The use of electronic means of payment advances with each passing year. In 2006, the number of credit cards grew 16.2% and amounted 79 million. The number of credit cards also increased from 45 million to 79 million, with a number of transactions that almost doubled in that period (FEBRABAN, 2006). Among the indicators of financial inclusion, the expansion of delivery channels was mainly concentrated in the ATM network and the banks correspondents, from 2003 to 2007 (Table 6.2). According to FEBRABAN, in 2005, 82.94% of Brazilians who use the services of the bank correspondents earned up to 3 times the minimum wage.

The public retail bank Caixa Econômica Federal (Caixa), taking advantage of its experience in dealing with lower income population, initiated operations with simplified bank accounts in May 2003, totalizing, in December 2004, 2.5 million new accounts. The public retail bank Banco do Brasil created a separate bank, the Banco Popular do Brasil, in order to implement a segmentation strategy including the low income market (Madi and Gonçalves, 2007). Afterwards, the strategy of expanding the financial access was also followed by the private retail banks that enhanced, through competition, the incorporation of the market segments of lower income clients. At first, the private retail banks

Table 6.2 Banking sector: delivery channels, 2003–2007

	2003	2004	2005	2006	2007
Bank Branches	16,829	17,260	17,515	18,067	18,308
Traditional Points (1)	10,045	9,837	9,527	10,220	10,427
ATMs (2)	24,367	25,595	27,405	32,776	34,790
Bank Correspondents (3)	36,474	46,035	69,546	73,031	84,332 (3)
Total	87,715	98,727	123,993	134,114	147,857

Notes: (1) Include advanced points of attendance (PAA), points of banking attendance (PAB), points of cooperative attendance (PAC), points of micro-credit attendance (PAM), advanced points of rural credit (Pacre), points for collection and payment (PAP), points to buy gold (PCO) and administrative units;(2) Automatic Teller Machines; (3) Non-financial agents of banks.

Source: Adapted from Gonçalves et al. (2009a)

privileged short-term credit strategies centered on the expansion of personal loans with higher spreads (Oliveira and Carvalho, 2007). After 2004, the banking system also expanded personal loans at lower interest rates due to the guarantees based on the future wages and pensions (consigned loans). As a result, the participation of consigned credit in total personal loans increased at the rate of 10.0% in the period between May 2004 and May 2005. In this new credit scenario, millions of Brazilian households that belong to classes D and E introduced almost 20 new products in their consumption baskets, and class C almost 16, such as food and clothes items, but also cars, mobile phones, households durables and electronic devices (Madi and Gonçalves, 2007).[2] Despite the legal and institutional changes, the development of microfinance in Brazil, mainly oriented to productive activities, remained below the government expectations (Madi and Gonçalves, 2013b). In addition, the bancarization process has enabled cooperative banks to increase their activities in number, although their participation remains low in terms of the total assets – almost 1.28% in 2003 (Gonçalves et al., 2009a). Indeed, the new institutional set up contributed to shape new types of credit contracts in the retail banking system and also affected the standards of credit risk management less-strict requirements in terms of income certification in the context of segmentation strategies aimed at foster financial inclusion (Gonçalves and Madi, 2013b). While in December 2003, the total credit in relation to GDP (Gross Domestic Product) was 24.60% of GDP, as of December 2007 this indicator amounted 35.17% (Table 6.3). At the end of 2007, the total credit oriented to household in relation to GDP was almost 16%.

The legal and institutional changes turned out to diminish the risk for banks, contributed to the reduction interest rates, the lengthening of the period of financing and the increase in the volume funded. Thus, the percentage of personal loans in relation to GDP grew from 9.33% to 15.98% in the period between 2003 and 2007 (Table 6.3).

The legal and institutional changes, in truth, helped to shape the expansion of loans to households. First, the introduction of consigned loans not only

Table 6.3 Total credit in relation to GDP: personal loans and total, in %

Year/December	Personal loans in relation to GDP	Total credit in relation to GDP
2003	9.33	24.60
2004	10.51	25.69
2005	12.29	28.27
2006	13.79	30.92
2007	15.98	35.17

Source: Adapted from Mora (2014)

Table 6.4 Personal loans by type, 2005–2007, in %

Year	Vehicles	Credit cards/overdraft	Consigned loans	Others
2005	32.7	14.3	20.4	32.6
2006	33.1	13.1	25.1	26.7
2007	34.0	12.6	26.8	26.6

Source: Adapted from Mora (2014)

caused a reduction in the cost of borrowing but enhanced further increase in the participation of this type of personal loans in the period between 2005 and 2007.

Second, there also was an increase in the participation of credit oriented to vehicles between 2005 and 2007 due to institutional changes, more specifically to the improvement of the system of guarantees where the buyer becomes the owner of the vehicle only after having paid the full debt (Mora, 2014).[3]

Third, long term credit loans also rose due to the growth of real estate credit oriented to households, mainly after 2005 (Table 6.5). Institutional changes also positively affected the real estate market, reducing the risks in these operations because of the system of guarantees (Mora, 2014).[4] Besides, as already highlighted before, the scenario of high rates of employment and income growth helped to increase the level of credit demand.

Evolution of personal loans after the global crisis, 2008–2013

Taking into consideration the immediate impacts of the global crisis in the Brazilian economy, the deterioration of private expectations provoked a fall in the levels of production and new jobs; an increase in the levels of stocks; a fall in the investment levels; and liquidity constraints in the domestic credit and capital markets. The first effects of formal job losses were especially felt in manufacturing and construction. Regarding the level of occupation soon after the global crisis, negative variations were observed for both men and women

Table 6.5 Real state credit: total loans and loans to households in relation to GDP, 2003–2007, in %

Year/December	Loans to households in relation to GDP	Total loans (households and corporations) in relation to GDP
2003	1.47	1.47
2004	1.34	1.69
2005	1.39	1.77
2006	1.54	2.01
2007	1.74	2.40

Source: Adapted from Mora (2014)

Table 6.6 Brazil: gross domestic product (GDP) and consumption of families, 2000–2014

Year	GDP annual growth (in %)	GDP per capita (current $US)	Consumption of families as % of GDP
2000	4.11	3,766.20	64.59
2004	5.76	3,623.05	60.20
2005	3.20	4,770.18	60.50
2006	3.96	5,860.15	60.43
2007	6.07	7,313.56	59.87
2008	5.1	8,787.61	59.73
2009	−0.13	8,553.38	61.95
2010	7.53	11,224.15	60.22
2011	3.97	13,167.47	60.27
2012	1.92	12,291.47	61.41
2013	3.00	12,216.90	61.72
2014	0.50	12,026.62	62.95
2015	−3.77	8,757.20	63.84

Source: World Bank, http://data.worldbank.org/indicator/NY.GDP.PCAP.CD/countries?page=1; ata.worldbank.org/indicator/NY.GDP.MKTP.KD.ZG/countries?page=1, update 2/08/2017

(Madi, 2016). These tensions shifted to the political sphere and led to economic policy responses in order to support economic growth (Gonçalves and Madi, 2013b).

As the unfolding impacts of the global crisis on the Brazilian economy, the federal government stimulated domestic demand levels and supported the continuation of the process of income distribution (Gonçalves and Madi, 2011). As a result, positive rates of households' aggregate consumption supported the macroeconomic growth (Table 6.6).

Indeed, the level of domestic consumption was stimulated by a reorientation of monetary and fiscal policies. Aware of the political threaten of unemployment, the government extended the period of granting unemployment benefits and increased its value. In this scenario, the government supported programs oriented to formal job creation and income redistribution (Gonçalves and Madi, 2011). Specific job creation programs oriented to young people – such as the First Job – were expanded all over the country. In addition, the government enlarged the coverage of the cash transfer program 'Bolsa Familia' that targets families under the poverty or extreme poverty lines. At the end of 2009, the number of families included in this program achieved almost 2 million and reached 12.4 million people (Sicsú, 2011). In this setting, the increase in the real minimum wage has been considered an important instrument to promote income distribution since it also impacts the income of a little more than two-thirds of those receiving Social Security benefits (about 27 million people). Besides, domestic consumption also continued to be buoyed by a set of fiscal policies, such as the reduction in the tax on industrialized products (cars, motorcycles, capital goods and construction materials) and changes in the consigned loans in order to enlarge the share of income flows potentially committed to debt (Madi and Gonçalves, 2014).

In the aftermath of the crisis, anti-cyclical credit policies sought to preserve the expansion of consumer loans in Brazil. In this setting, the role of public banks (Banco do Brasil and Caixa Econômica Federal) was relevant to cushion the effects of the global crisis on the Brazilian economy (Gonçalves and Madi, 2013a). Against a backdrop of retraction of the total amount of consumer credit operations in the domestic private financial sector, the rates of growth of consumer loans increased in all regions of the country on behalf of the Brazilian public banks' new credit strategies – also oriented to residential purposes. The credit scenario was characterized by the growth of the participation of public institutions in total credit in relation to GDP. This participation grew form 14.7% in 2008 to 28.1% in 2013 (Paim, 2013).

Among the relevant indicators of financial inclusion, the number of ATMs (Automatic Teller Machines) per 1000 adults in Brazil increased 81% from 2006 to 2010 and turned out to be almost 40% higher than the number of ATMs in developed countries and 350% greater than in other developing countries (Table 6.7).

In addition to the expansion of the ATMs, the number of bank correspondents jumped from 83,777 in 2005 to 151,523 by 2010 – presenting a rate of growth that amounted 81% (Table 6.8). These bank correspondents were

Table 6.7 Indicator of financial inclusion: number of ATMs per 1000 adults, 2010

	Number of ATMs per 1000 adults
Developed countries	9.4
Developing countries	2.9
Latina American and the Caribbean	3.1
Brazil	12.8

Note: ATMs: Automated Teller Machines

Source: Banco Central do Brasil (2011)

initially oriented to transaction activities related to means of payment, such as deposits, payments and tax collection. However, without abandoning these transaction activities, the bank correspondents started to also expand the sale of personal loans and credit cards mainly to people who earned up to three times the minimum wage (Gonçalves et al., 2009a, b).

After the mid-2000, the big retail banks, in truth, stimulated the expansion of the bank correspondents in order to implement their strategies toward financial access and personal loans. As as of 2009, the public banks Banco do Brasil and Caixa Econômica Federal got together a great number of the bank correspondents while, among the private banks, banco Bradesco developed the most proactive strategy towards the expansion of this kind of delivery channel (Table 6.9).

Taking into account other indicators of financial inclusion, the number of borrowers revealed the continuous growth of consumer loans, even in the aftermath of the global crisis, increasing from 17,927 million people, as of December 2008, to 30,159 million in December 2010 (Table 6.10).

As a result of the government anti-cyclical strategies, the nominal amount of personal loans increased 104.4% in the period between January 2008 and December 2013 (DIEESE, 2014) and, as a result, the total loans oriented to households increased their participation in relation to GDP (Table 6.11).

Between 2008 and 2013, some features of the credit market oriented to households can be highlighted. First, there was an expansion of credit cards. Second, there was an expansion of the volume of consigned loans. Indeed, the

Table 6.8 Retails banks in Brazil: delivery channels, 2000, 2005–2010

	2000	2005	2006	2007	2008	2009	2010
Bank Branches	16,396	17,627	18,067	18,572	19,142	20,046	19,813
Bank Correspondents	13,731	83,777	101,038	122,090	128,280	145,142	151,623

Source: Banco Central do Brasil (2011)

Table 6.9 Big retail banks: number of bank correspondents (physical points), 2009

Big retail bank	Bank correspondents
Bradesco	22,184
Caixa Econômica Federal	13,773
Banco do Brasil	13,645
Hsbc Brazil	7,198
Unibanco	3,173
Real	2,453

Source: Madi and Gonçalves (2013)

Table 6.10 Indicators of financial inclusion 2005–2010

Year/December	Consumer credit loans, in %	Number of borrowers (millions)
2005	21.46	10,580
2006	21.08	12,509
2007	24.71	15,146
2008	19.91	17,927
2009	15.16	22,233
2010	16.95	30,159

Source: Adapted from Gonçalves and Madi (2013b)

Table 6.11 Evolution of total loans and loans to households, in relation to GDP, 2008–2013, in %

Year/December	Total loans in relation to GDP	Loans to households in relation to GDP
2008	40.7	17.63
2009	43.85	19.36
2010	45.43	20.59
2011	49.1	22.2
2012	53.8	24.4
2013	56.5	26

Source: Adapted from DIEESE (2014)

consigned loans grew at a fast speed between 2009 and 2011 and, thereafter, the growth rates practically returned to the levels of 2008. Third, there was a reduction in credit oriented to vehicles and overdrafts (DIEESE, 2014). Four, the volume of credit oriented to the real estate market grew 5.7 times between 2008 and 2013, according to the Central Bank. Several factors influenced this substantial growth, as the outcomes of the anti-cyclical policies and the strategies of private banks besides, the role of the public bank Caixa Econômica Federal (Caixa), which holds almost 70% in total loans, and the federal government program 'Minha Casa, Minha Vida' (My House, My Life). Indeed, the government played an active role in the real estate credit expansion through, a) the operations of the public bank Caixa at lower interest rates, b) the regulation of funding oriented to real state credit and c) the expansion of the program 'Minha Casa, Minha Vida' oriented to low income people (Mora, 2014). Five, the high level of profitability of the retail banks was mainly based on the performance of credit revenues nurtured by high spreads centered on personal loans (Table 6.12).

In this setting, the growth of the indebtedness of the Brazilian households in relation to their income increased form 32.5 in January 2008 to 45.0 in 2013, according to the Central Bank. It is worth noting that, at the end of

Table 6.12 Brazilian banks: average spread in personal loans, 2003–2012, in %

Year/December	Average spread in personal loans*
2003	50.9
2004	43.9
2005	42.7
2006	39.6
2007	31.9
2008	45.0
2009	31.6
2010	28.5
2011	33.7
2012**	30.5

Note: Fixed rate operations in personal loans (free resources) are considered.
* The spread level is obtained from the difference between the rates of funding and credit operations.
** May.

Source: Adapted from Gonçalves and Madi (2013b)

2010, Brazil followed new international trends and established the national strategy for financial education (ENEF), with the publication of Decree No. 7379/2010, which aims to: a) promote financial education and social security; b) increase the ability of citizens to perform conscious choices about the management of their resources; and c) contribute to the efficiency and soundness of the credit markets, capital markets, insurance, pension plan and capitalization (ENEF, 2011). With the creation of the ENEF, the financial education turns out to be a permanent public policy. In its institutional design, there is the involvement of private and public (at the federal, state and municipal levels) institutions for the realization of free actions of public interest (Madi, 2017).

Financial education, in truth, has won the status of public policy in several countries, mainly after the global financial crisis (Martins, 2013). The OECD has led this process globally with the creation of the international network of financial education (OECD, 2005). Within the OECD guidelines, the importance of financial education as an object of public policy is justified on the basis of the growing complexity of financial products and services, demographic changes and on reducing the State's role in social protection policies. Among the OECD concerns there is the urgent need to increase the individual responsibility in financial decisions.

Considering this institutional framework, the recent actions of the Central Bank have shown concern with the financial decision-making on the part of families, since the spending planning and the management of budgets increasingly involve choices relative to financial services. Thus, the Central Bank has been involved in fostering the financial education among the population, as a way to prevent excessive risk-taking by bank customers, to encourage saving and to promote financial stability (BACEN, 2016).

Taking into account this background, the Brazilian Central Bank created the program named 'Financial Citizenship', aimed at the promotion of financial education and access to information about the national financial system. Thus, the financial citizenship emerges as a concept concerning the rights and duties of the Brazilian citizens regarding their financial lives. This program aims to ensure the protection of consumers of financial services in order to improve the quality of the citizens' relationship with the financial institutions. Within the guidelines of the Central Bank, the financial education contributes to the full development of citizenship. In this way, such a program is aligned to the national strategy for financial education and operates on three fronts: a) personal finance management with focus on savings and responsible credit habits; b) the relationship between citizens and financial institutions with emphasis on information, training and guidance on financial products and services, delivery channels and resolution of conflicts; and c) the relationship between financial institutions and citizens in order to induce good practices in the supply of products and services.

The ENEF, in fact, might actually favor the interests of the financial institutions in the current configuration and operation of the public policy of financial education (Martins, 2013). In other words, the strong presence of institutions and associations linked to the national financial system in the formulation of the ENEF's strategies and actions might have contributed to reinforce the asymmetric power between banks and consumers (Madi, 2017). This assymetric power turned out to reinforce the maintenance of high interest rates in credit loans and the high levels of profitability among the big retail banks in Brazil throughout the recent process of financial inclusion.

Recessive trends and indebtedness of families

If we look at the Brazilian credit downturn in terms of the lessons learned, the outstanding features of the Brazilian consumer credit market could be understood as a result of the structural changes oriented by the process of financial inclusion. Both private and public banks have turned out to encourage the expansion of personal loans, for 2003 to 2013, with rising banks' net interest incomes and, in the average, low credit losses. As highlighted, the relevant growth of the market share of public banks turned out to happen in the later part of the up-cycle. Throughout the credit expansion, banks adjusted capital requirements to risks in order to manage credit and liquidity risks, following the guidelines of the Basel Accords (Madi, 2013).

From the Keynesian tradition, Hyman Minsky (1986) considered the role of credit in the business cycle and developed the financial instability hypothesis which states that credit crisis are endogenous to the capitalist economy. In truth, profit-seeking banks promote adjustments of assets and liabilities on behalf of expected risks and returns. The active role of banks, through innovations and institutional changes, fosters the expansion of financial fragility because of the growth of the current value of the debts in relation to income flows. According to Hyman Minsky (1986), the strategies of banks oriented to credit expansion affect the spending decisions in the real sectors. When the pace of economic growth begins to decline, banks usually increase the restriction on new credit flows while liquidity preference increases in their asset management. When profits decline, the volume of new loans shrinks and this happens to increase the financial vulnerability of households and corporations to interest rates and other features of the new credit contracts.

In Brazil, the signs of domestic stagnation became clearer in late 2014 while a wave of strikes all over the country revealed social and economic tensions in the labor market. Considering the business environment, growing macroeconomic instability – in gross domestic product, inflation and interest rates – dampened the expectations surrounding the sustainability of economic growth. In this scenario, private banks turned out to be increasingly selective in personal loans due to the reversal of expectations about economic growth, employment and real aggregate consumption. Indeed, the growth of GDP was 0.3% in 2014 and it turned out to be -3.9% in 2015 while the level of inflation surpassed 10% per year in 2015.

Taking into account the recessive trends, in mid-2014, a set of measures adopted by the Ministry of Finance still considered as relevant the role of public banks in maintaining the consumer credit expansion and the levels of aggregate consumption. At the end of this year, the federal Government encouraged the expansion of consigned loans through the lengthening of the amortization period of this type of credit for retired people and pensioners of the National Social Security Institute (INSS) and for federal civil servants.

As a result of the macroeconomic and institutional environment that favored economic recession, inflationary pressures and the decrease of the purchasing power of households, the credit scenario was characterized by the following features:

- There was a continuous reduction of the volume of credit oriented to vehicles: the annual variation was -4.5% in 2014 and -12.7% in 2015.
- There was an increase in the volume of consigned loans that has been demanded to payback other types of more expensive loans, such as credit cards and overdrafts.
- Despite the volume of real estate loans oriented to households growth at rate of 30% in 2014, this rate was lower than the previous years (ABBC, 2014a).
- The annual variation of total credit to households showed a reduction of the rhythm of credit growth. The annual variation of total loans to households- including loans was 11.3% in 2014 and 7.3% in 2015, while the annual variation of total loans to households – excluding consigned loans – was 5.5% and 2.5%.
- Although there was credit expansion in in all the regions of the country, in the period between 2007 and 2014, the rate of growth of the total credit

oriented to households grew 92.5% in the average. While the Southeast region presented the lowest rate of credit growth oriented to households between 2007 and 2014 (85.6%), the Middle-West region had the highest rate of growth (1002.0%), followed by the Northeast region (101.4%), the South region (97.25%) and the North region (93.45%) (BACEN, 2015).

- Considering the real state credit expansion in in all the regions of the country, in the period between 2012 and 2014, the Southeast region presented the lowest rate of credit growth (62.0%), the North region had the highest rate of growth (95.2%), followed by the Northeast region (85.1%), the Middle-West region (80.7%) and the South region (69.6%) (BACEN, 2015).

Indeed, the actual reversal of credit strategies in public banks was decisive to the evolution of the consumer credit market. Selective credit strategies were adopted by both private and public banks in a context of recession where there was observed an increase in non-performing operations in the bank's portfolios from 4.4% in 2014 to 5.3% in 2015. In spite of the new credit strategies, the levels of profitability of the five biggest retail banks were very high in 2014 and 2015 (Table 6.13).

The recent bank strategies were also affected by the expectations about the default levels of corporations and the political environment. In this context, the management of credit risk was associated with further credit restrictions, besides increased interest rates and spreads charged on loans. As a result, the expansion of consigned loans and the renegotiation of debts have been stimulated by the government and banks to avoid the expansion of non-performing loans.

The main concern refers to the financial fragility of the Brazilian banking system, mainly after 2013. After a period of fast credit expansion, as Minsky (1986) warned, financial fragility tends to grow due to increased indebtedness of families and corporations. Considering the relevance of the access to credit in the Brazilian model of economic growth, from 2003 to 2015, the concerns about the level and composition of household's debts in a context of recession put in question the sustainability of the growth model (Table 6.14).

Table 6.13 Profitability of the biggest 5 retail banks, 2014 and 2015

Bank	2014	2015	Annual variation 2014/2015, in %
Itaú Unibanco	24.0	23.9	−0.1
Bradesco	20.1	20.5	0.4
Banco do Brasil	14.2	16.1	1.9
Santander	11.5	12.8	1.3
Caixa Econômica Federal	15.2	11.4	−3.8

Note: Profitability is measured by the volume of net profits in relation to equity.
Source: DIEESE (2016)

Table 6.14 Indebtedness of families: level and composition by credit, 2007–2015, in %

	2009	2011	2013	2014	2105
Total indebtedness	35.4	41.8	45.0	45.9	44.6
Real estate loans	6.6	10.8	15.5	18.0	18.8
Other loans	28.8	31.1	29.4	27.9	25.8

Note: Indebtedness of families = ratio between the current value of debts of families with the National Financial System and the household income accumulated in the last 12 months.

Source: Banco Central do Brasil

Conclusions

The recent performance of the Brazilian consumer credit market appears as highly significant not only because of the size of this market but also on behalf of its impacts on the Brazilian society (Gonçalves and Madi, 2013b). Among other relevant issues, this experience has revealed the decisive role of the legal and institutional changes led by the federal government in the early 2000s. These changes have been decisive both to shape and to enhance the expansion of the credit market oriented to personal loans. Besides, they affected the banks' credit risk, particularly because of the creation of credit guarantees (both in the acquisition of vehicles and the real estate operations) and of the consigned loans. However, the evolution of microfinance loans remained low despite the legal and institutional changes led by the federal government that aim to expand the micro-credit oriented to productive activities.

Taking into account the expansion of personal loans, the degree of market concentration in the Brazilian financial system favors high levels of operational revenues in personal loans due to high spreads charged on loans since the biggest 5 retail banks concentrate almost 90% of assets and deposits. In this scenario, the huge growth of the number of bank correspondents has supported the delivery of financial services, mainly oriented to low-income people, all over the country. Despite the advance of the enlargement of the access to financial services all over the country, the regional inequality in the process of financial inclusion is still a challenge. Among other issues related to the dynamics of the banking sector, the countercyclical role of government-controlled banks has been crucial to support the maintenance of the expansion of personal loans till mid-2010.

As a result of the expansionary period of loans oriented to households, the financial fragility of the household's debt structure will certainly condition the evolution of the credit markets in the near future. In the current conjuncture, the federal government seems to have lost room of manoeuvre to find short-term solutions in order to support economic growth by the expansion of personal loans.

The comprehension of the challenges of the recent personal credit expansion in Brazil and its social impacts is decisive to any transformation in institutions and policy making in order to promote economic growth with social inclusion. Indeed, the attempts toward financial education policies should be articulated to behavioral supervision strategies by the financial regulators to ensure customer protection and financial stability. In particular, the current vulnerability of the Brazilian economy, characterized by a recession and a high level of unemployment, raises important social and economic risks related to the debt capacity of households and, therefore, requires increasing attention from the federal government and the Central Bank regarding the evolution of the consumer credit crunch.

Notes

1 Under this type of personal credit contract, the monthly payments aimed to the amortization are directly deducted from the borrower's pay check itself.
2 Considering the average nominal value of the exchange rate between real and dollar as of 2014, Classes D and E have a monthly monetary earning up to US $460; Class C has a monthly monetary earning between US $460 and US $1,150 (Madi and Gonçalves, 2007).
3 The system of guarantees related to vehicles is legally known as fiduciary alienation (Law No 9514/1997).
4 The system of guarantees related to real estate operations involves two relevant legal innovations known as fiduciary alienation and the segregated estate regime (Law No 10931/2004).

References

Associação Brasileira de Bancos Comerciais e Múltiplos (ABBC). *O Crédito imobiliário e as instituições financeiras de médio porte*. São Paulo: Apresentação, 2014a.
Associação Brasileira de Bancos Comerciais e Múltiplos (ABBC). *Termômetro do crédito*, 2014b. www.abbc.org.br/images/content/Term%C3%B4metro%20do%20Cr%C3%A9dito%20-%20Maio%202014.pdf
Banco Central do Brasil (BACEN). *Relatório de Inclusão Financeira*, 2. Brasília: Banco Central do Brasil, 2011.
Banco Central do Brasil (BACEN). *National Partnership for Financial Inclusion. Action Plan to Strengthen the Institutional Environment*. Brasília, 2012a.
Banco Central do Brasil (BACEN). *Relatório de Inclusão Financeira*, 3. Brasília: Banco Central do Brasil, 2015.
Banco Central Do Brasil (BACEN). *O Programa de Educação Financeira do Banco Central*. Brasília, 2016. www.bcb.gov.br/?BCEDFIN.
Departamento Intersindical de Estatísticas e Estudos Socioeconômicos (DIEESE). A evolução do crédito na economia brasileira 2008–2013. *Nota Técnica 135*, São Paulo, 2014.
Departamento Intersindical de Estatísticas e Estudos Socioeconômicos (DIEESE). *Desempenho dos Bancos*. São Paulo: Rede Bancários, 2016.
Estratégia Nacional De Educação Financeira (ENEF). *Programa do Governo Brasileiro*. 2011. www.vidaedinheiro.gov.br/Imagens/Plano%20Diretor%20ENEF.pdf.
Federação Brasileira de Bancos (FEBRABAN). O Papel do Sistema Financeiro no Desenvolvimento Nacional. *Workshop*, Brazil, 2005.
Federação Brasileira de Bancos (FEBRABAN). *O setor bancário em números*. Research Report, São Paulo, 2006.

Gonçalves, J. R. B., Krein, J. D., and Madi, M. A. C. Labour and Trade Unions in the Financial Sector: Challenges and Perspectives in Contemporary Brazil. *Global Labour University Conference*, Mumbai, India, 2009a.

Gonçalves, J. R. B., Madi, M. A. C., and Krein, J. D. Bank Workers and Trade Unions in the Brazilian Financial Sector. Paper presented at *ABET Conference*, Campinas, Brazil, 2009b.

Gonçalves, J. R. B., and Madi, M. A. C. Private Equity Investment and Labor: Faceless Capital and the Challenges to Trade Unions in Brazil. In M. Serrano, E. Xhafa and M.Fichter (Eds.), *Trade Unions and the Global Crisis: Labour's Visions, Strategies and Responses*. Geneve: Intenational Labour Office, 2011.

Gonçalves, J. R. B., and Madi, M. A. C. Federal Public Banks in Brazil: Their Role and Importance in Credit Expansion, 1952–2008. In G. Chichilnisky, M. A. C. Madi, C. F. Yee, M. Kennet and M. G. de Oliveira (eds.), *The Greening of Global Finance*. Reading: The Green Economics Institute, 2013a.

Gonçalves, J. R. B., and Madi, M. A. C. Global Economic Integration, Business Expansion and Consumer Credit in Brazil, 1994–2010. *International Journal of Green Economics*, v. 7, n. 3, 2013b. https://doi.org/10.1504/IJGE.2013.058164

Madi, M. A. C. Global Finance: Banking Dynamics, Regulation and Future Challenges. In G. Chichilnisky, M. A. C. Madi, C. F. Yee, M. Kennet and M. G. de Oliveira (eds.), *The Greening of Global Finance*. Reading: The Green Economics Institute, 2013.

Madi, M. A. C. *Small Business in Brazil Competitive Global Challenges*. New York: Nova Publishers, 2016.

Madi, M. A. C. (2017). Educação Financeira e Regulamentação Comportamental. In A. von B. Dodl and L. R. Troster (Eds.), *Sistema Financeiro Nacional: o que fazer?* Rio de Janeiro: Elsevier.

Madi, M. A. C., and Gonçalves, J. R. B. Corporate Social Responsibility and Market Society: Credit and Banking Inclusion in Brazil. In A. Bugra and K. Agartan (Eds.), *Market Economy as a Political Project: Reading Karl Polanyi for the 21st Century*. London: Palgrave MacMillan, 2007.

Madi, M. A. C., and Gonçalves, J. R. B. Banks and Labor in Brazil: Recent Changes in Employment and Working Conditions. In G. Chichilnisky, M. A. C. Madi, C. F. Yee, M. Kennet and M. G. de Oliveira (eds.), *The Greening of Global Finance*. London: The Green Economics Institute, 2013a.

Madi, M. A. C., and Gonçalves, J. R. B. Entrepreneurship and micro-credit in Brazil: social challenges in the context of the productive reconfiguration, 1994-2010. In G. Chichilnisky, M. A. C. Madi, C. F. Yee, M. Kennet and M. G. de Oliveira (eds.), The Greening of Global Finance. London: The Green Economics Institute, 2013b.

Madi, M. A. C., and Gonçalves, J. R. B. Banks in Brazil: Challenges After the Global Crisis. *International Journal of Research in Commerce, Economics & Management*, v. 4, n. 3, March 2014.

Martins, A. Q. N. *A Formação da Estratégia Nacional de Educação Financeira do Governo Brasileiro*. Dissertação (Mestrado) – Escola Nacional de Saúde Pública Sergio Arouca, Rio de Janeiro, 2013.

Ministério da Fazenda, Brasil. Microcrédito e Microfinanças no Governo Lula. Presentation by Gilson Bittencourt, Brasília, 2005.

Minsky, H. P. *Stabilizing an Unstable Economy*. New Haven, CT: Yale University Press, 1986.

Mora, M. A Evolução do Crédito no Brasil entre 2003 e 2010. *Texto para Discussão* 2022, IPEA, Brasília, 2014.

OECD. *Recommendation on Principles and Good Practices for Financial Education and Awareness*. 2005. www.oecd.org

Oliveira, G. C. And Carvalho, C. E. O componente "custo de oportunidade" do spread bancário no Brasil: uma abordagem pós-keynesiana. *Economia e Sociedade*, Campinas, v. 16,

n. 3 (31), p. 371–404, dez. 2007.Paim, B. O crédito e o papel dos bancos públicos. *Carta de Conjuntura*, FEE, v. 22, n. 11, 2013.

Secretaria de Política Econômica, Brasil. *Principais avanços na implementação da agenda de poupança e investimento*. Brasília: Ministério da Fazenda, 2002.

Sicsú, J. *Lições da crise de 2008–2009: o que o Brasil deve fazer agora?* 2011. www.diap.org.br/index.php/noticias/artigos/18845-licoes-da-crise-de-2008-2009-o-que-o-brasil-deve-fazer-agora

Stockhammer, E. Some Stylized Facts on the Finance-Dominated Accumulation Regime. *Competition and Change*, v. 12, n. 2, pp. 189–207, 2008.

Stockhammer, E., and Wildauer, R. Debt-Driven Growth? Wealth, Distribution and Demand in OECD Countries. *Cambridge Journal of Economics*, v. 40, n. 6, pp. 1609–1634, 2016. https://doi.org/10.1093/cje/bev070

World Bank. *Brazil: Access to Financial Services*. Report no. 27773-BR, World Bank and Oxford University Press, Brazil, 2004.

7 Hits and misses of public investment strategy in Brazil*

Cristina Fróes De Borja Reis

Public investment has a strategic role for economic development and distribution.

First, as correctly specified in its name, it is an investment, and may not be misunderstood as public spending. The public investment constitutes capital accumulation, bringing productive capacity to the economic system either by the acquisition of machines and equipment or by building construction. It necessarily means gross capital formation, while the public spending encompasses expenditures on education, health, pensions, etc. that do not involve productive capital accumulation in *stricto sensu*.

Second, moreover, from the Keynesian and structural macroeconomic point of view, public investment may enhance private investment, presenting *crowding-in* effects (Auerbach, 1990). This happens due to its effects both on demand and supply sides of the economy. The demand effect happens basically through its multiplier spending effects and through the expansion of the internal market, especially provided by investments in infrastructure.[1] The supply effects arise by the reduction of production costs and by the increase in productivity, and through the structural shift to new productive activities afforded by public procurement policies (Reis, 2008). The degree of virtuous impacts in this process depends on the public investment's quality of planning and execution, and of other external and domestic conditions that affect the macroeconomic regime. If properly executed and redirected to innovative technologies and sectors, public investment can maximize its effects towards economic development – what Mazzucato (2013) calls *dynamizing-in* effects.[2]

Third, public investment is strategic due to its universal nature, whether planned by policy makers of governmental institutions or administration, or by state-owned enterprises, it enables projects and enterprises that are important to the country or the region.[3] Particularly, it may be directed both to business activities that trigger private investment and generate employment and income, and to public infrastructure that enhance people's quality of life.

> Infrastructure activities or services shape basic requirements for the sustainable development of an economy; moreover, its universal availability for the population as a whole is an element that expresses advanced levels of

civilization. Indeed, infrastructure composes, in addition to the macroeconomic ordination, the political-institutional system and the socioeconomic characteristics of national markets, which are the roll of systemic factors of international competitiveness.

(Maciel, 2006, p. 277)

Consequently, and fourth, public investment constitutes and changes demands and supply conditions that have geographical, sectorial, market, functional, and personal distributive impacts. Public investment can entirely modify the balance of power and wealth in place. Thus, it is necessarily a political decision with strong socioeconomic implications; its profile and trajectory depend on the groups of interests in power and, analogously, on the macroeconomic regime adopted by them.

So, it is not difficult to imagine that public investment brings up strong controversies and deepen distributive conflicts of a society, especially when often public investment decisions are not as democratic as people would like for them to be. On the one hand because complex institutional mechanisms are needed to capture the private sector and population's desires of capital formation with equanimity (furthermore, those desires and demands may not be clear or consolidated). On the other hand, due to behavioral problems that emerge in this kind of situation, such as *rentism* and corruption (Tanzi and Davoodi, 1990). Although rent-seeking behavior can be related to collective or cultural issues, in general its main roots are the monopolistic structures in private markets and the unequal wealth distribution that strongly influences public administration.[4] Anyhow, the effects of public investments unevenly benefit some sectors, markets, and companies, as well as regions, communities, families, and social classes or groups.

In Lula's Brazil, public investment had been significantly leveraged, triggering the debate about its effects on economic dynamics, but also about the controversies just mentioned. It can be safely attributed to public investment the epicenter of the political and economic crisis that came in the second mandate of President Dilma Rousseff. As is demonstrated in the present chapter, between 2003 and 2014, in Brazil, the political coalition supported the increase in public investment and other expansionist economic policies that benefited the growth of private investment, and therefore of the gross fixed-capital formation (GFCF), industrial production and the gross national product (GDP). In this process, the rise of state-owned enterprises (SOE) and infrastructure projects were crucial. Political and judicial decisions enabled more investment of state-owned enterprises, especially of Petrobras (Petroleo Brasileiro S.A), and the enlargement of their domestic production chains. In addition, heavy infrastructure projects were put in motion, mainly by public-private partnerships, though not enough to close the historical gap in this area. Once the investment in infrastructure provided selective competitiveness for industries and services, its revamp improved some productive conditions, mainly for the tradable sector of the economy. But it was not enough to raise the GFCF ratio to GDP close to the international average of middle-income countries.

The objective of this chapter is to analyze the political economy of public investment in Brazil between 2003 and 2014 from a structural and Keynesian approach.[5] In the first section, the key institutions in the trajectory of public investment are examined, both from public administration and from state-owned enterprises. The second section analyzes structural changes and macroeconomic results in light of the institutions and dynamics of public investments in the period. Finally, the third section brings some conclusions on the political and economic struggles, both internal and external, that were triggered and/ or intensified by public productive investment in Brazil, connecting them to the economic and political crisis faced by the country just after 2014.

Institutional changes for public investment's in Lula's Brazil in historical perspective

During the 20th century, especially between 1950 and 1979 – the Brazilian 'developmental period' – the State applied aggressive policies to enhance domestic demand and productive capacity, mainly through its productive enterprises. A couple of hundred state-owned companies were established, not only in infrastructure (energy, transport, communication, and mining) but in manufacturing and financial sectors as well (IBGE). Political and juridical decisions facilitated public investment by legally authorizing mechanisms that transferred taxes and tariffs' revenues to SOEs' budgets, and also to the public administration's institutions, such as ministries and bureaus.[6]

In parallel, the macroeconomic regime enacted policies in favour of domestic investment's growth, such as a selective exchange rate, expansionist fiscal policy, and a monetary policy with low interest rates and high rates of credit allowance. The tripod of the Developmental State was then shaped as an industrial structure convenient for the national and international interest groups in power (Chibber, 2004). One leg was the public sector, the leader in basic industry and infrastructure production. The second leg was big national corporations, acting in labor intensive activities such as food and beverages, textile, and metal-mechanic. Finally, the third leg was foreign multinational companies, dominating high capital and technologically intensive sectors such as chemical, electronics, and automobile.

However, the economic model was dependent on external funding allowed by the excess of liquidity of the seventies, which over-indebted[7] developing countries. This flow was cut in 1979 when the international interest rates were raised following the FED's decision (Serrano, 2002). Financial outflows from Brazil and exchange rate devaluation generated a balance of payment's crisis. The harsh economic scenario was handed down by new power coalitions to transform the State's political economy, promoting neoliberal reforms for trade and financial openness.[8] They changed the domestic logic of accumulation and, hence, the public investment profile. Such as Jessop (1991) accurately envisaged, internationally the productive paradigm of Fordism was being replaced,[9] pressuring for the end of welfare and developmental states, respectively in the center and in the periphery, and strengthening the financial sector.

> The "Washington-Wall Street complex" (and its leadership over the World Bank and the International Monetary Fund) established itself as the center of political power and of the ideology not only of globalized American capital but also of globalized capital in general. Despite its rhetoric concerning a minimal state and market efficiency the establishment of neo-liberalism as a doctrine led to a new strategy of accumulation and a new hegemonic project widening the dominance of capital in general and finance capital in particular over other fractions and interests. These transformations were triggered through a widespread attack on the unions and on the welfare state. It also corresponded to a new U.S. trade offensive to open the hitherto regulate internal market of the new industrialized exporting nations.
> (Medeiros, 2011, p. 49)

Due to the desire to reduce the Brazilian State and to open its economy, there were two remarkable institutional changes on public investment in the neoliberal period in Brazil: one in the beginning of the eighties, and the other all throughout the nineties. The first institutional change happened to attend the International Monetary Fund (IMF)'s borrowing conditionality in the eighties. After 1981, public finance started to measure the Public-Sector Borrowing/Lending Balance (NFSP),[10] including state-owned enterprises, which were not constraining public debt before. In order to hold the investment of the state-owned enterprises, its growth was legally limited. Additionally, in the Federal Constitution of 1988, the pass through of federal government revenues to social expenditures except infrastructure sectors hindered public investment's administration. Moreover, lower economic growth and fiscal adjustments promoted further investment cuts, especially in some funds previously directed to the budget of SOE (Silva, 2006).

The second was the privatization process, attending the request of the Washington Consensus (Williamson, 1993). The National Privatization Program (Programa Nacional de Desestatização) in 1991, triggered a sharp decline in the investment share of government-owned enterprises in relation to the GDP. Later the government of President Fernando Henrique Cardoso (FHC) speeded up the privatizations, in parallel to macroeconomic policies of free financial flows, appreciated exchange rate and super high real interest rates during its inflation stabilization plan Real, which was begun in 1994 (Filgueiras, 2006). There was a significant reorganization of the financial sector, which became dominated by a few private banks, though public participation remained important.[11] This drastic institutional change transformed power coalitions, increasing the influence of the financial private sector in the political arena, especially in Federal and State governments. It urged for more reforms to open capital and goods markets in order to diminish the role of the State in the economy, such as in the international capitalist context.

So, under the spirit of transforming the State from interventionist to regulative, the regulatory system was improved during FHC's privatization process. According to the World Bank's privatization database, including 139 developing economies, from 1988 until 2002, there were 176 privatization deals in Brazil, corresponding to 22% of the developing world value proceeds of privatization in the period. In particular, in 1995 the Brazilian government proposed a modification in the Constitution that used to forbid the Union to sell or to give a concession of oil & gas exploration. In 1997 this began to be legally accepted in the Petrol Law (Lei do Petroleo), which created the ANP (National Agency of Petroleum, Natural Gas and Biofuels) to set its regulatory system. But in oil & gas, as Schutte (2016, p. 22) asseverates, "in the case of Petrobras, there was no political accumulation to proceed with a privatization tout court. What happened was a gradual but decisive diminution of its political weight and economic control".[12] Nonetheless, the company lost its previous commitment to industrial and economic development, especially regarding local content of its suppliers' contracts. In addition, a controlled opening of its bonds had started in 2000, focused on the US market. The Federal Union kept the majority over the voting capital (56%), but not of the social capital (32%) (Schutte, 2016). Despite the expenditures to structure the regulatory system in many fields, mostly in infrastructure, obviously the privatization process made SOE's investment fall in the nineties.

Not only the public investment from SOEs was contracted before Lula's government, but also of public administration. More generally, the low economic growth and its consequent reduction in tax revenues prevented public investment. But also, as just argued, investment in fixed capital was the preferred item targeted by fiscal adjustments, especially after the adoption of the inflation target regime in 1999[13] – due to the compulsory pass through of tax revenues to social expenditures other than infrastructure. Furthermore, in 2000, the Fiscal Responsibility Act (Lei de Responsabilidade Fiscal – LRF) was issued, "establishing public finance standards focused on responsible fiscal management", including the investments of both public administration and enterprises. In practice, its downsizing stimulus was directed to the investments of public administration, government-owned enterprises, and controlled companies.[14] As a result of this new legal framework, the creditors of the public debt came to be prioritized meanwhile the expenditures in infrastructure were neglected to avoid deep deviations of net public result from its surplus target (Reis, 2008).

In real terms[15] from 1951 until 1981 public GFCF annually grew on average 10.3%, being that public administration's GFCF annual average growth was 5.2% and SOEs' 25.3% (Table 7.1). Public participation of total GFCF was 33% on average in 1950–1981, and peaked at 47% in 1976. In terms of GDP, public GFCF represented on average 6.7% in this period, with SOEs responding with about 40% of it (Chart 7.1). Differently, from 1982 until 2002, public GFCF dropped annually 1.1% on average, recording positive real variation only in 1985, 1986, 1990, 1991, 1996, 2000, 2001, and 2002. Public GFCF represented on average 24% of total GFCF or 3.8% of GDP between 1982 and 2002, so that SOE now accounted for 44% of the total on average. In

Table 7.1 Variation of gross fixed capital formation in Brazil, 1950–2013, private and public sectors – public administration and federal state-owned enterprises, R$ 1980 (in %, real figures calculated by GDP and GFCF deflators)

	Total GFCF (%)	Private GFCF (%)	Public GFCF (%)	Public Administration GFCF (%)	Federal SOEs GFCF (%)
1950–1981	8.1	7.1	10.3	5.3	25.4
1982–2002	0.5	1.5	–1.1	3.3	–0.5
2003–2013	6.0	5.1	9.5	8.3	12.5

Source: Elaborated by Reis (2008) and Reis, Araujo & Gonzalez (2016) based on data from IBGE, IPEA and DEST. Data for 1965–1967 and 2014 is not available in R$ 1980.

1999, public GFCF reached its lowest level of the historical series in real terms, 1.91% of GDP, finishing the period in 2002 at 2.5%. Many studies[16] demonstrate that the reduction in public GDP had caused the decline in private investment and contributed to reduce GDP growth in the neoliberal period (see Section 2).

In contrast, in Lula's Brazil public investment was revamped, especially of the state-owned enterprises of the energy sector. Indeed, the government proposals of Lula were explicit in saying that it would work for an integrated energy planning, improving the dynamics of hydroelectricity, gas & oil, nuclear energy, alternative sources (wind, solar, and biomass), etc. – which should be delivered not only by market forces, but neither by an authoritarian and centralized force (Sauer, 2015). Notwithstanding, its era is often called 'neo-developmental', led by a power coalition arguably more nationalistic than in the nineties, though still elitist.

> Lula da Silva's victorious candidacy in the 2002 presidential election came to represent a set of important modifications of Brazilian politics, modifications that were consolidated over the course of his two terms (2003–2010) and Dilma Rousseff's presidency (2011–2016). First of all, there was a change in the power bloc. The Brazilian internal grande bourgeoisie—the fraction of the capitalist class that maintained its own basis for capital accumulation and vied for position with international financial capital—underwent a political ascent at the expense of the interests of a different fraction of the grande bourgeoisie, the fraction that was integrated into international capital. The interests of large-scale international capital and of its domestic allies had guided the action of the Brazilian state under the governments of Fernando Collor de Mello (1990–1992), Itamar Franco (1993–1994), and Fernando Henrique Cardoso (1995–2002); these interests now found themselves displaced from the uncontested hegemony that they enjoyed during the 1990s. Having gone so far as to oppose the

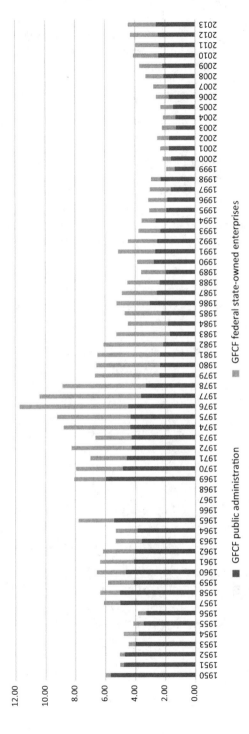

Chart 7.1 Gross fixed capital formation in Brazil in terms of the gross domestic product, 1950–2013, public administration and federal state-owned enterprises, R$ 1980 (in %, real figures calculated by GDP and GFCF deflators)

Source: Elaborated by Reis (2008) and Reis et al. (2016) based on data from IBGE, IPEA and DEST. Data for 1965–1967 and 2014 is not available in R$ 1980.

government of the Partido dos Trabalhadores (Workers' Party— PT) altogether, they came to occupy a subordinate position. Second, this change was connected to a broader mutation in national politics. The political rise of the internal grande bourgeoisie became possible only because of the creation of a political front that brought together, alongside it, the primary sectors of the popular classes. This political front, which we could call a "neodevelopmentalist front," is marked by heterogeneity and plagued by contradictions.

(Boito and Berringer, 2014, p. 96)

So, in the neo-developmental period, from 2003 until 2013, public GFCF grew annually 9.5% on average, peaking at 25% in 2008. Public GFCF represented on average 21% of total GFCF or 3.3% of GDP, so that SOE now accounted for 1.3% of the total in average in this period – according to Reis et al. (2016). Despite the improvement, public investment in Brazil remained too low in international comparisons, among the bottom ten countries in 2010–2012 according to data from the World Bank.[17]

Considering the actual financial alternatives for long term investments, new ways to finance public investments emerged, especially in infrastructure, most of them as public-private partnerships (PPPs).[18] 'Aggressive' (in comparison to previous Brazilian infrastructure programs, though weak compared to international experiences) infrastructure programs were announced by Lula's government, specifically, the Growth Acceleration Program (Programa de Aceleracao do Crescimento – PAC) in 2007. It consisted of investment in infrastructure and institutional measures. Infrastructure investment was subdivided in logistics, energy, and social and urban development, estimated initially at R $503 billion for 2007/2010 – what would correspond to 20% of total GFCF in nominal terms of the period. "The institutional measures are geared towards the relief and improvement of the tax system, encouraging credit and financing, improvement of the investment environment and long-term fiscal measures" (TCU, 2009).

The second phase of PAC came in 2010, during the first term of President Dilma Rousseff (2010–2014). PAC 2 expected to enhance infrastructure investment to R $955 billion in 2011–2014. It had more resources and partnerships with states and municipalities to execute infrastructure projects. In 2013, the Program for Investment in Logistics (Programa de Investimento em Logística – PIL) was launched, promoting concessions for Brazilian highways, railways, ports, and airports to prepare the country for the upcoming mega-events of the World Cup and the Olympics (Ministry of Planning, 2014a). It counted on the Fund of Investment in Infrastructure shares that was responsible for facilitating credit conditions to infrastructure investors (Ministry of Planning, 2014b).

In combination with the PACs, the macroeconomic and STI policies (science, technology, and innovation) where taken to sustain investment during the international financial crisis. Some remarkable achievements were funding policies of private sectors investment in the components of GFCF, as it was said, machines & equipment (M&E) and civil construction. Key institutions that led those funding policies were the National Bank for Economic and Social Development (Banco Nacional do Desenvolvimento Econômico e Social – BNDES); Banco do Brasil for agriculture machines, and Caixa Economica Federal for housing (De Paula and Ferrari Filho, 2011).[19] In addition, there was the cut in the Long Term Interest Rate (TJLP) of BNDES' loans, brought to the lowest level in history in the words of Cunha et al. (2011). For M&E, BNDES launched in 2009 the funding Program for Sustaining Investment (PSI) to stimulate the production, acquisition and export of capital goods and technological innovation. In 2007, Caixa Economica Federal started to manage the newborn investment fund of 'Fundo de Garantia do Tempo de Serviço' (FI-FGTS) that focuses on infrastructure investments in the energy, highway, railway, port, and sanitation sectors in Brazil. In 2009, CAIXA was responsible to conduct the loans of 'Minha Casa Minha Vida' (my house, my life) – an expressive public program for housing that enhanced GFCF in civil construction and its productive value chain (Ministry of Planning, 2014b).[20]

Other important policies that explain the rise of public investment in late 2000s and in the beginning of 2010s are related to Federal government's decision to empower the Petrobras and Eletrobras groups. Although the privatization process of state-owned enterprises was continued during Lula's governments,[21] these companies had conditions to leverage its investments. Petrobras and Eletrobras were taken out from the calculation of the primary balance in 2009 and 2010, respectively, by the Decrees n. 6867 and n. 7368. This attitude was in accordance to international experiences and relieved both the government's effort to reach the primary net lending target and the investments and spending of those companies. In a note, the Brazilian Financial Bureau affirmed:

> With the announcement of the Law Project of Budgetary Guidelines Bill ([Projeto de Lei de Diretrizes Orcamentarias] PLDO-2010), the government is giving specific treatment to Petrobras by withdrawing it from the calculation of the fiscal result of the public sector. This implies in the withdrawal of inventories of assets and liabilities of the company from the calculation of the Public Sector Net Debt ([Divida Liquida do Setor Publico] DLSP), so that the future transactions flows of the company will cease to affect the DLSP and the Public Sector Borrowing/ Lending Needs. This action was already under study by the government and we are implementing it now, in line with the methodology and international practices of most countries that recognize the specific situation of companies that are not fully public. In the case of Petrobras, the Union holds only 1/3 of the share capital, the remainder belonging to the private sector. This treatment is also in the context in which new private accounting rules enter into force. . . .
>
> (Ministry of Finance, 2009, our translation)

Criticisms and press retaliation emerged from it, based on the mainstream economics' view of the crowding out effect, and the pervasive consequences of uncontrolled increases of public spending towards inflation. Basically, it was argued that public investment would artificially increase domestic demand, leveraging consumption and investment, deflagrating inflation and increasing the risk of public debt – which would further grow (Andreoni, 1993). Then the interest rate would grow, preventing private investment and jeopardizing the growth dynamics (Reinhart and Rogoff, 2010). Furthermore, the neoclassic position was that out of the fiscal surplus target, public companies' investment could be uncontrolled, driving more investment crowding out and agency problems (Florêncio, 2016). This was actually the 'technical argument' chosen to justify the impeachment and its higher objective of changing the ideology and practice of State action. Nevertheless, it is not theoretically neither empirically consistent – both because public investment is able to enhance private investment, as it is defended in this chapter, but also because agency problems arise in private markets too, especially if they are oligo or monopolies.

Supported by a power coalition that listened more to industrial[22] and labor sectors than in the nineties during Lula's and Dilma's years (but that never really was opposed to the financial interests), Petrobras had grown and increased profitability, becoming one of the largest groups in the global oil sector.[23] In the middle of the decade, the discovery of Pre-Salt became world-widely known,[24] leveraging not only its productive capacity, but its market value and international relevance in the energy' geopolitics. Law n. 12351, 2010, regulated the exploration and production of oil, natural gas, and other fluid hydrocarbons, under the production sharing regime, in pre-salt areas and in strategic areas. It also created the Social Fund for health and education and provided some amendments to the Oil Law of 1997. The law put Petrobras as the sole operator of the pre-salt fields, with a mandatory participation of at least 30% in the groups of exploration and production. The idea was to guarantee national energy sovereignty and public usage of the revenues from natural resources (Rosa, 2016).

The institution that started the process of fostering local content and domestic value chains was the Program for Mobilization of the National Industry of Oil and Natural Gas (*Programa de Mobilização da Indústria Nacional de Petróleo e Gás Natural*, PROMIN) in 2003 – coordinated by the Ministry of Mining and Energy, then directed by Dilma Rousseff.[25] Other programs were its subsidiary such as Transpetro's Program for Modernization and Expansion of Fleet (Programa de Modernização e Expansão da Frota, PROMEF) in 2004, and the Funding for Mercantile Marine (Fundo de Marinha Mercantil, FMM), based on the pass through of freight taxes and BNDES funding. After the Pre-Salt discovery, there were several initiatives to address the production and exploration challenges in terms of technology, management, logistics, and finance. In 2010 there was its market capitalization, which aimed to enlarge funding possibilities.[26] So that progressively Petrobras would become both private and public during the course of the 21st century.[27] But Petrobras's financial health was very jeopardized, first, by the price control policies from 2011 until 2014, and since 2014 by the drop in international commodities prices. In the first case, oil and gas price control was defined by its administration council, managed at the time by the Federal Ministry of Finance – whom had the crucial concern in keeping inflation in the band admitted by the regime of inflation targets, such as 'markets' wanted.

Eletrobras System was very challenged, too. In terms of institutional reforms, previously in the nineties there were important changes in the utilities sector, from which Aguiar Filho (2007 p. 1) underlines five: i) the creation of the Brazilian Electricity Regulatory Agency (ANEEL) – which separated the functions of regulator and granting power; (ii) the de-verticalization movements of generation activities, transmission, and distribution, with reduction of intra-sectoral subsidies opposed to competition; (iii) the surge of the independent producer of electric energy, concessionaires of the exploitation of hydroelectric plants and thermoelectric plants with the prerogative for free commercialization of the energy produced; (iv) free trade market and the surge of the agent of commercialization, liberalizing large consumers to contract energy directly from the producer agent, located in any region of Brazil, since it is connected to the system; and (v) the creation of the National System Operator (ONS), for the coordination of centralization of energy dispatch and regulation of access to transmission networks.

From this point, the first government term of Lula started with the 'moral' commitment to avoid another blackout and power rationing that happened in 2001. According to Sauer (2015) the basic cause for that crisis was the incapacity of guaranteeing investments in expanding the generation capacity as fast as the consumption was growing, in order to become more autonomous in relation to favorable conditions of the hydrological behavior. In 2004, the new model for the electric sector in Brazil was defined by laws n. 10.847 and 10.848 pursuing objectives of planning, supply security, regulation and inspection over generation, transmission, distribution, and trade of electric energy. In generation, there was controlled competition; in transmission and distribution – natural monopolies – there were bids and concessions; and trade had competitive market (Aguiar Filho, 2007). Later came some amendments in the laws. Particularly, law n. 12.783 in 2013 allowed the reduction of electricity tariffs paid by final consumers; and in 2015 different tariffs were introduced, according to the conditions of electricity generation (Espinasa et al., 2016). Thus, as in the case of oil and gas prices, the general intentions of those measures were reducing inflation, avoiding the fiscal primary result to surpass the inflation targets, and improving cost conditions in several economic sectors, especially manufacturing industries – what could positively affect employment and income levels, such as argued by its leaders. Moreover, changing rules in 2013 had a strategic dimension in which the State wanted to increase its control over the concessions.

The fact is that from 2003 to 2013, GFCF of Brazilian state-owned enterprises alone grew more than four times, reaching R $113.7 billion in 2013 or about 10% of national GFCF. Almost 90% corresponded to Petrobras (Afonso and Fajardo, 2015). In 2014, however, the state investments fell to R $95 billion, R $82 billion from Petrobras. And in 2015, another fall happened, bringing

Petrobras' investments to the level of 2008. According to Cerqueira (2016), Petrobras investments on average dropped 21% per year in 2014 and 2015.

Clearly, from 2014 on the investment dynamic of Petrobras and Eletrobras, and so of public investment, were tied by serious financial and political troubles. Furthermore, the national macroeconomic regime went wrong, many infrastructure plans and projects were still unfinished, and class struggles deepened as expressed by massive public demonstrations (for Brazilian standards). Even winning the election in 2014 based on a pro-labor developmental campaign, Dilma Rousseff's second term adopted conservative economic policies, especially fiscal ones. Even though she tried to cherish the markets, she could not avoid her impeachment, or more precisely, the coup d'etat. The employment rate and GDP had three consecutive years of decline (2015, 2016, and 2017). The political reasons behind the economic policies in motion mirror financial and international capital interests to change the nature of the Brazilian State – disguised by a convincing, though wrong, technical argument of fiscal austerity.

Public investment and structural change in Lula's Brazil

The contrast in public spending between the developmental (1950–1981) period and neoliberal (1982–2002) period was diminished in Lula's Brazil (Chart 7.1), achieving better economic performance. From 1950 until 1981, the GDP grew at an average of 7% per year in Brazilian currency as of 1980, being that 1981 there was the only negative variation of the historical series (-4.4%, which happened again in 1983, and then only in 2015, 2016, and 2017). Furthermore, in this period GFCF grew 8% per year, and so did manufacturing value added.[28] Nonetheless, in the period 1982–2013, GDP annual real growth was 2.8%; considering the first two decades, from 1982 until 2002, annual growth was 2.4%, and 3.5% in 2003–2013 in reals as of 1980, in market prices. By its turn, the GFCF annual average growth rate was 2.4% in 1982–2013 and manufacturing was 0.1%. In 1982–2002, GFCF grew on average every year 0.5% and manufacturing value added -0.5%, while from 2003 to 2013 GFCF rose annually 6% and manufacturing value added 1.25%. GDP growth dynamics from 1982 and 2013 was not pushed by GFCF neither by the manufacturing sector. However, Chart 7.2 shows that after 2003, the GFCF/GDP ratio recovered from its bottom level of 12.9% up to the level of 17.6% in 2012, like at the end of the eighties. The remaining government-owned enterprises (federal government) increased their contribution to the GFCF between the first and second decades of this century, increasing from 0.8% of the GDP in 2002 to 1.9% in 2013 (in reals as of 1980 values).

Infrastructure investment especially had a dramatic drop comparing the developmental, the neoliberal and the 'new developmental' ages. From 1950 to 1982, average public GFCF ratio to GDP in mining, transport, communication and energy was 1.3% in reals as of 1980, reaching its highest levels in the seventies, around 3% on average. Its growth was consistent to urbanization and industrialization processes that rapidly transformed the country into

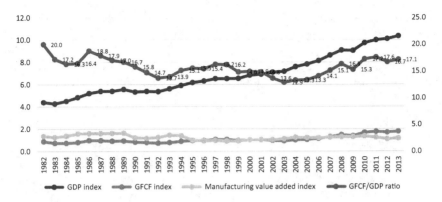

Chart 7.2 GDP/GFCF, GDP index, GFCF index and manufacturing value added index (reals as of 1980), 1982–2013

Source: Elaborated by Reis (2008) and Reis, Araujo & Gonzalez (2016) based on data from IBGE, IPEA and DEST

a middle-income industrialized economy. Though this process was continued in the next decades, public GFCF in infrastructure ratio to GDP fell to 1% on average from 1982–2002, and achieved its lowest ratio in 2000: 0.2%; therefore investment in infrastructure was lower than that.

Differently, after 2003, infrastructure programs launched in Lula's Brazil, especially PAC 1 and 2 enabled new investments in other sectors of the economy, increasing the supply of jobs and income.[29] In accordance with a report given by the Ministry of Planning (2010), the first phases 2007–2010 were successful:

> The results achieved by the PAC in these four years show the correctness of the decision to launch the program. The average expansion of the Brazilian economy is expected to reach 4.6% per year in 2007–2010, a significantly higher rate than in previous periods. Public investments doubled between 2007 and 2010, from 1.62% of GDP in 2006 to 3.27% of GDP in the 12 months ending October of this year. One of the factors that contributed to the increase in investments was the increase in credit, with lower interest rates and higher payment terms. Job creation continues to expand. The net result of job creation accumulated in PAC's period is a record, 8.2 million. The unemployment rate in October this year is the lowest in the IBGE's historical series: 6.1%. The PAC was also instrumental in curbing the impacts of the financial crisis that plagued international markets in 2008 and 2009. In Brazil, unlike most countries, the Federal Government did not reduce investments. On the contrary, the PAC, together with the strength of the domestic market, was able to significantly minimize the impacts of the international economic crisis. All Brazilians have won with the PAC, in large part because they are directly benefited by the works

being carried out and also because of the extremely positive effect that PAC has had on the economy, ensuring continued growth in our country.
(Ministry of Planning, 2010, p. 3, our translation)

The report affirms that 94% of the estimated investments were concluded by the end of 2010. Likewise, the 11th report of PAC 2 celebrated many achievements:

Continued investments in power generation and transmission, oil and natural gas exploration and refining, and revitalization of the naval industry ensure quality fuel, sustainable economic development and keep Brazil in a select group of countries that own and improve technology for the entire chain of deep-water oil exploration. With more than 40,000 projects in all regions of Brazil, investments made in PAC 2 will reach more than R $ 1 trillion by the end of 2014. This figure represents 96% of what is expected for 2011–2014. It is also more than 72% higher than the PAC 1 investments. By December 2014, the PAC 2 will conclude R $ 802.9 billion in works, which corresponds to 99.7% of the expected between 2011–2014.
(Ministry of Planning, 2014a, p. 3, our translation)

Regarding infrastructure areas, PAC 1 placed 45% of the investments in energy, 40% in social and urban, 15% in logistics (Amann et al., 2016). Those investments provoked a certain sectorial rearrangement in the manufacturing industry, with an increase in the relative importance of capital goods (Puga et al., 2010). Furthermore, it improved the external competitiveness by reducing operation costs in logistics and energy, positively impacting exports. More importantly, it reduced infrastructure costs to the population and improved public goods, especially housing. Minha Casa Minha Vida benefited more than 9.4 million people from 2014 until 2015, with 2,539 thousand housing units delivered by the end of 2015, 3,509 thousand contracted.[30] However the second phase of PAC 2 channeled 66% of the investments to energy, 22% to social and urban (which includes MCMV), and 12% to logistics (Amann et al., 2016; Ministry of Planning, 2010, 2014b).

Indeed, energy became the most important aisle of PAC 2 during the government of President Dilma Rousseff. This is thanks to, first, the geopolitical strengthening of Petrobras and, second, its soaring importance to the domestic growth dynamics. In 2010, it was the main Brazilian company and one of the top 20 most powerful and wealthy companies of the world. In 2010, Petrobras had already doubled its oil and gas reserves, refining capacity, production, and R&D activities.[31] To a large extent, Petrobras assumed a 'forced march', in the words of Schutte (2016), in the sense that its protagonist was intentionally led by the State. Abroad, its' contributions in developing national technology, naval and defense industry, logistic integration, and so forth, was in line with Brazilian international relations' efforts to strengthen Brazil in South-South and BRICS relations. "In the eyes of the world, not only has Brazil proved to be rich in oil, it has become a regional economic power that has replaced a submissive alignment with a more sovereign performance" (Centro de Altos Estudos Brasil Seculo XXI, 2015, our translation).

Domestically, Petrobras strengthened her ability to enhance supply and demand of new and settled markets. On the supply side, its ascension pushed several capital-intensive sectors of industry, notably the Brazilian shipbuilding[32] and machines and equipment industries. By the way, Pre-Salt achievements were based on its own technology and work in collaboration with suppliers, universities, and research centers (Petrobras, 2017), so that its investments had a key endogenous technological and innovative dimension as well. The company was important, on the demand side, for investment, exports, and imports. From the data of Afonso and Fajardo (2015), in 2013 the company had a weight equivalent of 9.3% of the Brazilian GFCF, or 1.9% of GDP, apart from its effects in the investment and production of other sectors. Its products represented more than 10% of exports in 2014 (Atlas of Economic Complexity). Therefore, the reduction of Petrobras investment, activities and revenues was so dramatic to the economy that it represented around 2 to 2.5 out of 3.8 percentage points of the drop in the Brazilian GDP in 2015. In the beginning of 2016, the market shares' prices of Petrobras (PETR3 and PETR4) were pushed down to a level lower than in 2003 – when the company had a much lower productive capacity, assets, revenues, etc. Thus, Petrobras' bonds depression in financial markets had a grievous speculative component, which befits the interests of rentiers and of states and companies that dispute the geopolitics of energy – so that it cannot be explained only by business performance.

In sum, Petrobras rise and fall for sure revolved around many national and international interests. From the geopolitical point of view, it was not interesting to the US, mainly, but also to the Great Powers[33] in general, a stronger alignment of BRICS (Brazil, Russia, India, China, and South Africa). After all, it meant the empowerment of Russia and China (historically, strong poles in the international relations), especially in what concerns energy, raw material and food markets. The rising importance of Lula's Brazil in Latin America and Africa conflicted with the US' external relations policy of dominance in Americas.[34] Especially regarding the naval force and fossil fuels' markets (petroleum, coal, and natural gas) – which still correspond to more than 80% of the international energy matrix (data for 2011, Centro de Altos Estudos Brasil Seculo XXI (2016)). Notwithstanding, one of the first measures of Michel Temer, after the impeachment of Dilma Rousseff, was the approval of the law n. 13.365, in November 2016, modifying the Law of Petrol. Petrobras lost the condition of sole operator in oil shared activities, and lost its mandatory share of 30%; though the preference remained its own. A new leadership in the company less prompt to nationalistic commitments confronts some domestic manufacturing and services interests, in benefit of international companies and financial shareholders that will take profit of a stronger and more private Petrobras in the medium/long run.

But the dismount of Petrobras is due to internal and governmental issues, too. There is no doubt that the corruption scandal contributed to weaken the management and operation of the company, and consequently its financial crisis. Apart from corruption, the crisis can be attributed to administrative errors, too, both in internal and external markets of oil & gas. In summary, the expansion of productive capacity underestimated its vulnerability in relation to stocks, flows, and price conditions of a very concentrated market, controlled by a couple of powerful companies and states. Moreover, the governmental monitoring of energy prices, which artificially pushed them down in the domestic market, caused serious damages to the financial sustainability of the company. Likewise, price administration has jeopardized the sugar-cane/ ethanol industries and the Eletrobras System. The hydrological crisis since 2014 deepened the collapse in the electricity sector in Brazil, after all the installed productive capacity did not grow as it was promised (and no contracting auctions were organized between 2004 and 2012); it had to deal with high costs of alternative sources, mainly thermic energy; and the distributors were suppressed by elevated differences in liquidation prices (Sauer, 2015). Therefore, the government's credibility was ruined in the energy sector, giving more arguments in favor of Dilma's impeachment.

Anyhow, PPPs and concessions of PAC 2 increased the participation of the private sector in infrastructure investments, in comparison to PAC 1, including Petrobras and Eletrobras systems (Amann et al., 2016). So it is difficult to advocate for crowding in or out effects since 2007; after all the program was made to be accomplished mostly by the private sector. The public sector had, for its turn, to provide funding and the regulatory mark, coordinating the auctions, bids and concession rounds. Theoretically and in practice, this coordination was far from good. On the contrary, it was too bureaucratic, slow, disarticulated, and confused. On the one hand, this problem is attributed to the weak autonomy of the regulators, both from governmental political interference and from the influence of the infrastructure providers themselves (Amann et al., 2016). As a result,

> A characteristic to date of infrastructure investments in Brazil has been the comparative slowness with which they have been rolled out. The delays in implementation (especially regarding those embodied in the PAC), in particular, have been blamed on the complicated bureaucratic mechanism which has grown over many generations governing the release of public funds and the very cautious approach of the authorities in running bidding competitions, especially in the field of the novel PPP contracts. However, there is a growing consensus (see, for example Amann and Baer, 2006; Cunha and Rodrigo, 2012; De Paula and Avellar, 2008) that it is the nature of regulatory governance in Brazil, and its attendant regulatory uncertainty, that have long been holding back investment.
>
> (Amann et al., 2016, p. 73)

On the other hand, governmental policy makers had to deal with ambitious demands from the private sector: unreal guarantees, low loan interest rates, long amortization prompts, and other favorable conditions to put down risks and costs of infrastructure investment, leaving it to the public sector alone. In addition, arguably, there was lack of quality in engineering projects and business models. So that rentism and corruption is not a problem of the public sector itself, but of the influence of private sector towards the governments, as Operation Car Wash made it clear. Despite the undeniable importance of combating corruption, Operation Car Wash had negative impact in the Brazilian political economy as well. On the one hand, it was a smokescreen for the approval of many illegitimate changes in social and economic conquests of Lula's Brazil.[35] On the other hand, it was highly selective and specifically reached Petrobras and the private sector that supported Lula, Dilma, and their party. In this sense, some estimations of prestigious Brazilian economic consultants show that the fall in contracting companies' investment involved in Operation Car Wash meant 0.7 out of 3.8 percentage points of GDP reduction in 2015. Altogether, before 2015 Petrobras and contracting companies represented more than one third of the productive investment in Brazil (Costas, 2015).

Another important aspect of the political economy of public investment in Brazil was public funding. As said before, there were some initiatives during Lula's administration to enhance private investment in infrastructure, furthered afterwards in PAC 2. These policies came in response to the insistent demand from the Brazilian industrial private sector, pretty much present in power coalition during Lula's and Dilma's governments. For example, as Oliveira (2016) lists, the creation of debentures to fund investments with income tax exemption in 2011; the launch of a Brazilian Agency of Guarantors and Warranties Funds in 2012; the modernization of the law that regulates PPP in 2012 (which increased tax exemptions); the renewal of BNDES' PSI in 2013, and the arbitrary attempt of public banks to reduce interest rates and financial spreads – which was not followed by the private banks. Furthermore, BNDES' disbursement to the infrastructure sector grew from R $1.2 billion in 2006 to R $70.4 billion in 2013.

PSI and other programs of BNDES or other public banks were in part financed with loans from the National Treasury since the international crisis. From 2008 on, the National Monetary Council (CMN) waived the BNDES exposure limit to Petrobras – and later to Eletrobras and Vale.

> Such a system, maintained even after resuming economic growth, produced a vertiginous increase in the volume of credit concessions to official financial institutions: according to the BCB [Brazilian Central Bank], in the order of 8.7% of GDP, compared to 0.5% of GDP at the end of 2006 and 9.2% of GDP at the end of 2012. The nominal growth of R$ 406.9 billion in credits granted by the Treasury to public banks was basically directed towards the re-composition of BNDES funding, which received 91.3% (R $ 371.7 billion) of the volume of resources. The other portion of the current stock, equivalent to R$ 35.3 billion, was allocated to the other financial institutions, especially Caixa Econômica Federal.
> (Afonso; Biasoto Jr., 2014, p. 269, our translation)

Furthermore, since 2012 the government continued anticyclical measures to revamp private investment, expanding tax cuts and subsidized credit, which were supposed to put less pressure on inflation. Orair and Gobetti (2017) affirm that tax cuts went from BRL 43 billion in 2010 to BRL 122 billion in 2014, while subsidies went from BRL 31.3 billion to BRL 73.5 billion. But the results were despicable, and tax revenue had growth rates systematically below GDP for the first time in decades. As a remedy, there came spending cuts and more 'creative accounting'.

> Under this scenario, with lower revenue growth, while a significant portion of expenditures maintained their previous rate of growth (social benefits) or were even extraordinarily accelerated (subsidies), fiscal policy reached a crossroads. The fiscal space was brutally reduced, while the government was reluctant to change its fiscal target, kept above 3 per cent of GDP during 2011–2014 (Table 7.1). How to solve this dilemma? The solution that was found was a mixture of two paths: i) stronger budget 'locks' (budget contingency) on a small portion of discretionary expenses, liable to be compressed in the short term; and ii) the use of nonrecurring measures to artificially inflate fiscal results (one-off revenues, creative accounting, fiscal gimmicks such as the rollover of payments to public banks – known as 'fiscal pedaling' etc.) and increase the deduction margin of the target.
> (Orair and Gobetti, 2017, p. 9)

Whether fiscal pedaling would jeopardize public accounts and compromise economic growth (and leaving space for opportunistic behavior) was the main controversy in fiscal policies in Brazil since the beginning of the 2010s. The mainstream economists and financial markets' technical argument against the so called fiscal abuses were the deterioration of public finance, increasing debt, risk, and interest rate – finally, crowding out private investment and mining growth. The developmental and heterodox economists, together with a part of the industrial and labor sectors, defended the investments and the general development strategy led by the state in order to create employment and income sources that otherwise would never emerge, leaving to its multiplier effects the revenues' sources for the fiscal regime. And, there were more progressive positions – unfortunately, barely heard in the debate – that were against both strategies (especially the first), once they have limited concerns in terms of environmental and social development, income and power redistribution, and a real pro-poor and labor national project. Fiscal policy and public investment debate was insufficient not only for its theoretical or scientific dimension, and was not even for its broad social, economic or political consequences, but especially because it was taken as the route to compel the change in power correlation forces – the true essence of a coup d'etat.

Actually, from 2003 until 2014 (Table 7.2), economic growth was accompanied by a remarkable decrease in the unemployment rate, which then reached its lowest level (circa 4%), as well as the wage participation in GDP achieved

Table 7.2 Economic activity, aggregate demand and fiscal policy 2004–2014 (annual growth in %, constant values BRL 2010)

	2004–2010: Lula I and II	2011–2014: Dilma I
Economic Activity		
GDP	4.5%	2.2%
Formal employment (millions)	1458	829
Unemployment rate	9.0%	5.4%
Aggregate demand		
Consumption of families	5.3%	3.3%
Consumption of public administration	3.2%	1.8%
Investment	8.0%	2.1%
. Machines & equipment	12.3%	−0.7%
. Civil construction	5.8%	2.8%
Exports	5.2%	1.6%
Imports	13.4%	4.1%
Fiscal Policy		
Fiscal primary result/GDP	3.2%	1.7%
Revenues of federal government	6.8%	1.2%

Source: SERRANO & SUMMA, 2015, p. 38

its higher participation in three decades (38%). The growth dynamics rescued about 36 million people from absolute poverty, and extinguished famine (FAO, 2014). But, clearly, from 2011 onwards the productive dynamic of the 2000's lost breath. On the demand side, in Lula's Brazil investment, consumption and exports grew significantly – as well as imports[36] – but all components reduced its growth path in Dilma's government. In particular, investment and exports cooled the most, due to the fall in commodity prices in the second case. On the supply side, the sector that grew most in Lula's governments were financial intermediation, however in Dilma's it was among the weakest performers. But the most affected sector was manufacturing, the only sector that presented negative growth in 2011–2014. As a result, the index of utilization of installed capacity in the manufacturing sector fell in last period to lower levels than in 2008, when there was the financial crisis. In this scenario of idle capacity and no expectations of growth in the effective demand, no wonder that private investment in machines & equipment would fall that much.

On the one hand, the manufacturing production and investment drop is explained by the increase in imports and the losses in international

Table 7.3 Value added annual growth of GDP, 2003–2014 (average in %, current volume)

	2003–2010	2011–2014	Ratio Dilma/ Lula growth
TOTAL	3.9	2.2	0.6
01 Agricultural	3.5	3.4	1.0
Industry	3.5	1.0	0.3
02 Mining and quarrying	4.7	1.8	0.4
03 Manufacturing industry	3.2	−0.5	−0.1
04 Production and distribution of electricity, gas, water, sewage, urban cleaning	4.1	1.5	0.4
05 Construction	4.3	3.4	0.8
Services	4.1	2.5	0.6
06 Trade	4.9	2.2	0.4
07 Transport, storage and post	3.6	2.6	0.7
08 Information services	4.3	5.7	1.3
09 Financial intermediation, insurance and supplementary pension and related services	7.6	2.2	0.3
10 Real estate activities	4.2	3.2	0.8
11 Other services	3.4	2.9	0.9
12 Public administration, health, education, social security	2.6	1.4	0.5

Source: Own elaboration from IBGE data

competitiveness of Brazilian manufacturing exports, mainly related to the appreciation of the exchange rate. On the other hand, there were structural and institutional reasons from both macro and corporative scenarios that prevented further domestic investment and reinvestment. Some key ones are: the multinational companies' logics of value allocation of global productive chains in general excluded Brazil from the high value-added activities; the uneven concentration in markets, domestic technological gap, and strong resistance to strengthen profit margins and rate in Brazil. Last, the 'Brazilian cost', usually highlighted by the national bourgeoise (and super emphasized by Brazilian media), which means labor costs, heavy tax burden, complex bureaucracy related to companies' operation and management (especially micro, small, and medium ones), high interest rates, and infrastructure deficiencies – especially in logistics and energy prices, electricity in particular.

And it was also to put in motion the so-called FIESP agenda (Federation of the Industries of Sao Paulo State), that the public investment dynamic presented in this chapter took place. Despite its geopolitical character, something that goes beyond the industrial demands, Lula and Dilma's governments tried to cherish the domestic manufacturing sector, providing incentives to production and exports, such as: tax reductions and subsides; special credit lines and long term interest rates to consumption and investment from public banks, including an attempt to reduce the reference interest rates of national debt; fostering state-owned enterprises' investments; reduction in energy prices; and the infrastructure investments presented before. However, the minimum wage valuation policy went against all these efforts, in the sense that it raised salaries and income in the economy and enlarged the wage rate in many sectors, as well as labors' bargaining power.[37] This was tolerated by businessmen while total revenues and profits were growing, but this was not true anymore after 2014, especially after the adoption of austerity policies in Dilma's second term.

> The third sub-period (from 2015 onwards) has been characterized by the radical shift in fiscal policy, now driven by the hypothesis of expansionist austerity, and by the worst recession ever recorded in the country's history. This shift towards austerity started with the fiscal adjustment of 2015, which was coupled in the following year with an expectation that investors' confidence and economic growth would be regained by furthering liberal structural reforms.
>
> (Orair and Gobetti, 2017, p. 18)

At that moment, the government was criticized by all political groups, from left to the right; by all sectorial classes, especially industrial and financial ones; and by workers and capitalists. People in general were very unsatisfied with the fall in production, employment and income, and with the quantity and quality of public goods. Although it expanded in Lula's Brazil, especially in education and health compared to the two previous decades, it was far from good. Moreover, though income and wealth inequality remained very high, its improvements in Dilma's II were rapidly vanishing. Mass media and the general public simply resumed the explanations for the economic crisis in State's corruption and incompetence, centered on the fiscal policy and public investment dynamic. Therefore, and unfortunately, this was the perfect opportunity to kick the president out, seriously injuring democracy.

Conclusions on the political economy of public investment and economic development in Brazil

Public investment has historically been positive and directly impacts economic development in Brazil. From 2003 until 2014, the government created and shifted institutions to foster public investment, and then private, driving economic growth. All sectors developed during Lula's governments, especially the services and financial sector. Domestically, public investment contributed to the economic dynamics, from the supply and demand sides of the economy, supported by public banks, infrastructure programs, and state-owned enterprises. The macroeconomic regime, although tied by the inflation target, had fiscal space to enhance consumption and investment, leveraging employment and income. Exports also grew, taking advantage of the rise in demand and process of commodities, which led to a change in its profile towards specialization in primary products. The neo-developmental strategy, in contrast to the previous salvage neoliberal view of State action, empowered the country in international relations, betting high on the investment capacity of Petrobras.

That strategy counted on industrial, technological, and innovation policies, too, fostering industrial growth, but part of the stimulus was transferred to imports. In Dilma's Brazil, the economic cycle turned down, performing worse than the international capitalist system. Public investment continued to be fostered in Brazil, and the state-owned enterprises and public banks were compelled by performance to an anticyclical role thanks to specific institutions. Theoretically, this strategy had the intention of sustaining the economic cycle that could have been worse in its absence. But its execution showed planning, coordination and operational problems, such as in the regulatory framework, price administration, loans from the Treasury to public banks, and creative accounts.

For sure, the choices about public investment between 2003 and 2014 have privileged particular foreign and national interest groups, notably some companies in the manufacturing industry and civil construction. It also benefited the export agroindustry complex and services providers oligopolies, especially of the financial system in Lula's governments. Banks were the main winners, due to the expansion of national income and public indebtedness that were also related to public spending and investment. The Brazilian inflation target regime consistently established high and odd interest rates, allowing for speculative operations in the exchange markets and international capital flows, too. The unique attempt by the public sector to reduce interest rates in 2012/2013 was not accompanied by the private sectors, and triggered their withdrawal of political support. Last, the employment creation and minimum wage valuation policies and initiatives, as well as cash-transfer and social programs, benefitted the poor and working population. Undeniably, there were important social conquests in terms of fighting poverty and hunger, leveraging consumption standards, the supply of public goods and services enabled by the rise in public spending and investments. And despite the fact that average income levels have improved in Brazil, regional, functional (between salaries and profits/rents and interests), and personal income distribution have shown little progress.

Therefore, the Brazilian society experienced modernization without deep structural changes in Lula's and Dilma's years. The complex and contradictory neo-developmental economic model, managed by a broad coalition between classes and sectors, was rapidly demolished when the economic growth cycle reverted. Industrial and financial elites reunited against social-democratic conquests, supported by international interests, urging for the change in the nature of the State. Corruption and incompetence in the public sector were then transformed as the main argument for Dilma's impeachment, based on the controversial evidence of fiscal pedaling. Thus, the criminalization of fiscal policy, in what regards public investment especially, served to push reforms and conservative austerity economic policies. So, the impeachment in 2016 was a consequence of Lula and Dilma's governments hits and misses. Hits in relation to social conquests and rising power in international relations, though still weak and fragile. And misses in relation to its internal operation, contradictory macroeconomic regime and, more importantly, its inability to truly improve the distribution of wealth and power in Brazil.

Notes

* I thank Andre Barroso de Souza and Pedro Chadarevian for their precious comments on this chapter.
1 "Infrastructure is fundamental for the advancement of the systemic conditions of business competitiveness, especially industrial business, as noted by Coutinho and Ferraz (1994). It provides positive externalities to companies that are primarily associated with a reduction in production costs, increasing the profitability of private investments. Thus, infrastructure investment, which is generally public or made through public-private partnerships (PPPs), raises aggregate supply and demand. Likewise, infrastructure can be a special way of introducing technological innovations and, therefore, growth in productivity" (Reis et al., 2016).
2 "And this is the punchline: when organized effectively, the State's hand is firm but not heavy, providing the vision and the dynamic push (as well as some 'nudges' – though nudges don't get you the IT revolution of the past, nor the green revolution today) to make things happen that otherwise would not have. Such actions are meant to increase the courage of private business. This requires understanding the State as neither a 'meddler' nor a simple 'facilitator' of economic growth. It is a key partner of the private sector – and often a more daring one, willing to take the risks that business won't. The State cannot and should not bow down easily to interest groups who approach it to seek handouts, rents and unnecessary privileges like tax cuts. It should seek instead for those interest groups to work dynamically with it in its search for growth and technological change" (Mazzucatto, 2013, p. 11).
3 Chang (2003) ranked five main reasons for the existence of state-owned enterprises (SOEs). The first one is the verification, in capital markets, of absolute and comparative advantages in activities in which the minimum efficiency degree is too high to attract private investment. The second reason is the natural monopolies, which are very common in the infrastructure sector. The third one is the fact that they have an important strategic character, in order to enable activities that generate interesting externalities or spillovers for the economy's development. The fourth one is the domestic technology production and accumulation, which reduces the dependency on external capital. Finally, SOEs' investments and price policies may be a mechanism of income redistribution (Reis, 2008).
4 For a critical review of mainstream's theoretical foundations for privatization and reduction on public investment, see Bayliss (2006).
5 "In accordance with a perspective based on the demand and on the historical-structural tradition, investment is the key variable of growth dynamics and capitalist structural change. The demand induces and creates – through the Principle of effective Demand – the supply, which adjusts itself both in the short and long run to variations of demand's autonomous components (funding standards, consumption, competition and the social relations between capital and labor) and induced ones (accelerator mechanism that adjusts the capital stock). Economic development is a process of structural change led by capital accumulation which increases the productivity of the whole economy, sustaining high growth rates in the medium and long run" (Reis, 2011, p. 78). Development

is necessarily related to a more complex productive matrix, better income and living standards, and more equanimity in power and wealth distribution. In our approach, furthermore, there is causal reciprocity in the processes of historic and material evolution, and of dynamic institutional changes. "The most general interaction that institutions specify is the one between economic and political processes. At the most general level, the formal and informal property right structures provide incentives and *simultaneously* specify asset distributions" (di John, 2009, p. 136, underlined by the author). Establishing and enforcing property rights are challengeable. It is not possible to separate issues of incentives and efficiency from issues of distribution and equity.

6 Because of this, in Brazil, the main public investors are the public administration and the state-owned enterprises (SOEs).

7 "In fact in 1870, 1920, 1970, or 1990 the supply of financial flows (loans and bonds) led by expansion cycles in developed countries, finance innovations and changes in the interest rates in the world financial centers brought about massive loans and capital inflows to LAC [Latin American countries]. These loans and capital flows created a situation of loan frenzy to public and private sectors in LAC. This external over-borrowing generated by its turn a current account deficit not checked by exchange rate devaluation. The reluctance to adjust the rate of exchange to domestic prices and the defense of high covered interest rates have generated a period of real appreciation of the exchange rate and an import boom were common consequences. A pro-finance and pro-commodity strategy associated to these flows has stimulated an internationalization of private domestic assets. This cycle has been normally reverted by external shocks with an increase in the rate of interest of a major financial center and a collapse of commodity prices. The collapse of the exchange rate has been followed by the impossibility to meet all debt commitments in foreign exchange generated contraction and defaults. Property transferences, de-nationalization and empowerment of mobile international asset holders have been some common political and economic outcomes of this pattern. These cycles resulted in real exchange rates with strong volatility and a tendency to depreciate against the strongest currencies" (Medeiros, 2008, pp. 85, 88).

8 "In the immediate aftermath of the debt crisis, it did seem that the drive toward liberalization and privatization had acquired an irresistible force in the developing world. There was an ineluctable quality to the dismantling of the policy apparatus handed down from the years of development planning, enough to make even the mention of "national projects' seem somewhat quaint. But matters are different today. After the dismal economic record of the quarter-century under neo-liberal hegemony, the experience of the 1950s and 60's has gained respectability – as indeed it should. For despite its somewhat ignominious end, the developmental era out-performed its successor on most every measure. Politically, the dismal record of neoliberalism has meant a steady loss of legitimacy in the South" (Chibber, 2004, p. 1).

9 "The details of the 'post-Fordist' system are still unclear and it will obviously share some features with Fordism. But two key differences concern the re-organization of production and the re-composition of the labor force. Firstly, post-Fordism sees an increasing emphasis on flexibility in organizing the labor process, internal and external labor markets, relations among firms, and so forth. This is not just a question of the enhanced flexibility due to the expanding role of electronics, the micro-processor, and information technology in producing goods and services but also of the increased flexibility of social relations. Secondly, post-Fordism is accompanied by changes in occupational structures. Whereas Fordism was characterized by the key role of the affluent mass worker (or semi-skilled worker), post-Fordism is likely to see a growing polarization of the workforce into a full-time skilled core and an unskilled periphery often engaged only part-time and subject to new forms of Taylorization. This will extend beyond areas where flexible manufacturing is established and also occur in the tertiary or service sector. Here the introduction of more flexible word- and data-processing machinery has been

Hits and misses of public investment strategy 155

accompanied by more flexible work practices including work from home as well as flexible part-time and shift-work" (Jessop, 1991, p. 90).
10 NFSP covers all public sector, that is, central government (National Treasury, Central Bank and Social Security), state administration, and public companies in the three levels of the federation (Silva, 2006)
11 "However, a different path was taken by the banks owned by the federal government (from now named federal public banks), which kept the property of Banco do Brasil (BB), Caixa Economica Federal (Caixa), Banco da Amazonia (BASA) and Banco do Nordeste do Brasil (BNB), both regional banks, and Banco Nacional de Desenvolvimento Econômico e Social (BNDES), as the name shows, a development bank. It is important to notice that, almost all of these banks (except for BNDES) were capitalized by the federal government recently (late 1990's and early 2000's), and all of them are under the same regulatory framework as the private banks and are managed according to governance principles. It means that they have to face a complex range of objectives: to reach their social mission and obtain good micro results measured by efficiency and profitability ratios. The Brazilian public financial system is composed, besides the banking institutions, by compulsory saving funds, which are not the only sources, but that provides stable institutional funding, essential for the long term operations: FAT (Workers Support Fund), FGTS (The Guarantee Fund for Time of Service) and Constitutional funds" (Sarti and Mendonca, 2016, p. 14).
12 "In the governments of Collor and Itamar [1989–1993] there was privatization of some subsidiaries, in particular Petroquisa and Fosfértil. Then, in the Real Plan, imports of [oil and gas] derivatives were liberalized, although it had no practical effect. Then the Constitutional Amendment n. 9 of 1995 opened the sector to other companies. And, lastly, there was the sale of a large portion of Petrobras' shares on the New York and São Paulo stock markets in 2000. Petrobras should lose its position, not only as executor of the national petroleum policy, but as a formulator. Law n. 9478/1997 determined in its article 26 that the concessionaire would own the oil extracted: "if successful, produce oil or natural gas in a particular block, granting ownership of these goods, after extraction." It would be up to the ANP to organize the bids in which the interested companies compete for the blocks available. It is worth remembering that President FHC was forced to make a commitment not to include Petrobras in the privatization program in order to get PEC approval, which in a way shows the strength maintained by the nationalist vision" (Schutte, 2016, pp. 22–23, our translation).
13 "Since mid-1999, after the introduction of the inflation-targeting system, the Brazilian monetary authority has pursued a single official objective, the control of inflation, which must remain inside a pre-defined range around a center value in each calendar year (defined since 2005 as 4.5% a year plus or minus 2%). After a period in which inflation was above the upper limit of the inflation target range in almost every year (1999–2003), since 2004 the central bank has been successful in keeping inflation within the target range every single year. However, from 2010 to 2014 inflation got very close to the upper limit" (Summa and Serrano, 2015, p. 1).
14 Government-owned enterprises 'receive financial resources from the controlling entity for the payment of expenses related to personnel or general or capital expenses, excluding, in the latter case, those expenses arising from increased shareholder participation'. Controlled companies are those 'whose majority of share capital with voting rights belongs, directly or indirectly, to the entity of the Federation' (LRF, art. 2, our translation).
15 The inflation variation was discounted by the gross fixed capital formation's deflator, R$ 1980, provided by IPEA. See database in Reis (2008) and Reis et al. (2016).
16 For a review, see Reis et al. (2016).
17 Brazil had a low participation rate of public investment, a maximum of 2.3% on average between 2010 and 2012, according to World Bank data (calculated by the difference between total GFCF/GDP and private GFCF/GDP, US dollars), for about 100

economies. In Latin America and the Caribbean, the average public GFCF just after the international was around 4.2% of GDP (and average private GFCF of 16%), 5% in developing countries in Europe and Central Asia (private GFCF of 17%), and in developing countries on the Pacific side of East Asia, public GFCF reached 18.2% (and GFCF of private sector is on average 23%).

18 According to the World Bank Public-Private-Partnership in Infrastructure Resource Center, "Public Private Partnerships (PPPs) take a wide range of forms varying in the extent of involvement of and risk taken by the private party. The terms of a PPP are typically set out in a contract or agreement to outline the responsibilities of each party and clearly allocate risk." There is none or low private participation when the public owns and operates assets, such as in utility restructuring, corporatization and de-centralization, or civil works and service contracts. PPP are usually applied for managing and operating contracts, leases, concessions, build-operation-transfer projects, design-build-operate projects, and joint venture/ partial divestiture of public assets.

19 The public share in total credit in Brazil rose from 35% to 41% in 2010 compared to 2008, according to Almeida (2011).

20 "Launched by the federal government in 2009 with the objective of overcoming the country's housing shortage of over seven million units (National Household Sampling Survey -PNAD- data, 2009), the 'Minha casa, minha vida' program drives the production and acquisition of new housing units or the refurbishment of urban properties, as well as the production and refurbishment of rural housing for low-income families by means of subsidies/discounts. The program also has a positive impact on local economies by encouraging civil construction." (Caixa Economica Federal, 2016, p. 59). At the end of 2015, 84.42% of the MVMV operations were contracted through Caixa (IDEM, p. 59)

21 Gobetti (2010) affirms that approximately 110 federal and 28 state government-owned enterprises were completely or partially privatized between 2003 and 2009. From 2010 until 2014, the number of state-owned enterprises remained around 135, 48 direct and 87 indirect – being 27% in the sector of oil & gas and 22% in electricity (Dest, 2016).

22 Industrial interests must be understood in the context of financialization, so that industrial and financial interests are not antagonist.

23 According to the Forbes list of the 2000 biggest companies of the world, in 2010 Petrobras was the 18th, the largest Brazilian company in the ranking, with US $140 billion in sales, US $16 billion in profits, US $198 billion in assets, and US $190 billion in market value. In 2014 Petrobras was ranked in 32nd, and in 2017 she was the 399th, the 7th Brazilian company after Itau, Bradesco, Banco do Brasil, Vale. Eletrobras was the 610th in 2017, much worse than its 235th rank in 2010.

24 According to the company, "The discoveries made in the pre-salt are among the world's most important in the past decade. The pre-salt province comprises large accumulations of excellent quality, high commercial value light oil. A reality that puts us in a strategic position to meet the great global demand for energy. Daily oil output at the pre-salt progressed from the average of approximately 41,000 barrels per day, in 2010, to 1 million barrels per day in mid-2016. A nearly 24-fold increase" (Petrobras, 2017).

25 "The legal obligations of local content, through nationalization indexes established by the ANP [National Petrol Agency], were therefore intended to create opportunities that would not be created by the market dynamics itself. And, consequently, to reduce the growing dependence of Brazil on the purchase of equipment and services in dollars in the foreign market. It is important to emphasize that this policy was focused on generating employment and income in Brazil regardless of the origin of capital. Moreover, it also encouraged multinational companies to settle in Brazil, especially to get access to technology. In Lula's government, the local content clause went through quantitative and qualitative changes" (Schutte, 2016, p. 31, our translation).

26 "The main focus was on raising new funds for Petrobras to meet its investment needs both directly (new money) and indirectly, by increasing its borrowing capacity. Part of

this process was the onerous transfer through which Petrobras was granted the right to undertake exploration and production activities in given Pre-Salt areas, at a limit of up to 5 billion barrels of oil and natural gas. The value of this onerous transfer was assessed in accordance with market practices and paid to the Union by the company. The proposed law allowed Petrobras to pay the Brazilian government using public debt securities. The Federal Government shared in the capitalization by using federal public debt instruments. Petrobras then used the debt instruments to pay the Government for the 5 billion barrels of oil. Total capitalization was US$ 72 billion, (± R$ 120 billion), and the onerous transfer was priced at R$ 74 billion, which means that 'only' R$ 46 billion in new money was raised. This operation was the largest capitalization of a public company in history (as a comparison, Facebook's IPO raised US$ 16 billion)" (Schutte, 2013, p. 60).

27 In 2010 the Union had 55.7% of ordinary bond, plus 1.9% of BNDES. Private shareholders have 61% of preferential bonds, according to Fuser (2011, p. 55).

28 Data for manufacturing production is in Brazilian real as of 2000, basic prices, according to the IPEA.

29 The governments of Luiz Inácio Lula da Silva, even with the international economic crisis of 2008/2009, achieved a fortunate process of economic growth with increases in balance of payment surplus, higher levels of activity and revenue, declining unemployment, falling interest rates, and a decrease in the public debt. Manufacturing industry was triggered by the greater dynamism in global demand before the crisis that had a positive impact on the profitability of exporting sectors such as steel, paper and pulp, and mining. The domestic expansion of consumption broadened the cycle of investments to consumer and intermediate goods, as well as debt (Puga et al., 2010). See Chapters 3–6 of this book to learn more about the mechanisms of growth dynamics in Lula's Brazil.

30 "Of these, 38.94% went to families with an income of up to R$ 1,600; 50.14% to families with an income between R$ 1,600.01 and R$3,250.00; and 10.91% to families with an income from R$ 3,250.01 to R$ 5,000" (Caixa Economica Federal, 2016, p. 59, our translation).

31 "The discovery of the Pre-salt led the Country to become one of the world's great producers. There are estimates that the reservoirs will exceed 60 billion barrels. And productivity continues at an excellent pace: according to Petrobras, since 2010, the annual average daily production of Pre-salt has grown more than 12 times," hitting new records in 2015 and 2016 (Centro de Altos Estudos Brasil Seculo XXI, 2016, our translation).

32 Campos Neto (2014) shows that the offshore oil and gas production activity, in the extent of the decision to contract vessels with increasing percentages of local content, allowed the growth of formal employees in the naval industry from 1.9 thousand in 2000 to 71 thousand in 2013.

33 Polayni, 1944.

34 "Besides the unique and unrepeatable personal leadership that had a tremendous international impact [Lula], the expansion of Brazil in the first decade of the century, both inside and outside South America, had a double advantage in relation to the others [Latin-American countries]. In the first place, paradoxically, Brazil enjoyed the status of unarmed power, because in fact it is located in the unconditional atomic protection zone of the United States. And, second, whether it wants to or not, Brazil has enjoyed the status of candidate-heir to the condition of power, formed from the same cultural and civilizing matrix as the United States" (Fiori, 2011, pp. 30–31).

35 "Given the spectacle created by the press in the so-called 'fight against corruption', the dominant interests widely represented in the Brazilian Congress take advantage to impose their regressive agenda on the country. Instead of seriously discussing and passing a political reform which is the basis of the structure of the Brazilian political system, being at the root of the current scandal, Congress members opportunistically submit already defeated conservative ideas on bills (PL), proposals for constitutional amendments (PEC)

and Senate draft resolutions (PRS) for approval under the emergency regime. A quick examination of some of them shows how they undermine national sovereignty, democracy and human rights in Brazil" (Reis et al., 2016, p. 2).
36 Note that the economic surplus generated by the expansion of aggregate demand in Lula's government was not entirely domestically absorbed. Indeed, part of the surplus was transferred abroad via trade, services and income balances, especially after the world financial crisis. However, as Schincariol (2017) clarifies, high foreign direct investment flow in Brazil, especially in portfolios, enabled surplus in the Brazilian Balance of Payments after 2007. However, current accounts have remained negative since then, too, not due to deficit in the trade balance, but in services and incomes – especially correspondent to machines' rental payments and remittances of profits and dividends, respectively.
37 First formalized in a decree in 2007 and in Law 12382/2011, the valuation of the minimum wage was a long-term strategy in which it is annually adjusted to inflation, with a one-year lag, and with the GDP growth of the economy, with a lag of two years. From 2002 to 2013, the minimum wage increased more than 70% (in real terms), provoking increases in the earnings of social security and assistance benefits, with beneficial effects on the labor market and income distribution.

References

Afonso, José Roberto, and Biasoto Jr, G. Política fiscal nos Pós-crise de 2008: A credibilidade perdida. In Geraldo Biasoto Jr, Rafael Cagnin and Luiz Fernando Novais (Org.), *A economia brasileira no contexto da crise global*, 1st ed. São Paulo: Imprensa Oficial SP, 2014, v. 1, pp. 251–280.

Afonso, José Roberto, and Fajardo, Bernardo. Evolução da taxa de investimentos e a indução pelo setor público. *Nota técnica IBRE/ FGV*, Rio de Janeiro, April 2015.

Aguiar Filho, Fernando Luiz. *Modelo institucional do setor elétrico brasileiro: análise da capacidade de atração de capital privado para investimentos em geração de energia hidrelétrica*. Dissertação de Mestrado em Engenharia. Escola Politécnica da Universidade de São Paulo, 2007.

Almeida, Julio Sergio Gomes de. Como o Brasil superou a crise. In Desdobramentos da crise financeira internacional. *Brazilian Journal of Political Economy*, v. 31, n. 2, pp. 315–335, 2011.

Amann, Edmund, Baer, Werner, Trebat, Thomas, and Lora, Juan Villa. Infrastructure and Its Role in Brazil's Development Process. *The Quarterly Review of Economics and Finance*, v. 62, pp. 66–73, 2016.

Andreoni, J. An Experimental Test of the Public-Goods Crowding-Out Hypothesis. *The American Economic Review*, pp. 1317–1327, 1993.

Auerbach, David Alan. (1990) *Public Investment and Private Sector Growth*. Economic Policy Institute, Washington, 1990.

Atlas of Economic Complexity. *Harvard's Center for International Development*. atlas.cid.harvard.edu

Bayliss, Kate. Privatization Theory and Practice: A Critical Analysis of Policy Evolution in the Development Context. In B. Fine and K. S. Jomo (Eds.), *The New Development Economics: Post Washington Consensus Neoliberal Thinking*. London: Zed Books, 2006.

Boito Jr., Armando, and Berringer, Tatiana. Social classes, neodevelopmentalism, and Brazilian foreign policy under Presidents Lula and Dilma. *Latin American Perspectives*, n. 41, pp. 94–109.

Caixa Economica Federal. *Caixa 2015 Sustainability Report*. Brasília, DF, 2016.

Campos Neto, Carlos A. Investimentos e Financiamentos na Indústria Naval Brasileira 2000–2013. In Campos Neto and Pompermayer, Fabiano (orgs.), *Ressurgimento da Indústria Naval no Brasil (2000–2013)*. Brasília: Instituto Pesquisa Econômica Aplicada, 2014.

Centro de Altos Estudos Brasil Século XXI. A crise da Petrobras à luz da geopolítica. *Brasil Debate*, June 16, 2015.

Cerqueira, Braulio Santiago. Política fiscal, demanda agregada, crescimento e crise: o investimento federal e o investimento da Petrobras no período 2003–2015. *Textos para discussão* n. 7, IE/ UFRJ, Rio de Janeiro, 2016.

Chang, H. *Globalization, Economic Development and the Role of the State*. London and New York: TWN, Zed Books, 2003.

Chibber, V. Reviving the Developmental State? The Myth of the National Bourgeoisie. *Theory and Research in Comparative Social Analisys*, Paper 20, University of California Los Angeles, 2004.

Costas, Ruth. Escândalo da Petrobras 'engoliu 2,5% da economia em 2015'. *BBC Brasil*, São Paulo, December 2, 2015.

Coutinho, Luciano; Ferraz, Joao Carlos. (orgs.) (1994) *Estudo da competitividade da indústria brasileira*. Campinas: Papirus, 1994.

Cunha, André M., Prates, Daniela, and Ferrari-Filho, Fernando. Brazil Responses to the International Financial Crisis: A Well Succeed Example of Keynesian Policies? *Panoeconomicus*, v. 58, n. 5, pp. 693–714, January 2011.

de Paula, Luiz F., and Ferrari Filho, Fernando. Desdobramentos da crise financeira internacional. *Review of Political Economy*, v. 31, n. 2, pp. 315–335, 2011.

DEST. *Departamento de Coordenação e Governança das Empresas Estatais*. Perfil das Empresas Estatais Federais, 2014. Ministério do Planejamento Desenvolvimento e Gestão – Brasília: MP/SE/DEST, 2015, 2016.

DEST. *Departamento de Coordenação e Governança das Empresas Estatais*. Ministério do Planejamento, Orçamento e Gestão [Department of Coordination and Governance of State Owned Enterprises. Ministry of Planning, Budget and Management]. Statistics. www.planejamento.gov.br/assuntos/empresas-estatais/dados-e-estatisticas

di John, Jonathan. *From Windfall to Curse? Oil and Industrialization in Venezuela, 1920 to the Present*. Pensilvânia: Pens State University Press, 2009.

Espinasa, R., Teixeira, A., and Anaya, F. Energy Dossier: Brazil. *Techinical Note IDB* n. 1121, Inter American Development Bank, November 2016.

FAO. *The State of Food Insecurity in the World 2014: Strengthening the Enabling Environment for Food Security and Nutrition*. Roma: FAO, 2014.

Filgueiras, Luiz. O neoliberalismo no Brasil: estrutura, dinâmica e ajuste do modelo econômico. In *Neoliberalismo y sectores dominantes. Tendencias globales y experiencias nacionales*. 2006, pp. 179–206.

Fiori, José Luís. Brasil e América do Sul: o desafio da inserção internacional soberana. *Textos para Discussão*, n. 42, CEPAL-IPEA, Brasília, 2011.

Florêncio, P. The Brazilian 2010 Oil Regulatory Framework and Its Crowding-Out Investment Effects. *Energy Policy*, v. 98, pp. 378–389, 2016.

Forbes. *The World's Biggest Public Companies* 2010, 2013, 2017. www.forbes.com/global2000

Fuser, Igor. *Conflitos e contratos – a Petrobras, o nacionalismo bolivariano e a interdependência do gás natural (2002–2010)*. Tese de Doutorado em Ciência Politica, FFLCH/ USP, 2013.

Gobetti, Sérgio W. Estatais e ajuste fiscal: uma análise da contribuição das empresas federais para o equilíbrio macroeconômico. *Economia e Sociedade*, Campinas, v. 19, n. 1 (38), pp. 29–58, April 2010.

Instituto Brasileiro de Geografia e Estatística (IBGE). *National Accounts, Estatísticas do século XX (XX Century Statistics), Estatísticas das Empresas Públicas e Estatísticas da Administração Pública (Statistics of Public Companies and Public Adminsitration)*. www.ibge.gov.br

IPEA. *Base de dados do Instituto de Pesquisa Econômica Aplicada: National Accounts and GFCF Deflator Historical Series*. www.ipeadata.gov.br

Jessop, B. *The Welfare State in the Transition From Fordism to Post-Fordism*. In Jessop et al The Politics of Flexibility: Restructuring State and Industry in Britain, Germany and Scandinavia. Edward Elgar,, 1991.

Maciel, C. Políticas de regulação de setores infra-estruturais no governo Lula (2003–2005). In R. Carneiro (org.), *A Supremacia dos Mercados e a Política Econômica do Governo Lula*. São Paulo: Unesp, 2006.

Mazzucato, Mariana. *The Entrepreneurial State: Debunking Public vs. Private Sector Myths*. Londres: Anthem Press, 2013.

Medeiros, Carlos A. Financial Dependency and Growth Cycles in Latin America. *JPKE*, v. 31, n. 1, pp. 79–101, Fall 2008.

Medeiros, Carlos A. The Political Economy of the Rise and Decline of Developmental States. *Panoeconomicus*, v. 1, pp. 43–56, 2011.

Ministry of Planning. *11o Balanco Completo do PAC*. Brasilia, October 2010. www.pac.gov.br/sobre-o-pac/publicacoesnacionais

Ministry of Planning. *Estatais brasileiras batem recorde de investimentos em 2013*. February 2014a. www.planejamento.gov.br/conteudo.asp?p=noticia&ler=10930

Ministry of Planning. *11o Balanco Completo do PAC2*. Brasilia, October 2014b. www.pac.gov.br/sobre-o-pac/publicacoesnacionais

Ministry of Finance. Tratamento da Petrobrás no cálculo do resultado primário. *Noticias*, April 15, 2009. www.fazenda.gov.br/noticias/2009/abril/r150409b

Oliveira, Alexandre Silva. O papel anticíclico do BNDES na crise econômica internacional. *Textos de Economia*, Florianópolis, v. 19, n. 2, p. 39–59, June 2016.

Orair, Rodrigo, and Gobetti, Sergio. Brazilian Fiscal Policy in Perspective: From Expansion to Austerity. *Working Paper n. 160 Institute for Applied Economic Research (Ipea) and International Policy Centre for Inclusive Growth* (IPC-IG), Brasilia, August, 2017.

Petrobras. *Pre-Salt*. 2017 www.petrobras.com.br/en/our-activities/performance-areas/oil-and-gas-exploration-and-production/pre-salt/

Polayni, Karl. *The Great Transformation: The Political and Economic Origins of Our Time*. Boston, MA: Beacon Press, 2001 [1944].

Puga, Fernando P., Borça Júnior, Gilberto, R., and Nascimento, Marcelo. O Brasil Diante de um Novo Ciclo de Investimento e Crescimento Econômico. In A. C. Além and F. Giambiagi (eds.), *O BNDES em um Brasil em transição*. Rio de Janeiro: BNDES, 2010.

Reinhart, Carmen; Rogoff, Kenneth S. Growth in a Time of Debt. M. *American Economic Review*, v. 100, n. 2, pp. 573–78, May 2010.

Reis, Cristina F. B. Os Efeitos do Investimento Público sobre o Desenvolvimento Econômico: análise aplicada para a economia brasileira entre 1950 e 2006. In *XIII Prêmio Tesouro Nacional*, ESAF, Brasília, 2008.

Reis, Cristina F. B. Public Investment for Economic Development and Poverty Reduction: Theoretical and Empirical Analysis. In Alicia Puyana Mutis and Samwel Okuro (eds.), *Strategies Against Poverty: Designs From the North and Alternatives From the South*. Buenos Aires: CLACSO-CROP, 2011.

Reis, Cristina F. B., Araujo, Eliane Cristina, and Gonzalez, Erica A. Public Investment Boosted Private Investment in Brazil Between 1982 and 2013. In *VI LAPORDE – Latin-American Program on Rethinking Development Economics*, University of Cambridge/ FGV, Sao Paulo, 2016, January 2017.

Reis, Cristina F. B., Carlotto, Maria C., and Berringer, Tatiana. What Is at Stake in Brazil Today? *Revista Fevereiro*, v. 9, p. 26, 2016.

Rosa, L. P. Energia e setor elétrico nos governos Lula e Dilma. In E. Sader (ed.), *10 anos de governos pós-neoliberais no Brasil: Lula e Dilma*. São Paulo: Boitempo; Rio de Janeiro: FLACSO Brasil, 2013, 2016.

Sarti, Fernando, and Mendonca, Ana Rosa R. Challenges for Brazilian Development: Investment and Finance. In *28th Annual Meeting of the Society for Advanced of Social-Economics*, University of California, Berkeley, CA, June 24, 2016.

Sauer, Ildo L. A gênese e a permanência da crise do setor elétrico no Brasil. *Revista USP*, n. 104, pp. 145–174, janeiro/fevereiro/março 2015.

Schincariol, Vitor Eduardo. *Brasil, Economia e Política Econômica: 2011–2014. Uma história político-econômica da primeira administração de Dilma Rousseff*. São Paulo: Tricontinetal, 2017.

Schutte, Giorgio Romano. Brazil: New Developmentalism and the Management of Offshore Oil Wealth. *European Review of Latin American and Caribbean Studies/ Revista Europea de Estudios Latinoamericanos y del Caribe*, n. 95, pp. 49–70, October 2013.

Schutte, Giorgio Romano. Petrobras em marcha forçada. *Discussion Papers of the Centre of Strategical Studies on Democracy, Development and Sustainability* (NEEDDS), n. 1, April 2016, UFABC.

Serrano, F. Do ouro imóvel ao dólar flexível. *Economia e sociedade*, n. 20, 2002.

Silva, V. A. (2006) *Financiamento do investimento público: debate teórico e alternativas para o caso brasileiro*. Dissertação de mestrado não publicada, UFRJ, 2006.

Summa, Ricardo F., and Serrano, Franklin L. Distribution and Cost-Push Inflation in Brazil Under Inflation Targeting, 1999–2014. *Revista Circus: Revista Argentina de Economía*, July 2015.

Tanzi, Vito, and Davoodi, Hamid R. Corruption, Public Investment, and Growth. *IMF Working Paper*, October 1997, pp. 1–23.

TCU – Tribunal de Contas da Uniao. *Simplified Version of the General Government Accounts of the Republic – Year 2009 Growth Acceleration Program*. 2009. https://portal.tcu.gov.br/lumis/portal/file/fileDownload.jsp?fileId=8A8182A24F0A728E014F0ADB071A1873.

Williamson, J. Democracy and the 'Washington Consensus'. *World Development*, v. 21, n. 8, pp. 1329–1336, 1993.

World Bank. *Privatization Transaction Data, World Development Indicators, Private Participation in Infrastructure Database*. www.worlbank.org

8 Sovereign or dependent integration into the world economy? The Brazilian external sector[1]

Marcelo Milan

Introduction

This chapter compares the Brazilian external sector over two periods: the neoliberal period (1989–2002) and the progressive period (2003–2010). Using the Marxian circuits of capital as its theoretical framework, it seeks to address the question of whether or not there have been major qualitative and quantitative changes regarding the mode of articulating the domestic economy with the world economy in the second period. Additionally, it aims at interpreting the nature of those changes, in the case that they are identified. In this regard, the chapter addresses issues regarding the dependent status of the Brazilian economy and the possible changes in that status over the two periods. The hypothesis of the chapter is that there were significant quantitative modifications in the form of integration of the Brazilian economy with the world economy, on the one hand, but, on the other, these changes were also regressive from a qualitative point of view, mainly from a developmental perspective, regarding the nature of Brazilian capitalism. In order to accomplish that, the chapter presents data about trade and capital flows, balance of payments, net revenue flows, and international reserves, using the concepts of the Marxian circuits of capital to highlight how they reflect or not changes in the articulation domestic-world economy.

The chapter is organized as follows: the first section after this introduction discusses the overall trends in the world capitalist economy from the 1990s to the 2000s using the circuit of industrial capital as an analytical device. It stresses the changing role of the periphery in the restructuring of the world economy. Thus, this first section presents the general conditions of capitalist accumulation in the world economy, in which national economies, both developed and underdeveloped, are inserted, albeit in a hierarchical form. The second section brings forth an analysis of the Brazilian economy in this general setting, emphasizing the role of Lula's government in possibly promoting changes in the way that the Brazilian capitalism makes up the world capitalist economy. In this regard, it must be stressed that the external accounts reflect structural links between domestic capital accumulation and global capital accumulation. The section discusses also the insertion of the Brazilian economy into the world economy, underlining the different segments of the circuit of industrial capital. The final section concludes, answering the question about whether or not the changes under Lula's government were effective and represented a major change in the historical pattern of dependent integration or if it was a deepening of the previous trends.

The world capitalist economy and the changing international division of labor

One can think about the world capitalist economy in terms of the Marxian circuit of industrial capital, starting from the view of money capital:

$$M \quad C \, \{LP, MP\} \ldots P \ldots C \quad M$$

The self-expansion of capital described by that circuit is scattered along different nations, regions, and territories. Some circuits are fully restricted to the national borders. Or even to the regional level. The capitalist state may play a role in this relative isolation, or spacial specialization, by means of taxes, national content of government purchases, regulations and so on. But the internal capitalist dynamics, intertwined with pre-capitalist structures, may also explain a circuit that is geographically constrained (lack of competitive capacity by the bourgeoisie or lack of interest in expanding the circuit beyond the region by influence of archaic modes of production). On the other hand, the level of development of productive forces (technological change reflected in labor productivity), plus the interactions between the advanced capitalist sectors and the capitalist state in in the international scene, highlight the role of each territory or region in the global circuit. As Marx described in the Communist Manifesto (Marx and Engels, 2017 [1848]), the capitalist economy would tend to become more and more 'globalized', that is, the different national flows and stocks that make up the segmented circuit would be more and more integrated into a single circuit, with less and less national differentiation (Soederberg et al., 2005). This means that it is less likely, under globalization, to find regionally isolated circuits, with all metamorphoses circumscribed to a single region or territory.

Thus, with the advance of the formation of a world market and the consolidation of a global circuit of capital, the analytical starting point, money, for example, could be obtained by banks and other monetary and financial institutions at different parts of the globe, originated mainly in profits but also in wages earned in farther away nations. Considering commodity capital, commodities, both means of production and means of subsistence, new and old, are also increasingly produced on different territories and traded in distant markets. Regarding industrial capital, production is increasingly scattered among different nations and territories by means of outsourcing and multinational corporations. Each part of the labor process is carried increasingly out on different places. This modifies the existing technical, social, and international divisions of labor, and creates new ones. Technologies are developed to combine constant and variable capital, and develop new forms of production and new commodities, but technological transfers tend to be restricted both by legal means and by capitalists' competitive strategies. Finally, commodities are sold around the world, not necessarily where they are produced, realizing the crystallized surplus values far away from where they were produced. Since part of the labor process is carried out by capitals from different nations, this generates flows of interest and profits between countries. All these different circuits create the need for organized foreign exchange markets to transform foreign currencies into national currencies. The same institutions that appear on the first movement of capital reappear here, with different forms and roles. Since all these different movements are recorded in the balance of payments of different nations, the circuit of capital can be understood, in its global expression, by the external accounts of the countries involved in the accumulation of capital on a world scale.

Of course, the circuit does not proceed smoothly. It is interrupted by recurrent crises that may start on a single or a couple of *loci* for capital accumulation, and on any of the circuits of the three basic types of capital, and then generalize to the capitalist world economy or remain limited to a single country or region. But there is a growth trend intrinsic to the nature of capital, value in self-expansion, in which all capital metamorphoses happen on an increased scale. Capital seeks to self-expand in terms of value by breaking political and economic barriers, between the different metamorphoses and within them. Capital tends to overcome political frontiers. For example, labor relations that constrain the ability of capital to buy and use labor power induce capital flight to countries in which labor laws are nonexistent or weak. The same is true regarding monetary and financial regulations, trade regulations, state-owned enterprises that limits the ability of capital to produce and appropriate surplus value, and so on.

From a logical-historical perspective, neoliberalism, which characterizes, with a few exceptions, most of national capitalist experiences from the 1970s on, represents the very attempt to free capital to self-expand on an unseen velocity and across different places (Köse et al., 2007; Plehwe et al., 2006, Petras and Veltmeyer, 2011). This boils down to deepening the global circuit and bringing new places, local, regional, national, or international, to it, increasing the competition and forcing national and regional capitals to become more internationalized, and state-owned enterprises to become private, unconstrained profit-seekers. As a consequence, accumulation and realization crises are also more and more a global phenomenon. The world capitalist economy experienced an atypical period during the so called golden age after the Second World War, up to the 1970s, in which crises were relatively well managed (Marglin and Schor, 1990). Production proceeded at a rapid pace, with increased employment and at the same time higher productivity levels. The Fordist mode of regulation, to use a term developed by the French Regulation School, collapsed at that time. Profits were squeezed, profit rates fell steadily, and distributive conflicts caused prices to go up. Oil, a crucial element of circulating constant capital and therefore a central means of production, experienced high prices, transferring flows of value to oil-exporting areas.

Capital responded to its different crises by eliminating barriers to its own mobility, including the defeat of the workers' instruments in the class struggle, but also the capacity of the state to tame this very conflict, along with domestic-external capital disputes, creating the conditions for globalization. Indeed, Dreiling and Darves (2016) interpret globalization as a result of pressures of large corporations on policymakers. In the 1990s, a period that interests this work, these changes were hastened and imposed on most countries, using different mechanisms. For instance, the Washington Consensus was a set of rules that underdeveloped countries adopted to restore the lost growth by means of integration into the world economy, that is, to become part of the internationalized circuit of industrial capital. As expected, neoliberalism did not restore the golden age of growth and full employment, neither in the center nor in the periphery. On the contrary, it contributed to increased instability and the more frequent occurrence of crises, now also in the center of global capitalism. The instability of capital and its crises culminated with the subprime breakdown in 2007–2008 in the U. S. and the ensuing disintegration of different circuits of capital around the world.

The capitalist world economy, therefore, can be seen as an increasingly integrated circuit of industrial capital. However, as mentioned, nations and territories enter the circuit in different positions and hierarchies. The level of development of productive forces affects the ability to channel surplus to political and military uses, creating a power structure among countries and regions, a hierarchy that sustains itself over time. National governments attempt to obtain a better position in the global circuit by means of monopolizing segments of production, sources of raw materials, technologies, and complex labor processes (dependent on skilled workers). Monopolizing financial flows and stocks is also a way to get the upper hand in the competitive capitalist world economy. As a consequence, not all labor processes, commodities, and capitals will be available to all or most countries. The Economic Commission for the Latin America and the Caribbean (ECLAC) was perhaps the first to note that specialization in specific branches of production, raw materials or industrial output, would generate a growing gap in global incomes. This approach has been vindicated today by the study of the complexity of economic activity (Hausmann et al., n.d.). Producing raw materials and less processed commodities regarding the circulating capital, and foodstuff regarding means of subsistence, and commodities without technological sophistication, has lead to loss of capital competitiveness in the world capitalist economy, subjecting those producers to the low ends of the global hierarchy.

During the Golden Age, import substitution represented perhaps the first systematic attempt by some peripheral countries at changing the international division of labor without abandoning the integration into the capitalist world economy. A number of countries in Latin America, Africa, and Asia tried to industrialize by substituting previously imported industrial commodities, that is, internalizing part of the global circuit by absorbing its most dynamic – with higher levels of surplus - productive activities. These dynamic labor processes were characterized by relative surplus value extraction and technologically sophisticated commodities. Besides the production, the realization of surplus value would also depend more and more on the internal markets and less on the world markets. This would require changing the main sources of means of production and of subsistence. Geopolitical elements caused parts of Asia, mainly the Southeast, to industrialize, with the realization of surplus value taking place in developed countries, specially the U. S. In the later case, realization would be dependent on the external markets, and what was going to change were the commodities produced, with an increasing role for the manufactured ones. As a consequence, the international division of labor changed, China raised as a major capitalist power, following the other successful cases of integration into the world capitalist economy by means of export-driven industrialization (in the cases of Japan and the New Industrialized Countries of Asia).

With specific manufacturing capital moving to a few underdeveloped countries, the advanced capitalist economies displayed a changed economic structure, with services growing, and, within services, financial activities. This is part of the phenomenon of financialization. Instead of exporting commodities, industrialized or not, advanced capitalist countries exported industrial capital and finance capital. This modification in the world capitalist economy required institutional changes in the underdeveloped countries, like privatization, liberalization, and lifting up the constraints to the formation and circulation of money and finance capital to foreign capitals. The circuit of money capital therefore became central to the accumulation, but, as mentioned, caused the overall circuit to be increasingly plagued by crises and disruptions. And the increasing international flows of interest income became a relevant feature of the capitalist world economy and an indicator of integration into it.

The Brazilian economy in the progressive era: a changed pattern of integration into the world economy?

Regarding the role of Brazilian capitals in the global circuit of industrial capital, the structural crisis of capitalism in the 1970s also marked the end of the so-called Brazilian Miracle, a short period of time (1967–1973) characterized by rapid growth and even faster income concentration, with an entrepreneurial-military dictatorship crushing the organized labor movement. This contributed to changes in the composition of the commodities produced, from nondurable to durable commodities regarding the means of subsistence. Multinational corporations provided most of the sophisticated commodities, showing a dependency of foreign capitals. State-owned enterprises provided the most important elements of circulating constant capital (electricity, oil, raw materials, and so on). National capital provided the residual commodities. The dictatorship (1964–1985) attempted at deepening the import substitution program, but with external financing provided by recycling of petrodollars by U.S. banks. This changed the pattern of financing of capital accumulation in Brazil, and therefore the integration of the Brazilian capitalism into the global circuit of capital. The new pattern of financial crisis was inaugurated with the external debt crisis in the 1980s (Baer, 2007).

After the dictatorship ended in Brazil, but before a formal democracy (voting was allowed only insofar as it brought about no major political changes) was implemented, a new Constitution was enacted in 1988. Only in 1989 the first direct election for President took place. Luis Inácio Lula da Silva contended with Fernando Collor de Melo (heretofore Fernando I for short), a right-wing offbeat candidate. After major manipulation by the leading commercial TV network in Brazil, Globo, Fernando I beat Lula da Silva. This election represented the first attempt of a late adoption of the neoliberal program of increased integration into the world economy in Brazil. Fernando I removed trade barriers with the hope of integrating the Brazilian capitalism into the more dynamic flows of commodity capital. Intra-oligarchical disputes caused the first impeachment of an elected President in the Brazilian history (Dilma Rousseff was the second, by means of a Parliamentary Coup in 2016 – see Milan (2016)), and Fernando I was replaced by Itamar Franco, a politician with a nationalist twist, but responsible for preparing a full neoliberal plan to Brazilian capitalism.

Major imbalances characterized the economy since the 1980s, and bourgeois economists blamed the State and the import substitution period for all of them, with no exceptions. Neoliberalism was thought as a redemption tool. In 1994 Fernando Henrique Cardoso (Fernando II for short) was elected with the mission of completing and deepening the neoliberal reforms began by Fernando I. The Washington Consensus was implemented *ipsis literis*. The diplomacy was targeted at favoring the interests of the U.S. The economic performance, however, was poor. Given the goals of this chapter, only the external sector will be considered in the analysis below to highlight that.

In order to emphasize the most important external sector outcomes, during the first part of Fernando II presidency, current account had growing deficits, which was not something new, given the chronic imbalances in terms of trading specialized services and in terms of flows of interest and profits. What is interesting to note is the deficit in the external trade of commodities (trade balance), something unusual in Brazilian history. In 1999 Brazil had to change its exchange rate regime, after a failed attempt at sustaining a crawling peg without enough reserves (trusting that the markets would abide by, since this was a market-friendly government after all) in order to back a monetary reform program. With the global circuit of capital being disrupted by the crises in Asia and Russia, capital outflows drained the shrinking reserves, and Brazil had to resort to the IMF, despite having the highest real interest rates in the world. (Baer, 2007).

After years of poor neoliberal economic performance, in 2002 Lula was elected, with a compromise of not deepening economic democracy and of not challenging the rule of capital. Vindicating Polanyi's thesis in *The Great Transformation*, this political change, although not profound, represented a reaction against market-induced destruction of jobs and the need to save society from the satanic windmill of neoliberalism (Lo, 2012; Went, 2000). So, Lula's government marked a new period, the progressive era. The results were so remarkably different from the neoliberal period, despite the Faustian agreement with capital, that some authors suggested a new economic miracle (this time under a somewhat democratic rule) (Amann and Baer, 2012). This, of course, could be seen only with hindsight. Some hurried accounts of Lula's government were dismissed by the later facts (Love and Baer, 2009). From the external sector perspective, there were major changes in the direction of external policy: an assertive external policy, seeking new and more trade partners, replaced the passive policy of 'whatever is good to the U.S. is good to Brazil' characteristic of neoliberalism.

Amorim (2010) and Zilla (2017) recount the major changes in the external policy under Lula's government. If these diplomatic changes were effective or not is a debatable issue. It seems that the BRICS were indeed important for the external economic performance of Brazil. Anyway, the data show a remarkable change in the external accounts. It is possible to use the circuit of capital to highlight the single most important ones.

Starting with the circuit of commodity capital (excluding services), Table 8.1, using data from the Ministry of Industry and Trade (MDIC, 2017) compares the neoliberal period and the progressive era.

The hard evidence makes it clear that, in the progressive era, the value of exports increased three times as much as during the neoliberal period, despite their confidence in the market miracle, that is, avoiding at all costs a managed trade by means of diplomatic tools. Imports increased by a factor of 2.6, and the average value of trade balance increased eight-fold. So, despite the alluded or rhetorical advantages of neoliberalism, in the Brazilian case it is more discourse than reality. Managed traded based on a new diplomatic turn proved to be more advantageous to the Brazilian capitalists (and workers in the exporting sector).

Table 8.1 Brazilian external merchandise trade in the neoliberal and progressive eras – Values

	Average Annual Value of Exports (US$ billion)	Average Annual Value of Imports (US$ billion)	Average Annual Value of Trade Balance (US$ billion)
Fernando I and Itamar Franco (1990–1994)	36.2	24.1	12.1
Fernando II (1995–2002)	52.5	53.6	−1.1
Neoliberal Era	**46.2**	**42.3**	**3.9**
Lula (2003–2010) – Progressive Era	**142.5**	**109.9**	**32.6**
Progressive Era/Neoliberal Era	3.08	2.6	8.4

Source: Elaborated by the author using the Brazilian Ministry of Industry and Trade data (MDIC, 2017)

Since the value of trade flows is equal to quantity x price, and conversion of prices requires the use of exchange rates, whose value is plagued by speculative activities, it is possible to make the same analysis using the weight of trade. Table 8.2 presents the results. Physical exports doubled in the progressive era, whereas imports increased by 30%. The physical trade balance was almost 2.5 times lower in the neoliberal period. So, opening up markets to foreign competition and 'leaving it to the market' is clearly not enough.

However, it is important to evaluate this increased trade flows. Could it be that the country was just learning to compete after years of protectionism (and by a divine coincidence, the learning was completed only under Lula)? In that case, it should export more goods for which it had a competitive advantage on. But if the trade basket changed, this means that it had to learn again (or every time it changed). Or it could be the case that the trade was imposed from outside, by the dynamics of global capitalism and the differential integration of the Brazilian economy into the global circuit of capital. Yet, Brazil had more trade partners in the progressive era, partners usually considered less important by neoliberal apologists (countries in Africa and Middle East, for example). So, the new diplomacy may have something to do with the increased trade flows. Tables 3 and 4 provide some additional information regarding exports. In the year 2000, the main destinations of Brazilian exports were the rich countries, with the exception of Argentina and Mexico. The U.S. participated with almost 24% of all merchandise exports. The top ten countries accounted for almost 2/3 of all merchandise exports. By the end of the progressive era, the top ten had a little more than half of all merchandise trade, showing a diversification. The U.S. now accounted for less than 10% of all exports, much to the dismay of neoliberals, notwithstanding a considerable growth in the export to that country. And among the most important partners there were four poor countries:

Table 8.2 Brazilian external trade in the neoliberal and progressive eras – weights

	Average Annual Weight of Exports (millions of tons)	*Average Annual Weight of Imports (millions of tons)*	*Average Annual Weight of Trade Balance (millions of tons)*
Fernando I and Itamar Franco (1990–1994)	14.7	5.8	8.9
Fernando II (1995–2002)	19.6	7.5	12.0
Total Neoliberal Era	**17.7**	**6.8**	**10.9**
Lula (2003–2010) – Progressive Era	**35.7**	**9.1**	**26.5**
Progressive Era/ Neoliberal Era	2.0	1.3	2.4

Source: Elaborated by the author using the Brazilian Ministry of Industry and Trade data (MDIC, 2017)

Table 8.3 Main destination of Brazilian merchandise exports (year 2000, US$)

United States	13,180,528,710	23.93%
Argentina	6,232,745,675	11.31%
Low Countries	2,796,181,752	5.08%
Germany	2,525,750,862	4.59%
Japan	2,472,374,403	4.49%
Italy	2,145,853,323	3.90%
Belgium–Luxembourg	1,867,040,679	3.39%
France	1,731,644,480	3.14%
Mexico	1,711,340,831	3.11%
United Kingdom	1,498,417,242	2.72%
Total	55,085,595,326	65.65%

Source: Elaborated by the author using the Brazilian Ministry of Industry and Trade data (MDIC, 2017)

Table 8.4 Main destination of Brazilian merchandise exports (year 2010, US$)

China	30,785,906,442	15.25%
United States	19,307,295,562	9.56%
Argentina	18,522,520,610	9.17%
Low Countries	10,227,723,216	5.07%
Germany	8,138,465,358	4.03%
Japan	7,140,831,782	3.54%
United Kingdom	4,634,526,237	2.30%
Chile	4,258,362,263	2.11%
Italy	4,235,337,908	2.10%
Russian Federation	4,152,040,877	2.06%
Total	201,915,285,335	55.17%

Source: Elaborated by the author using the Brazilian Ministry of Industry and Trade data (MDIC, 2017)

China, Argentina, Chile, and the Russian Federation. The formation of the BRIC in 2009 may explain part of those changes. So, the integration of the Brazilian capitals into the global circuit was modified, quantitatively and qualitatively.

On the other hand, the changes in the circuit of global capital and the division of labor modified the pattern of Brazilian trade, that is, the pattern of the integration of Brazil into the circuit of commodity capital. Brazil started exporting more raw materials (soybeans, iron ore, foodstuff, etc.) and less manufactured commodities (cars, planes, electronics, etc.). This represented a reprimarization of exports (Cypher, 2015). China became increasingly important for realizing the surplus value produced by the Brazilian primary sector and for supplying industrialized commodities to the country. Thus, behind the quantitative gains when compared to the neoliberal years, dependency was actually reinforced. The policy changes were just enough to overcome the poor performance of neoliberalism, not to provide a major structural change in the way that Brazilian capitals would integrate into the world capitalist economy.

Looking at the circuit of productive capital, foreign direct investment (FDI) represents the way in which multinational corporations produce commodities in countries other than their homeland. Under global capitalism, accumulation occurs on a world scale, and flows of FDI represent the insertion of national capitalisms into the global chains of capital accumulation. The Brazilian Central Bank (BCB) data about reserves start on 1995 (Brazilian Central Bank, 2017). So, there are no figures about the government of Fernando I. This means that the neoliberal period will be considered by looking only at the period of Fernando II for analyzing the circuit of productive capital. Here again the evidence goes against neoliberalism in Brazil and in favor of the progressive era policies. The data were adjusted to exclude inter-company loans (which, in the Brazilian case, is just another form of interest-bearing capital). So, only participation in capital was considered for comparing FDI flows. Under full neoliberalism, FDIs increased by a factor of four. It is not totally wrong to assume that a large chunck of these inflows was targeted at cheaply sold (quasi-donations) state-owned enterprises under privatization-donation programs.

FDI was lower during Lula's first year, but increased by a factor of eight during the progressive era. Overall, average FDI in the latter period was 39% above the average in the former. This happened despite the reduced amount of salable assets during the progressive era (or the political decision not to privatize the remaining major state assets). Hence, in the progressive era the integration of Brazilian capitals into the global capital accumulation circuits was deeper than in the neoliberal period. Yet, again, these flows were directed at sectors producing for the internal market, creating potential problems for the external accounts (lack of imperialist currencies) or to the sectors more dynamic from

Table 8.5 Inflows of FDI (excludes inter-company loans) (US$ billion) – 1995–2010

Fernando II	
Average (A)	19
First year (B)	4.2
Last year (C)	17.1
C/B	4.1
Lula	
Average (D)	26.2
First year (E)	9.3
Last year (F)	75
F/E	8.1
D/A	1.39

Source: Elaborated by the author using data from the BCB (Brazilian Central Bank, 2017)

the perspective of external trade – exports of raw materials, which reinforces dependency. It does not seem either that Brazil became a powerful developer of new technologies by entering into the circuit of productive capital by means of appeals to FDIs, failing at increasing the complexity of its domestic commodity production. This seems to validate the initial hypothesis.

Considering the circuit of money and mainly interest-bearing capital, data about foreign portfolio investment (FPI) provides information regarding the additional sources of foreign financing of capital accumulation besides the profits of multinational enterprises investing (and reinvesting) in Brazil. Now inter-company loans (wrongly considered FDI by international organizations) are included in the analysis. Table 8.4 shows the results. Annual averages more than doubled in the progressive era. Despite an expected reduction of FPI in the first year of Lula, it increased faster in the following years. It is interesting to note that during the last year of Fernando II's government there was a negative number (capital flight, both foreign and domestic). One explanation for that was the eminent victory of Lula in the elections, given the substandard economic performance of Fernando II. If Lula's compromise to promote socioeconomic inclusion through better income distribution, i.e. to reduce inequality, was the reason, this was clearly a misguided move, since by all different measures the macroeconomic performance under Lula was much better than during the neoliberal period, and his policies did promote social inclusion and better income distribution.

As a consequence of the deepening of the integration of Brazilian capitals into the global circuit of produtive and money capital, interest and profit flows also increased. Table 8.7 presents data about income flows for capital (profits and interest) and Table 8.8 provides information about income flows for labor. In the progressive era, average outflows of capital income more than doubled. A comparison in terms of last year over first year is also favorable to the progressive era. From a labor perspective, employees' earnings were also more favorable under the progressive era than under the neoliberal one. Compensation of Brazilian workers abroad on average increased by a factor of eight. Fernando II started with deficits on that account, meaning that foreign employees earned more income in Brazil than Brazilian workers abroad.

Regarding stocks rather than flows, unfortunately the Brazilian Central Bank has only quarterly data about the International Investment Position (IPP) starting on December of 2001. So, a comparison between the progressive era and the neoliberal era in terms of the composition of assets (claims on new value created) and liabilities (obligations to finance the realization of surplus value by the private and government sectors) cannot be carried out.

Another important measure of national capitals integrated into the global circuit of capital is provided by reserves. International reserves, representing universal abstract capitalist money, provide a synthesis of all different circuits of capital on a world scale in a given period of time. First, commodity capital, both tangible and intangible, generates inflows and outflows of commodities and money-capital. Second, the balance of incomes (mostly primary income)

Table 8.6 Inflows of FPI (US$ billion, includes inter-company loans) – 1995–2010

Fernando II	
Average (A)	10.2
First year (B)	10.5
Last year (C)	−5.3
C/B	–
Lula	
Average (D)	23.2
First year (E)	5.9
Last year (F)	85.1
F/E	14.4
D/A	2.27

Source: Elaborated by the author using data from the BCB (Brazilian Central Bank, 2017)

Table 8.7 Net flows of primary income for capital (US$ billion) – 1995–2010

Fernando II	
Average (A)	−15.9
First year (B)	−10.6
Last year (C)	−17.8
C/B	1.68
Lula	
Average (D)	−33.3
First year (E)	−18.2
Last year (F)	−67.5
F/E	3.71
D/A	2.09
(C/B)/(D/A)	2.21

Source: Elaborated by the author using data from the BCB (Brazilian Central Bank, 2017)

Table 8.8 Net flows of primary income for labor (US$ million) – 1995–2010

Fernando II	
Average (A)	44
First year (B)	−160
Last year (C)	102
C/B	–
Lula	
Average (D)	347
First year (E)	109
Last year (F)	498
F/E	4.57
D/A	7.9

Source: Elaborated by the author using data from the BCB (Brazilian Central Bank, 2017)

represents flows of interest, profits, salaries, and wages. Third, the finance account represents the different forms of finance capital, money capital, and interest- bearing capital. The average annual value of reserves under Fernando II was US $43.9 billion, and under Lula it was US $142.9 billion. A difference of almost US $100 billion! Figure 8.1 shows the annual evolution of reserves for the two periods.

The evidence is clear and in favor of the main hypothesis. Under full neoliberalism, reserves dropped for most of the years with data available, meaning that flows of imports, payments to external capital and labor, and outflows of capital were larger than the correspondent inflows. In absolute terms, they remained above US $60 billion in just a single year. It is interesting to note that the 'geniuses' who conducted macroeconomic policy had a managed exchange rate regime (crawling peg) from 1994 to the beginning of 1999. That is, at the same time that they opened up the external sector to foreign flows of capital, they barely had reserves to manage the exchange rate. In order to attract capitals, they had to maintain the highest interest rates in the world (and of course they were very glad to do so). Hence, despite the claim by vulgar bourgeois economists that under a full neoliberal program of privatization (mostly substitution of national, state-owned capital, for international, many times state-owned capital- given the structural weakness of Brazilian bourgeoisie – see Milan (2016)), commercial and financial openness (increased circulation of international capitals at home and the potential increased circulation of national capitals abroad – potential only because to fully realize it, there has to be an able bourgeoisie,

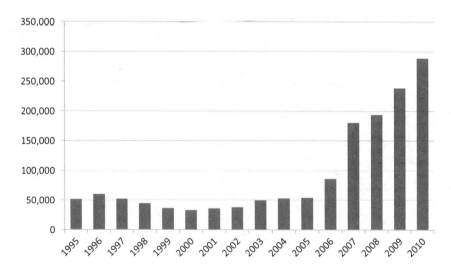

Figure 8.1 International reserves 1995–2010 (US$ million)

Source: Elaborated by the author, using BCB data (Brazilian Central Bank, 2017)

something lacking in Brazil), and liberalization (the State imposing fewer constraints on the circulation of capitals and commodities) the neoliberal paradise lost after the import substitution program would be found, the external macroeconomic performance was rather weak, partially confirming our hypothesis.

Conclusion: neoliberalism rejected but dependency renewed?

Soederberg et al. (2005) claim that national varieties of capitalism are declining. Brazil, under Lula, seemed to be an exception when it comes to the external sector. However, despite the undeniable quantitative gains when compared to the neoliberal period, confirming partially the main hypothesis, the policies implemented during the progressive era created the conditions for its own demise, completing the validation of our hypothesis. The model renewed and deepened dependency both on exports of primary, less complex commodities, and on international money, finance, and productive capital. So, the scale of integration into the global circuit of commodity capital was enlarged, but with a concentration on primary and raw commodities that were unlikely to provide a structural change that could move the Brazilian capitalism up the ladder of economic development in the global hierarchy. Dependency shifted from the U. S. to China. The same is true regarding the circuit of productive capital. FDI increased remarkably in the progressive era when compared to the neoliberal years. Nonetheless, the flows were directed to the production of commodities to the internal market or to export sector characterized by lack of technological deepening. This reinforces the dependency in terms of technological knowledge, reducing the competitive capacity of the Brazilian bourgeoisie, which is already very low. On the other hand, considering money and finance capital, there were also major changes under Lula. But, again, the changes were mostly quantitative. Reliance on short-term capital flows hinders the ability of economic policy to guide capital accumulation in a way that promotes autonomy and sovereignty. The Brazilian economy remains dependent. As a consequence, outflows of profits and interest surged. And labor income was not significant due to the very dependency of the Brazilian economy.

Neoliberalism was rejected at the policy level, but its most regressive results were encroached at the structural level, sustaining the Brazilian economy in the low hierarchical levels of global capitalism. Overcoming neoliberalism is difficult for a single country. However, to retrieve Petras and Veltmeyer (2011) subtitle, there is a word to win. And since neoliberalism has its intrinsic limits, it is going to be defeated by its own contradictions. But it has to be challenged. The challenge must be radical, though (Went, 2000). It is not enough to change policies at the State level. It is necessary to change the economic, political, and cultural structure of society, democratizing it. The recent crisis and the Parliamentary coup d'etat of 2016 are just the outcomes of this lack of daring policies to defeat neoliberal capitalism once and for all.

Note

1 The author would like to thank the editor, Pedro C. Chadarevian, for the opportunity of writing this chapter, and gratefully acknowledges his patience.

References

Amann, E., and Baer, W. Brazil as an Emerging Economy: A New Economic Miracle? *Brazilian Journal of Political Economy*, v. 32, n. 3 (128), pp. 412–423, July–September 2012.

Amorin, C. Brazilian Foreign Policy Under President Lula (2003–2010): An Overview. *Revista Brasileira de Política Internacional*, v. 53, Special Edition, pp. 214–240, December 2010.

Baer, W. *The Brazilian Economy: Growth and Development.* 6th ed. Boulder: Lynne Rienner Publishers, 2007.

Brazilian Central Bank. www.bcb.gov.br/htms/infecon/Seriehist_bpm6.asp, 2017

Brazilian *Ministry of Industry and Trade.* www.mdic.gov.br/index.php/comercio-exterior/estatisticas-de-comercio-exterior, 2017.

Cypher, J. *Structure, Development and Underdevelopment: Interpreting Contemporary Latin America Through the Hypotheses of Institutional Political Economy.* 2015. http://www3.eco.unicamp.br/posgraduacao/images/arquivos/Institutions_for_Development_and_Underdevelopment.pdf. Accessed July 23, 2017.

Dreiling, M. C., and Darves, D. Y. *Agents of Neoliberal Globalization: Corporate Networks, State Structures, and Trade Policy.* Cambridge: Cambridge University Press, 2016.

Hausmann, R., Hidalgo, C., Bustos, S., Coscia, M., Chung, S., Jimenez, J., Simoes, A., and Yıldırım, M. *Thee Atlas of Economic Complexity. Mapping Paths to Prosperity.* Center for International Development and Harvard Kennedy School, Harvard University, and Media Lab, Macro Connections, MIT. n. d. http://atlas.cid.harvard.edu/media/atlas/pdf/HarvardMIT_AtlasOfEconomicComplexity_Part_I.pdf

Köse, A. H., Şenses, F., and Yeldan, E. (eds.). *Neoliberal Globalization as New Imperialism: Case Studies on Reconstruction of the Periphery.* New York: Nova Science Publishers, Inc., 2007.

Lo, D. *Alternatives to Neoliberal Globalization: Studies in the Political Economy of Institutions and Late Development.* New York: Palgrave MacMillan, 2012.

Love, J. L. Love, and Baer, W. *Brazil Under Lula: Economy, Politics, and Society Under the Worker-President.* New York: Palgrave MacMillan, 2009.

Marglin, S., and Schor, J. *The Golden Age of Capitalism: Reinterpreting the Postwar Experience.* Oxford: Clarendon Press, 1990.

Marx, K., and Engels, F. *The Communist Manifesto.* London: Pluto Press, 2017 [1848].

Milan, M. Oligarchical Restoration and Full Neoliberalism Reloaded: An Essay on the Roots of the Twin Crises and the 2016 Coup D'etat in Brazil. *Austral: Brazilian Journal of Strategy and International Relations*, v. 5, n. 9, 2016.

Petras, J., and Veltmeyer, H. *Beyond Neoliberalism: A World to Win.* Burlington, VT: Ashgate, 2011.

Plehwe, D., Walpen, B., and Neunhöffer, G. *Neoliberal Hegemony: A Global Critique.* New York: Routledge, 2006.

Soederberg, S., Menz, G., and Cerny, P. G. (eds.). *Internalizing Globalization: The Rise of Neoliberalism and the Decline of National Varieties of Capitalism.* New York: Palgrave MacMillan, 2005.

Went, R. *Globalization: Neoliberal Challenge, Radical Responses.* London: Pluto Press/The InternationalInstitute for Research and Education (IIRE), 2000.

Zilla, C. Brazil's Foreign Policy Under Lula. *SWP Research Paper*, Stiftung Wissenschaft und Politik, German Institute for International and Security Affairs. RP 2, Berlin, March 2017. www.swp-berlin.org/fileadmin/contents/products/research_papers/2017RP02_zll.pdf. Acessed July 18, 2017.

Part III
The challenges of change

9 Dystonia as domination

How the Brazilian elites have put politics and power out of step

Félix Ruiz Sánchez

In order to discuss the destruction process of the democratic institutionality in Brazil it is necessary to combine several perspectives of analysis. First, we need to assimilate – as in the formulation of Antonio Gramsci – power relations.

When debating the relationship between the 'processes or organical movements from those short-term, occasional processes, immediate and near-accidental ones', the author calls our attention to the distinction between 'the organic phenomena (that) give place to the historical-social criticism which affects large groups of people beyond the people immediately responsible and besides the leading group' (Gramsci, 1978, pp. 187–196).

In the same way, it is a question of absorbing into the analyses the tendencies which determine the most present and the most active vectors of the historical process; Fernand Braudel's observations (1999, pp. 60–80) on the long term (or duration) points to the diversity of historical periods.

In this perspective, it is important to examine the constitutive process of the historical temporality of the society. Once we have fixed and determined the founding processes of the more permanent and longer temporality, it would be possible to approach the richness of the political conjuncture.

It is with this instrumental methodology that we will approach our object of study, the dystonia of domination.[1]

This idea, in one first conceptual approach, takes us to an analogy with a corporal disfunction that incapacitates one's muscular capacity. The designation of our thesis is also associated with the domination related to the breakdown of a situation, which, at a first glance, should be normal but, instead, presents itself as disturbed or deformed in a way that distances it from a more traditional framework which the political science literature would call crises.

In this very way, the Brazilian parliamentary coup of 2016 showed paradoxes related to the fact that it occurred in a political alliance scenario that was once built up in large political conflict for more than one decade.

The government cycle that began in 2002 with Luiz Inácio Lula da Silva's election was testing the limits of the statal domination and the democracy itself in Brazil.

This cycle, that has ended up, coincides with profound social and economic changes and, of course, with transformations in capitalist power.

This happened with the application of an economic policy that is, in the words of André Singer (2012), a mixture of weak reformism with the preservation of essential aspects of the neoliberal agenda implemented in the governments of Fernando Collor de Melo, in 1990; Itamar Franco, in 1992; and Fernando Henrique Cardoso, who ruled between 1994 to 2002.

Thus, what we saw in the Brazilian society was the emergence of what we could call 'presidentialist coalition' (Abranches, 1988). This type of presidentialism had the most prominent aspects during the governments of Luiz Inácio Lula da Silva and Dilma Rousseff, the latter ruling from 2010 to 2016, until the parliamentary coup.

The administration, between 2003 to 2016, and mainly after 2010, of this form of political regime has given place to what we call dystonia of domination.

This resulted in the parliamentary coup that deposed the constitutionally elected president Dilma Rousseff.

And, afterwards, her replacement in favor of her vice president, Michel Temer, was supported by a parliamentary basis achieved during the years of government of what some authors call the 'Lulist era', comprising both the government of Luiz Inácio Lula da Silva and of Dilma Rousseff.

The impeachment process had the involvement of a large sector of the business class and also the middle working class of the Brazilian civil society. This also explains the high percentage, 69%, of disapproval of Dilma Rousseff's government.

What happened with the Brazilian society? The destruction of the political regime of the military dictatorship, which lasted from 1964 to 1985, resulted, after years of democratic governments, in this coalition presidentialism.

This period has been marked by a political cycle of democratic advances, with the introduction, for example, of important law changes: for instance the universalization of the right to vote, unseen in the Brazilian Republic, and published, finally, in 1985.

After a hundred years of the implantation of the Brazilian republic, the illiterate and the poor coming from the old days of slavery and servile work – Brazil was the last country in the world to abolish slavery – just got their right to vote in the first national election after the dictatorship in 1989, one year after the promulgation of the Brazilian Constitution, in 1988.

It was in this same context, after a government brought out after a civil-military coup, that the Brazilian society recently found the hardships of a parliamentary coup.

What we have seen since August 31, 2016, when Dilma Rousseff suffered an impeachment in a tumultuous session of the National Congress transmitted all over the country, was the application of an ultra liberal program.

This political program was never debated, much less voted by the Brazilian electorate.

Until the present edition of this chapter, that is, in September 2017, this coup culminated, in addition to experiencing general setbacks in all areas related to human rights and the fight against poverty, along with the approval of a labor reform that removes rights and guarantees won by the working class over a century, plus a freeze on public spending that throws a spade of lime in the dream of a liberating education in Brazil. Therefore, this last political cycle shows the limits of the Brazilian Republic.

It is up to us, then, to connect our idea of dystonia to the Brazilian society itself, to inquire the meaning of these regressions in relation to the process of the formation of this society.

The path of Brazil, from its colonization in 1500, with the arrival of the said Portuguese discoverers, to its independence in 1822, promulgated by a member of the Portuguese royal family, to the elaboration of the Constitution as a Federative Republic in 1988, is marked by genocide and injustice.

First, in relation to the natives, we have to say that this group accounted for almost five million at the time of the arrival of the colonizers. After more than five hundred years, they were reduced to thousands, threatened by the alignment of the new and old government with the so-called ruralist group of agribusiness entrepreneurs.

Parallel to this indigenous genocide and slavery, there were four centuries of African slavery. This began in Brazil, in the mid-eighteenth century, until the declaration of abolition in 1888, and was responsible for the greatest human trafficking in history.

Finally, in terms of population, there was a strong current of immigrants, including Portuguese, Italians, Japanese, Chinese, Bolivians, and many other nationalities throughout Brazilian history and then in the twentieth century, who, if they were not killed by thousands, at least suffered the servile and almost slave-like reality of Republican Brazil.

The fracture of the democratic order in this country requires us to reflect on the historical debts of its trajectory.

We propose to discuss the dystonia of the process of domination by being an apparently – and only apparently – anomalous phenomenon.

We will point out hypotheses about this dystonia, that is, about the limits imposed on the republican political system in Brazil, in addition to its deformations behind the supposed normality of domination and the exercise of power of the Brazilian State.

It is a question of looking at paradoxes of a lineage of studies that characterizes a certain idea of the so-called state of exception (Agamben, 2004).

The Italian philosopher Giorgio Agamben writes that in modern democracy, totalitarianism can be defined as the establishment, through a state of exception, of a legal civil war that allows the physical elimination not only of political opponents but also of entire categories of citizens.

Agamben also tells us that the voluntary creation of a permanent state of emergency, even if not declared in the technical sense, has become one of the essential practices of contemporary states, even those democratic sayings.

The end of Lula and Dilma's cycle of government involved practically all the powers of the state, from violence outside and within institutions.

As, for example, in the emblematic violations of human rights with regards to forced removals from homes and repression of demonstrations, in the case of the 2014 World Cup.

Given this, the Brazilian case can be easily associated with the state of exception described by Giorgio Agamben.

The abuse of rights and the violations that occurred after 2014, once again in housing rights issues, street demonstrations, and violence against so-called minorities, constitute situations that update the debate on racism and the inhumane management of populations in social vulnerability.

As is the case of the indigenous, black, women, LGBT, and elderly people in Brazil today.

The state of exception appears more and more as a paradigm of government in contemporary politics.

In this perspective, it presents itself as a 'level of indeterminacy between democracy and absolutism' (Agamben, 2004, p. 13), thus expressing a technique of government and a paradigm of legal order.

This explains the preponderance of the actions of the Judiciary in Brazilian society to the detriment of the other two powers, Executive and Legislative.

These features of the current Brazilian political and economic crisis and parliamentary coup are related to the historical formation process of this society.

The recognition of the singularities of the formation of the national state, as well as slavery as a dominant form of production in capitalism in nineteenth-century Brazil, is necessary for us to continue.

In the same sense, the survival of the traditional rural, provincial, or even state oligarchies leads us to understand the power arrangements confluent with the regime of the 1988 Constituent, such as, as we have said, coalition presidentialism.

In the second part of this chapter will be presented, in a synthetic way, the links of the political history of the country, in 1964, 1989, and 2016.

These periods clearly show us the democratic and authoritarian and oligarchic deformations that characterize the attempt of democratic construction in Brazil.

The historical formation of society in Brazil indicates the exclusionary and statesmanlike character of its national state.

Authors such as Warren Dean (2013) look at the evolution of the country after Independence in 1822.

What happened, according to the author, was the formation of an 'archipelago' (Dean, 2013, p. 13) of territories formally constituted in the same national space. However, despite the unification, these integrated areas were permeated by tensions and contradictions.

Mike Davis, on the other hand, on the process of formation of the national state to the proclamation of the Republic, tells us,

> National integration meant little more than the San Pablo state citizens in the Congress from time to time to please other oligarchies. . . . Brazil until the early twentieth century was still an 'archipelago' economy, separated by the frightening internal cost of transportation. In fact, class interests were so discrepant that they raise serious doubts about the validity of using the nation as a unit of analysis.
>
> (Davis, 2002, p. 392)

As we have already said, these oligarchies and the regional market that was linked to them were in a social order dominated by slavery.

Brazil between the sixteenth and nineteenth centuries flourished under the dynamics of a capitalist market hungry for commodities, such as sugar, coffee, and cotton.

Nevertheless, in these territories there were also practically free forms of labor power, limited to survive in the gaps of slave society.

The Brazilian Republic, then, was a dense reality.

Already in the nineteenth and twentieth centuries, what we saw was a democracy without citizens, because it was initially restricted to the owners of the means of production.

Large land properties, what we call in Brazil 'latifúndio', and slavery thus combined in the history of Brazil, with the generation of a network of agrarian and extractivist oligarchies.

The transition to new forms of work other than slavery required access to an abundant production tool, such as land.

This happened in 1850, with the 'Lei de Terra', that is, the Land Law, and the importation of European, first, and then Japanese immigrant labor, along with the vast population of Brazilian slaves freed or in the process of liberation.

Without rights, or recognition, these populations made up the proletariat of Brazil with a developing economy.

In this sense, the work of Luís Cláudio Villafañe G. Santos (2004) discusses the phenomenon of Inter-American Politics and its effects on the process of formation of the states of the continent:

> The Brazilian singularity would begin to manifest at that moment, with the construction of an identity that, in a way, reaffirmed the (internal) relations of power of the colonial era. Contrary to what happened in its neighbors in Brazil, due to the continuity of the monarchy, independence did not translate into a rupture in the ideological and social order of the colonial period, its replacement by the ideas of popular sovereignty and nationality, and in the less partial, of the social relations inherited from the colony as in the rest of the continent.
>
> (Santos, 2004: 68)

On the other hand, as Benedict Anderson (2008) states, the new American states of the late eighteenth and early nineteenth centuries were the first models of the contemporary national state.

Luiz Felipe de Alencastro characterizes this truncated process of national and state formation of Brazil:

> The original circumstances surrounding the independence of Brazil marked the cultural identity of the country and the political legitimacy that still serves as a foundation for the ruling classes. . . . The end of the colonial period in Brazil appears more as a result of a struggle in the field of metropolitan power – a conflict aggravated by the economic and political influence that England exercised on Portugal – than as a result of a national and popular uprising. José Bonifácio de Andrada e Silva, the hero of our

> [Brazilian] independence, is a high official of the metropolitan government, a man of cabinet and negotiation.
>
> (Alencastro, 1987, p. 68)

The author points out later,

> In these three centuries the history of Brazil unfolds within and outside the current national territory that is part of a broader picture, the history of the South Atlantic. . . . I say more, I say that Angola's, Congo's and Benin's (formerly Dahomey) history is also that of Buenos Aires as one studies the history of the captaincies of Portuguese America, at the same time and in the same intensity, otherwise one can not understand the history of Brazil in all its complexity.
>
> (Alencastro, 2011: 239)

Another great valuable source of research is the work of István Jancsó (2003), who solidly defends the idea of the Brazilian State as the demiurge – like the Platonic idea of the divine artisan of the universe – of the nation.

This problem is debated by several researchers who, since then, have deepened the relationship between nation, state, and the singularities of the Brazilian and American process, such as in Marcia Berbel in her work of 2010.

In relation to slavery, its elimination did not depend on an anti-racist political and humanitarian culture in the nineteenth century, rather, as it was, by the commercial and economic defeat of the slave masters, who were obliged to give away to foreign impositions to break with slavery and expand the Brazilian domestic market.

When we elaborate a picture of the Brazilian state's power constitution, the strength of the bureaucracy as a driving force becomes clear.

In this respect, the following observations of Luiz Felipe de Alencastro are very relevant:

> The formation of the Brazilian State is articulated around two convergent processes. The first concerns the insertion of imperial institutions into the Lusitanian possessions of America. The second concerns the integration of the territory around the viceregal capital. From the outset, the power centered in Rio de Janeiro has neither the means nor the strength of the metropolis. Moreover, the real country – formed by the rural owners of the different American regions where Portuguese was spoken – had its lungs on another continent. [In fact, this Brazil was, in a sense], the reproduction of slaves in Africa.
>
> (Alencastro, 1987, p. 69)

The author continues his reasoning:

> Paradoxically, it is this inadequacy of economic spatiality to political spatiality that will facilitate the strengthening of imperial power. In fact, it is the

imperial bureaucracy – and it alone – that has the diplomatic and political means able to withstand British pressure, in order to maintain the slave trade between the African ports and Brazil until 1850. . . . The empire does not remove the prerogatives of the rural lords in the political and social framework of the populations. On the contrary, the emperor confirms and legitimizes the forms of private control – among them slavery – which the owners exercise over the inhabitants of the countryside. Even more. Not suppressing the slave trade, the central government gives owners something far more important than the legal recognition of slavery itself: recognition of the legitimacy of Atlantic piracy operations that allowed the reproduction of slave production . . . the second process of consolidation of the national state refers to the indispensable agreement that was to be established between the different regions covered by the political space that was structured under the tutelage of the imperial bureaucracy.

(Alencastro, 1987, p. 69)

This process of constitution of the State is also thematized by Florestan Fernandes in his classic study of the bourgeois revolution in Brazil, in which he recognizes the uniqueness of the process of class domination in the country.

In addition, the Brazilian author also recognizes the impact that this process has on the conformation of the bourgeoisie and the state bureaucracy, a line of reasoning similar to that of Luiz Felipe de Alencastro.

Elida Rugai Bastos, another theoretician who focuses on the Brazilian state, affirms that Florestan Fernandes' studies mark an advance in sociological thinking on the racial question and represent a break with Brazilian sociological reflection (Bastos, 1987: 140).

Florestan Fernandes' great contribution to understanding Brazilian society comes when he questions the supposedly racial democracy built as a theory after the 1930s, fundamental to bourgeois domination in the country.

Above all, the sociologist shows how the question is foundational to the bourgeois revolution itself in Brazil. Society's redemption of the family and the patriarchal sphere is one of the keys to rebuilding the industry pact with the rural oligarchy. At the same time it prevents the Brazilian blacks from taking a full place in Brazilian society.

The intensity of the transformation of the country was gigantic. At the same time that there was a demographic explosion in the large Brazilian cities, that is, from 1930 to 1980, Brazil went from 20% of urban population and 80% of rural population to the opposite (Wainwright, 2006, p. 54).

At the political-partisan level, the inclusion of the population in the budget discussion, within the political program of the PT, was also discussed.

The strength of this process lies in the capacity of the dominant powers in Brazil – both the high state bureaucracy and the provincial and regional oligarchies – to create a dynamic of national state building.

This concerns the setting up of a web of power capable of preserving the strength of inherited bureaucracies with the interests of agrarian oligarchies:

oligarchies with different economic vocations in relation to the body of each emerging province of that federation from the Declaration of the Republic in 1889 (Lynch, 2014).

This was a process of federalization but, at the same time, of separation. It was based on a coffee economy anchored in the authoritarian power of regional oligarchies. The universal citizen participation in the electoral process was restricted by the initiative of these same oligarchs:

> The strongly oligarchic character of the First Republic represents exactly the materialization of the timid democratic ideal developed during the Second Reign by the bulk of the political class. As is well known, it was the Spencerian republican and federative project that came to prevail with the fall of the monarchy in 1889. It is clear, therefore, its character, not democratic, but oligarchic, and that therefore had little or nothing to do with the empirical, real democracies that were built in the North Atlantic, with the rapid expansion of the urban and state electorate in the socio-economic field. The Brazilian republican heroes could not be more than 8.5% of the population, and in practice they were around 2.3% of the total population during the first twenty years of the Republic.
>
> (Lynch, 2014, p. 258)

The Revolution of 1930, deposing a constitutionally elected president and, last but not least, the Vargas movement that began at that time – that is, the one in which the dictator Getúlio Vargas, a symbol of caudilhismo to the Brazilian – ruled the so-called National Development Republic until 1964.

As we have said, these movements before the 1964 civil-military coup consisted of the double movement of centralization of the state and, at the same time, of autonomy of the regional and local oligarchies.

Even more serious, what characterizes the process of democratic construction in Brazil is its demophobic component.

Christian Lynch, in studying this trait of the country's political history, defines demophobia as

> the fear on the part of the social elites that the extension of civic participation beyond its circle, in a perspective of democratization of social life, would trigger disorder, subversion and would be the sign of decadence of the civilized political world. As a phobia, demophobia has been characterized by the exaggerated fear of crowds.
>
> (Lynch, 2014, p. 249)

This fear is expressed in moments of struggle of the working class, as in the political cycles that led to the civil-military coup of 1964, to the rise of the Fernando Collor government in 1989 – to which we will speak a little later – and to the coup against the Dilma government in 2016.

Vladimir Safatle (2016) has developed a set of reflections on demophobia.

He resumes the importance of affections in the construction of society and its institutions. For him,

> if it is not the tacit adherence to systems of norms that produce social cohesion, then we must turn to the circuits of affections that concretely play that role. They will allow us to understand both the nature of social behaviors and the incidence of political regressions also revealing how social norms are based on fantasies capable of continuously updating the same affections in situations that are materially different from one another.
>
> (Safatle, 2016, p. 16)

For this, the author points out lines of thought. First, he recognizes fear as a fundamental component of the relationship between affect and politics.

He also identifies the feelings of helplessness and recognition as other types of affections that allow the explanation of the construction of sociability.

Lynch's notion of demophobia thus gains the explanatory categories that allow its application to processes and different historical circumstances.

In this perspective of analysis, a society like the Brazilian one, crossed by contradictions of income concentration and social and ethnic-racial status, experiences a demophobic behavior on the part of its elites.

The political process leading to the parliamentary coup of 2016 explains its uniqueness in a society that accumulates impasses in its formation process and in the constitution of its State.

It is useful to return to two moments that show trends of demophobia and oligarchic authoritarianism.

The process of accelerated modernization of industrialization and urbanization after 1930 had a path that culminated in import substitution, much later in the 1950s, led by the government of Juscelino Kubitschek, in which the installation of an industrial park was tested.

The civil-military coup of 1964, in turn, brought back elements that limited the emergence of a democratic political regime that could have been strengthened by the growth of the number of workers due to this industrialization.

In the varguista regime the conditions were created for an industrialization based on strong state dirigisme.

This happened with the transformation of the high state bureaucracy that the national-developmental regime installed in strategic sectors of the economy – Companhia Vale do Rio Doce, Petrobras, and others.

Luciano Martins questions, from this, the meaning of the class formation process in Brazil:

> This by itself renders the process of sedimentation of dominant classes in 'bourgeoisie' with all the consequences that such a circumstance entails for the development by such classes of a historical project of domination . . . in

> a situation sui generis for the state and its bureaucracy in the process of capitalist accumulation.
>
> (Martins, 1985, p. 23)

These bureaucracies allowed the dynamization of the capital accumulation of the coffee economy, which allowed the support of what was called 'late Brazilian capitalism', a concept of João Manoel Cardoso de Mello, in his 1986 work.

Florestan Fernandes (1976) was able to capture what other authors have only intuited, namely, the connection of these perverse dynamics of the evolution of capitalism in Brazil, which was based on the colonial period of exploitation based on generalized slavery.

Umbilically associated with the process of formation of the absolutist dynastic state of Portugal, Brazil had progressively transformed itself into a patrimonial and absolutist state.

The national-developmental republic born under the leadership of Getúlio Vargas in 1930 overcame the deficiencies of the Old Republic with regard to its disruption with the centralization of the State. In addition, of course, this new government tried to promote conditions to develop the industrialization and urbanization of the country.

The process is based on the populist commitment that implements a state-assisted welfare policy directed to the urban industrial working class, to which essential social rights are recognized.

On the other hand, the non-recognition of the rights of the working population in the countryside was maintained, especially with regards to the right to land ownership.

Aspasia Camargo produced an important interpretation of this process. According to the author,

> If we could define the Brazilian political "model" . . . we would say that one of its basic characteristics is to have secreted a political class that is simultaneously linked to agrarian interests and to the performance of state functions.
>
> (Camargo, 1981, p. 123)

The pact of power of national-developmentalism, thus, was the result of the recognition of social rights by the population itself, under the tutelage of the regime.

One of the components of the civil-military coup of 1964 is precisely the crisis of the coup seceded in the Vargas regime.

In this regard, Camargo points out,

> Recalling that in the immediate post-30 period, the reformist content dissociates social democracy from political democracy, considered the latter irremediably contaminated by an irremovable short-term oligarchic inheritance. . . . In the 1960s, the diagnosis is no longer the same. The pressures to

improve the living conditions of the peasant population through Agrarian Reform will be reinforced by enlarging their political participation, with the vote of the illiterate and the union organization.

(Camargo, 1981, pp. 128–129)

In this sense, the struggles of the peasant leagues that arise in Pernambuco claiming their right to land, along with freedom of association and unionization, had spread throughout the country (Bastos, 1983).

This rupture of the oligarchic-industrial pact combined with a cycle of mobilizations of the urban working class that grows in organization, arriving at the realization of two general strikes in 1962 and one in 1963.

With the promise of adoption of the so-called 'Reformas de Base', among them, for example, the Agrarian Reform Law and the Profit Remittance Law – which provided a quantity fixed by the government as a limit for multinationals to send money abroad – by the government of João Goulart in 1963, the country plunged into an impasse between popular and nationalist reforms with greater state intervention on the one hand and, on the other hand, the conservative response of the oligarchies threatened by social mobilization.

The fear of the revolution mobilized the middle class of the cities in front of a supposed Cuban exit from the political crisis, that is, with the ghost of Che Guevara and Fidel Castro haunting Brazilian families' moms and inspiring middle class youth from all over Brazil.

The 'March for the Family with God for Freedom', a movement to the right in the political spectrum of that time, that called for the pacification of the country in the face of the supposed communist threat, a few days before the coup of March 31, anticipated the end of the crisis of the populist regime (see Skidmore, 1979; Gaspari, 2002; Dreifuss, 1981).

In the process that led to the civil-military coup, the most authoritarian features of the political order in the country were once again affirmed.

Florestan Fernandes (1987) characterizes the situation resulting from this coup as 'autocratic-bourgeois model of capitalist transformation'.

From this situation, on the specific demophobia concept, it is possible to identify a crisis of the oligarchic pact. This was because there was a growth of the peasant struggle, frightening the agrarian elites.

This combination, in our opinion, fueled the demophobia that was strengthened and exploded in the conjuncture that gave rise to the dictatorship in 1964.

It was up to David Maciel (2012) to redeem the period from 1985 to 1990 of the political history of Brazil.

He analyzes the rise of the New Republic, that is, the so-called democratic government following the civil-military government, in addition to the Constituent Assembly in 1988 and its 'center' – that is, the parliamentary base of support – reconstituted with different legends and parliamentarians, but with similar conciliatory intent, in the 2015/2017 biennium at the Brazilian political crisis.

In addition to these two phases of Brazilian politics, the author also makes a reading of the 1988 and 1989 elections, which consecrate back the bourgeois autocracy characterized by Florestan Fernandes as the solution in extremis of bourgeois domination in the face of the risk of it being shaken or succumb. The name of Fernando Collor de Mello came as a solution.

What is interesting to recall from David Maciel's analysis is the way the ruling elites of the Brazilian state transformed the troubled transition from dictatorship to democracy by reconverting their alliances into a new national agreement settled in the 1987/88 Constituent Assembly.

It led to the promulgation of the constitution called 'citizen' by Ulysses Guimarães, a charismatic figure of Brazilian politics at the end of the civil-military dictatorship and the president of the Constituent Assembly in 1987.

Then a new regime suited the interests of this new elite: that same coalition presidentialism that we discussed above.

The political regime established rules to improve the conditions of governability in which the Presidency of the Republic kept abreast of the necessary agreements for the composition of a government with majority in the two houses of the Legislative Power.

Its governability was guaranteed by the bicameral conformation of, first, a Senate with the attributions of a review chamber of the laws, then approved by the Chamber of Deputies and organized in order to guarantee the majority election of three titular members and two alternates with eight years each.

This parliamentary space became the space for the reconversion of oligarchies. With the Federal Chamber, called in Brazil the Chamber of Deputies, there was a distortion in the criteria of representation by setting a minimum number of representatives, eight for each state, in addition to a maximum ceiling of representatives, 70 deputies.

This made the presidency of the Republic truly the only democratic and direct election of the country at the time.

The left, then represented by the PT, did not subscribe to the 1988 Constitution.

Coalition presidentialism then functioned as an adequate tool to sustain a national state with a low introjection of popular and communitarian traditions, and with a strong continuity of oligarchic and authoritarian legacies.

This situation confirmed an authoritarian institutionality that Florestan Fernandes and David Maciel denominated as bourgeois autocracy.

José Correa Leite (2016) offers an interpretation on this point when he recalls,

> The theme of centralism and federalism is crucial in the history of Brazil, which maintained its territorial unity with a very strong central state, the only empire of the continent, in a succession of the Portuguese absolute monarchy. Federalism and the republic were the flags of the agrarian ruling classes against the 'tyranny' of central power. Empowered, they eliminated, in 1881, the right to vote for the illiterate, the vast majority of the population, formalizing their adherence to a liberal and elitist conception of

politics. The Republic, proclaimed in 1889 as revenge of the coffee farmers against the abolition of the slavery by the Empire, represented nothing progressive for the Brazilian people. There is a continuous and systematic demophobia rooted in the agrarian elites and ruling classes of the country, who treat the Brazilian population as that of a conquered country.

(Leite, 2017)

In a similar analysis, Benjamin Moser (2016) will call this process self-imperialism. That is, as a result of the ruling class treatment of their own country, the Brazilian people were, and are, today, treated almost as a conquered foreign population.

This process of reconversion of institutionality in the re-democratization of the country between 1985 and 1989 occurred in the midst of a crisis of domination.

This instability emerged in the form, first, of a hyperinflationary and economic crisis resulting from what was called a debt crisis: a result of Ronald Reagan's US interest-raising policy, when Paul Volcker of the Central Bank raised interest rates in 1979.

Second, instability emerged because of an economy that had undergone an intense process of industrialization in the five decades following the 1930 Revolution, plus the civil-military dictatorship with its economic miracle, and the growth of the Brazilian economy was high in all of those years. Peripheral Fordism, in addition, has produced an industrial park with the largest concentration of workers in the Latin American continent.

The third issue of the crisis and institutional process in the early years of the New Republic was the fact that our society was undergoing an important rise in the workers' struggles.

This movement began in 1978, leading to the reorganization of the trade union movement with greater independence from state tutelage, which resulted in the formation of the Unitary Workers' Union (Central Única dos Trabalhadores – CUT) in 1983.

Finally, the fourth and last issue is the founding of the Workers' Party in 1980, channeling the independent political organization of the working class.

Éder Sader (1988) characterized this party as the fusion of a dispersed left that had gone through the clandestine and the physical and political banishment in the years of the dictatorship, added to the authentic unionism, not protected by the state.

In addition to this equation were the Christians from the Basic Ecclesial Communities driven by Liberation Theology, which we can characterize as a religious philosophy to the left of what the official Catholic Church preached.

To the right of all this and of the PT foundations, was José Sarney, a Brazilian politician formed in the years of the civil-military dictatorship. He had privileges in terms of positions and was next to the military government. Later, he became vice-president of Tancredo Neves in the Democratic Alliance in full redemocratization of the Country.

This man came to a five-year term, practicing acts of corruption in the relationship with the Legislative, at the time dominated by the 'centrão', which we discussed above, which functioned as a conservative bloc in the 1987/88 Constituent Assembly.

The economic situation, in addition to the wear and tear accumulated by the parties that had formed this Democratic Alliance, arrived in 1988 in a profound delegitimization.

In the municipal elections of November 1988, the electoral calendar coincided with intense mass mobilizations and strikes, such as that of Companhia Siderúrgica Nacional, the repressed and with the death of striking workers.

A chain of solidarity was established nationally and the electoral result was a victory of the Workers' Party in important cities of the country, especially in those most industrialized in the State of São Paulo. Municipalities included São Paulo, Campinas, Santos, Diadema, São Bernardo, and Santo André.

The presidential electoral process of that time, scheduled for November 1989, found a high rejection of the electorate in the candidacies of the parties of the former Democratic Alliance, that is, Aureliano Chaves, of the Party of the Liberal Front, with 1% of intentions of voting, and Ulysses Guimarães, of the Party of the Brazilian Democratic Movement, with a scarce 3%.

The candidatures represented by the former governor of Rio de Janeiro, Leonel Brizola, and the metallurgist Luiz Inácio Lula da Silva, PT, from the left field, appeared in second and third place behind the candidacy of Fernando Collor de Mello, the species of Maharajah hunter quoted above.

The dispute of the first shift in November of 1989 places Fernando Collor and Lula in first and second place, respectively.

The 47 days that separated the holding of the second round of elections caused a sharp division in the country.

Fernando Collor won, at this stage, massive support from the business community and from all the parties that until then had served as support to the political regime in the country.

Luiz Inácio Lula da Silva won support from Leonel Brizola and from a wider front that includes even the Brazilian Social Democracy Party.

> Despite all the mobilization and the constitution of a broad front of the left and the democratic forces around Lula the victory was not possible. On the one hand, the late unification around a common candidacy, the opportunist behavior of the PSDB [Brazilian Social Democracy Party] and part of the PMDB [Party of the Brazilian Democratic Movement] and the PT and CUT's own inability to break with the politico-logical imposed by the democratic institutionality contributed to the defeat. In the second round, for example, there was a clear reduction in the number of strikes, not only because of the economic recovery, facilitating wage agreements and adjustments, but also because of the union leaders' own concern to reduce political radicalization to avoid turning the tide and to reduce the

resistance of the electorate to Lula (apud, Folha de S. Paulo Newspaper, Dec. 1989).

(Maciel, 2012, p. 374)

A real demophobic outbreak was set with the possibility of the people coming to power through the Workers' Party – Lula with an infinitely more radical platform than the one that elected him in 2002 – we have the declarations of Mario Amato, president of the Federation of Industries of the State of São Paulo, an employer's association who supported the parliamentary coup of 2016 – threatening, in the event of Lula's victory at that time, the escape of industrialists and investors from Brazil.

In addition, there was also a media campaign led by Rede Globo, a national communications conglomerate.

In this picture, Fernando Collor got enough votes to win.

This trajectory illustrates the process of the manipulation of fear by the dominant powers, leading to the demophobia of the richest part of the population.

At the same time, this process took place in a context where the feeling of helplessness in the segments of the marginalized working class, already discussed here through the ideas of Vladimir Safatle, gained an emancipatory dimension.

This was because, in 1988–1989, there was an influx of social actors into a vast social movement of the oppressed and exploited.

The period discussed became a unique moment in the history of the country, with the emergence of a new subject in Brazilian politics.

The problem of demophobia then reappears with intensity in the context of the June 2013 demonstrations that represent a milestone in Brazilian political history.

"The magnitude of the mobilizations has terrified the politicians of almost every party – in government, in the right-wing opposition and even in the extreme left" (Leite, 2016).

In June 2013, 24 million people, mostly young people, took to the streets in hundreds of cities unified by progressive flags of better transportation, education, and health services and against the corrupt political system.

They then updated the line of protests that spread around the world with major innovations, such as the Occupy Wall Street movement in the United States and the Arab Spring in the Middle East.

Demonstrators articulated their mobilizations through the internet and social networks. They occupied the public space and reaffirmed the social protest with appeal to the horizontality as a method of organization.

> The protests shaped the adhesion of progressive sectors of Brazilian society to the global wave of late reactions to the economic crisis of 2008 (Arab Spring, Indignados, Occupy Wall Street) emulated by their examples, sharing their demands, their methods of action and their rejection of the established political system.
>
> (Leite, 2016)

These demonstrations failed to promote change and had two important counterpoints.

The first of them is, in the second round of the 2014 presidential campaign, candidate Dilma Rousseff defeats PSDB candidate Aécio Neves in a polarized dispute that recovers the mobilization of the streets in 2013.

Moreover, the social polarization that had taken root with these manifestations advanced to the urban middle classes.

It then developed in this urban middle class, a line of conservative, racist, homophobic, and xenophobic protests.

This includes positions in Brazil that are based on the wage inequality between blacks and whites and, even more, between black women and white men, besides the large-scale murder of LGBTs and the hatred of the Brazilian ruling classes over Latin American immigrants, for example. And this even happens to interns, migrants from the area of northeastern Brazil by the inhabitants of the cities of the most developed part of the country, the Southeast.

These articulations found in the denunciation to the 'lulismo', to the 'petismo', and to the left preferential targets.

These sectors that moved in the elections of 2014 later were supported by the media propaganda and the businessmen.

A year and a half later, at the end of the first half of 2016, they led the big demonstrations calling for the impeachment of the former president Dilma Rousseff.

On the other hand, the hesitation of this same government, elected in 2014, broke with the speech of the mobilization moments of June 2013, as well as in October 2014.

The appointment of Joaquim Levy as Minister of Finance, an economist linked to the financial system and to the Brazilian banks, was a bucket of cold water in the proposals for changes brought by these waves of support and protection, even if they were fragile, in the new government of Dilma Rousseff.

What prevailed was a conservative mobilization that was openly demophobic.

Therefore, the bet on a strategy of alliance with the oligarchies and with the capital sectors revealed its inconsistency in the Brazilian case. The defense of class conciliation and a resumption of national development by Lulopetism clashed with the trench that the bourgeoisie erected to banish the people from all of this.

This was a hard lesson of this sad episode of dystonia of domination.

In the demophobia that reiterates and resigns, we are exposed to the urgency, in Brazil, to overcome the oligarchic heritage that devastates the lives of most Brazilians.

Note

1 Dystonia (*dys*, disturb, *tonia*, tonus) refers to the neurological disturb of the muscular movements characterized by involuntary contractions and spasms.

References

The references listed here are in the original language. Most of the material is available in full or in part in English or Spanish.

Abranches, Sérgio Henrique Hudson de. Presidencialismo de coalizão: o dilema institucional brasileiro. *Dados – Revista de Ciências Sociais*, Rio de Janeiro, v. 31 n. 1, pp. 5 a 34, 1988.
Agamben, Giorgio. *Estado de exceção*. São Paulo: Boitempo Editorial, 2004, 143 p.
Alencastro, Luiz Felipe de. O fardo dos bacharéis. *Revista Novos Estudos Cebrap*, São Paulo, n. 19, 1987.
Alencastro, Luiz Felipe de. História, política e cultura. *Revista de Estudos Avançados*, São Paulo, v. 25, n. 72, pp. 235 a 247, 2011.
Anderson, Benedict. *Comunidades imaginadas: reflexões sobre a origem e a difusão do nacionalismo.* Trad. Denise Bottmann. São Paulo: Companhia das Letras, 2008.
Bastos, Elide Rugai. *As ligas camponesas*. São Paulo: Vozes, 1983.
Bastos, Elide Rugai. *A questão racial e a revolução burguesa.* in D'INCAO, Maria Angela. *O saber militante – Ensaios sobre Florestan Fernandes.* Rio de Janeiro: Paz e Terra, 1987.
Braudel, Fernand. *La Historia y Las Ciencias Sociales.* Espanha: Alianza Editorial, 1999.
Camargo, Aspásia de Alcântara. A questão agrária: crise de poder e reformas de base (1930–1964). In Boris Fausto (ed.), *História Geral da Civilização Brasileira, Brasil Republicano – Tomo III – Vol. 10.* São Paulo: DIFEL, 1981.
Davis, Mike. *Holocaustos coloniais.* Rio de Janeiro: Record, 2002.
Dean, Warren. A economia brasileira, 1870–1930. In Leslie Bethell (Org.), *História da América Latina: de 1870 a 1930 – Volume V.* São Paulo: Edusp, 2013.
Dreifuss, René. *1964: A conquista do Estado.* São Paulo: Vozes, 1981.
Fernandes, Florestan. *A revolução burguesa no Brasil – Ensaio de interpretação sociológica.* Rio de Janeiro: Guanabara, 1987.
Fernandes, Florestan. *Circuito fechado.* São Paulo: Hucitec, 1976.
Gaspari, Elio. *A ditadura envergonhada.* São Paulo: Companhia das Letras, 2002.
Gramsci, Antônio. *Obras Escolhidas – Volume I.* São Paulo: Martins Fontes, 1978, pp. 187–196.
Jancsó, István (Org.). *Brasil: Formação do Estado e da Nação.* São Paulo/Ijuí: Hucitec, 2003.
Leite, José Correa. *O Partido dos Trabalhadores e a construção de uma sociedade neoliberal no Brasil,* Mimeo Platform, 2016.
Lynch, Christian Edward Cyril. *Da monarquia à oligarquia. História institucional e pensamento político brasileiro (1822–1930).* São Paulo: Alameda, 2014.
Maciel, David. *De Sarney a Collor. Reformas políticas, democratização e crise (1985–1990).* São Paulo: Alameda, 2012.
Martins, Luciano. *Estado capitalista e burocracia no Brasil pós-64.* Rio de Janeiro: Paz e Terra, 1985.
Moser, Benjamin. *Auto-imperialismo: Três ensaios sobre o Brasil.* São Paulo: Crítica, 2016
Sader, Éder. *Quando novos personagens entram em cena.* Rio de Janeiro: Paz e Terra, 1988.
Safatle, Vladimir. *O circuito dos afetos: Corpos políticos, desamparo e o fim do indivíduo.* São Paulo: Autêntica, 2016.
Santos, Luís Cláudio Villafañe G. *O Brasil entre a América e a Europa.* São Paulo: Edunesp, 2004.
Singer, André. *Os sentidos do lulismo.* São Paulo: Companhia das Letras, 2012.
Skidmore, Thomas. *Brasil: de Getúlio Vargas a Castelo Branco.* Rio de Janeiro: Paz e Terra, 1979.
Wainwright, Hilary. *No olho do furacão: repensando o futuro da esquerda.* São Paulo: Editora Xamã, 2006

10 Rain forests, land rent and the ecological contradictions of development in contemporary Brazil

Pedro Chadarevian

The dialectics of the capital-nature relation

We shall approach the environmental issue in contemporary Brazil from a radical political economy standpoint, following John Bellamy Foster's and other critical authors' account of the socialist tradition on the dialectical relationship between capital and nature as the background and starting point for this reflection (Foster, 2000; Foster et al., 2010; Harris-White, 2012).

Yet, for a long time, by virtue of the experience of real socialism under the iron curtain, Marxism was associated with a negligent system of thought towards the environment, from which came a process of socialist modernization as devastating to nature as capitalism itself. A negative environmental legacy of the communist countries that is not actually due to the Marxism's approach to nature, but to a negligent reading of the understanding of Marx and Engels – and of the critical thinkers who succeeded them – on the subject.

However, despite a rationale for a radical critique of the man-nature relationship, and particularly the capital-nature one, has been well established since the late nineteenth century, an environmental movement of national and global relevance would emerge only very recently. We had to wait 100 years for the capitalist system, whose crises from the 1970s came to bring vast environmental impacts, to face resistance from organizations, activists and political parties identified with the nature protection cause. The increasing environmental pollution of industrial chemical waste in the countryside and the uncontrolled emission of carbon dioxide in large urban centers, in addition to frequent nuclear leaks, were important triggers of this political process (Viola, 1984).

Environmental conscience at the present day is the result of this contradictory development of the man/capital-nature relationship, and it fights the dominant ideology of modernization which, on the left as well as on the right, places nature as a passive entity at the disposal of humanity and capitalism to provide the necessary inputs for their reproduction – and survival. Critical voices from nineteenth-century socialists concerning the human-nature relationship differ a great deal from the dominant ideology, including mainstream economics, which sustains that environmental destruction can be offset by punctual preservation actions, paradoxically creating even new markets to reach this end, such as carbon markets or sustainability bond markets.

Among the founders of 'scientific socialism', the critique of the human-nature relationship finds its place at several moments. Friedrich Engels very early stated, "The animal is limited to taking advantage of the external nature and in it produces changes simply by its presence; but man, with the modifications to which he submits it, compels nature to serve his own ends, reigns over it. Practice unequivocally demonstrates that every phenomenon has in nature its necessary foundation" (Engels, in: Sodré, 1968). Note the emphasis on the authoritative character of a relationship where one side must necessarily subordinate itself to the other, and become its subject.

On the other hand, the idea of nature as the foundation of social and economic phenomena was also advanced by Marx, in a scarcely quoted passage from *Capital*: "Use values, such as clothing, fabrics, etc., that is, embodied commodities are the combination of two elements: natural matter and labor. If we could subtract the sum of all the various useful works that are contained in clothing, fabrics, etc., there remains a material substrate that is there due to nature, without any intervention of man." Thus, not only must labor claim a fairer share of the wealth produced, but nature too, since only its transformation with human labor – 'the metabolism between man and nature' – will give rise to commodities and to the social product (Marx, 1993, pp. 48–49; 207).

This notion, which places nature in the genesis of the determination of the social product, goes back at least as far as the history of modern political economy is concerned, to the Earl of Lauderdale. In his critical assessment of Adam Smith's work, Lauderdale sees a limitation in his concept of wealth by not distinguishing public wealth from private riches. From the contradictory relation between these two mutually exclusive dimensions, arises what the author classifies as the paradox of wealth: the compulsion of the system for the constant increase of individual private riches at the expense of public wealth (including nature itself) (Lauderdale, 1804; Foster, 2009).

Réclus, an anarchist militant of the First International, stood out by his pioneering critical approach towards the environmental problem in capitalism. Many consider him as the founder of modern ecology. He foresaw, far ahead for his time, an imbalance in the man-nature relationship jeopardizing the sustainability of civilizations: "Among the causes that in the history of mankind have determined the disappearance of several civilizations in succession, one must first consider the brutal violence with which most nations treated the native nature. Forests were cut down, water sources allowed to dry and rivers to flood, the climates deteriorated, the cities surrounded of marshy and pestilential zones; moreover, when nature, profaned by them, became hostile to them, they faced it with hatred and, unable to return to the forest like the savages, became increasingly brutish by the despotism of priests and kings" (Réclus, 1866).

In the Soviet Union, which greatly contributed to the denial of the critical approach to the man-nature relationship, while the Bolshevik regime strongly advanced on the environment to extract the necessary inputs for its maintenance, official propaganda and its organic intellectuals defended the existence of a unique harmonious relationship between man and nature: "The degree of influence of society in the geographical environment and in nature is ultimately determined by the character of the social regime and by the level of development of production, technique and science. Particularly favorable are the conditions for influencing the nature that the socialist regime provides; the society acquires, for the first time in history, the possibility of transforming it in a conscious and harmonious way, in function of the workers's needs" (Afanasiev, in: Sodré, 1968).

It is worth noting, however, that this view is characteristic of a period of Soviet history in which long-held purges had eliminated any reminiscence of critical thinking in different sectors of society, including the environmental activism. It has not always been so, as Chattopadhyay (2014) shows. He disputes the existence of a purely productivist approach of twentieth-century socialism. The precursors of ecology, or conservationists as the author calls it, in pre-revolutionary Russia, won the sympathy of Lenin and ended up leaving as a legacy the demarcation of dozens of nature reserves in the country, despite their defeat in the confrontation with the Stalinist bureaucracy.

The appropriation for purely propagandistic purposes of the conservationist ethic only makes sense in view of the need for social legitimation of the Stalinist Soviet regime. The ideal of a harmonious relationship between man and nature, the core of this ethic, was already present in Engels and Marx, authors who, however hard he tried, Stalin could not hide: "The more this takes place [man's dominion of nature], the more men will not only feel, but will again know that they are part of nature, and the more it will become absurd and unnatural the idea of an opposition between spirit and matter, between man and nature, and soul and body, an idea that has spread in Europe since the decline of classical antiquity and which has known with Christianity its highest development" (Engels, 1975, p. 181). Meanwhile, Marx criticizes a productive system that focuses exclusively on his extractivist goals, hardly worrying about the environmental inheritance he leaves for the next generations that, in order to reproduce itself, exhausts its two only sources: labor and land (Marx, book III, chap. 46).

From these fundamentals, it is possible to put into practice a political economy analysis of the environmental problem. The process of capital accumulation on a global scale invariably results in an imbalance for nature, or in what is technically called a 'metabolic rift'. Capital extracts the maximum from the earth and nature, just as it does from labor, however, the replenishment and reproduction of the natural elements is not done in the same rhythm – as it occurs with the nutrients of the soil, for example, or the fauna and flora eliminated in the productive process. Entire ecosystems are exhausted in capitalist exploration in a process in which the inputs metabolize in surplus value, transferring the riches from the countryside to the cities, from the periphery to the center, at the expense of nature.

The eco-socialist perspective, or the radical political economy of the environment, considers that the endless movement of imperialist capital only materializes itself with the alienation of nature. A vision radically opposed to mainstream economics, which sees nature as a gift always available to capitalist exploitation, and possible imbalances such as pollution, a classic example to neoclassicists, as mere externalities. For this conservative standpoint, the solution to the ecological issue, just like to any other economic problem comes with a good management strategy and its transformation into yet another byproduct to be commodified (as the above mentioned carbon market).

"One must acknowledge, however, that within Economics there is a significant cut in how to understand issues related to environmental degradation. There is an orthodox view point, which attributes to the absence of certain market incentives the cause of major environmental problems. The theoretical construction, in this case, turns to the justification and suggestion of mechanisms (incentives) that allow the extension of the logic of the market to situations in which it still does not operate clearly or efficiently. Given the right incentives, it is believed, individuals would redirect their wasteful practices in a sustainable sense" (Medeiros and Barreto, 2013).

In addition to this, the overexploitation of marginalized peasant populations in the infinite imperialist movement of capital cannot be seen as displaced from the process of plundering nature, which is the most fundamental source of value, incurring an unquantified dimension of accumulation: the ecological debt (Bellamy Foster and Clark, 2004). Following these authors,

> A wide range of activities contribute, Third World critics contend, to the ecological debt: the extraction of natural resources; unequal terms of trade; degradation of land and soil for export crops; other unrecognized environmental damage and pollution caused by extractive and productive processes; appropriation of ancestral knowledge; loss of biodiversity; contamination of the atmosphere and oceans; the introduction of toxic chemicals and dangerous weapons; and the dumping of hazardous waste in the periphery.
> (op. cit.)

The eco-socialist perspective is therefore radically opposed to that of the mainstream economics, where nature is seen as a source always available for capital to monetize inputs, raw materials, and values (real or fictitious ones – in the latter case, speculative capitals).

The radical perspective in the analysis of the environmental problem is intended to be multidisciplinary and pluralistic, with a focus on class relations and conflicts that particularly present themselves as its determinants in the last instance. It is, therefore, an analysis based on the pillars of political economy, and enriched by instrumental legacies of other social sciences such as politics, history, geography, sociology and anthropology, without neglecting the central importance of the contribution of ecology itself and other natural sciences disciplines.

Capitalist development versus environmental protection: the 'Lula years' most fundamental contradiction

If there is a point at which left and right seem to converge in today's serious social and political divide in Brazil it is in relation to the critique of the environmental legacy of the 'Lula Years' – understood here as the 13-year period in which the country was ruled by the Workers' Party, or Partido dos Trabalhadores/PT (2003–2016). In fact, many were the inconsistencies of the PT model, whose axis of political support was the social pact that sought to include, from the very beginning, representatives of the broadest spectrum of factions of the productive system alongside social movements.

In the environmental area, this was manifested by the always conflictual coexistence between figures from the agribusiness with political and social leaderships associated with the defense of agrarian reform and national environmentalism. Although clearly hostage to the powerful lobby of the rural bourgeoisie group throughout the period of PT hegemony, it would be frivolous not to recognize the importance of a series of environmental policies introduced by the socialist government. They allowed, notably, a historical reduction in the rate of deforestation in both the Amazon and the Brazilian *Cerrado* (a unique ecosystem located in the center of the country).

As a hypothesis, we maintain here that two parallel movements eroded the axis of political support of the PT government. On the one hand, as a result of the contradictory and dialectical development of capital itself, the metabolic rift widens, giving rise to the race for new agricultural land. Which takes place in the context of introducing regulatory instruments that seek to

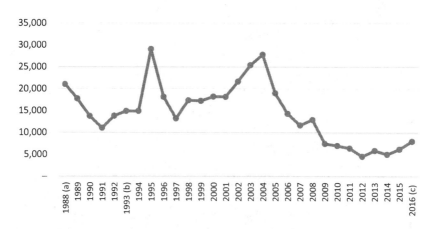

Figure 10.1 Amazonia annual deforetation rates (in km^2, Brazil)

(a) Mean of 1976 to 1988 period
(b) Mean of years 1993 and 1994
(c) Estimate
Source: Instituto Nacional de Pesquisas Espaciais

impose limits, however timid, on the devastation caused by the expansion of capitalist activity in the countryside, as we will analyze in detail in the next section of this chapter. These limits eventually introduced an internal pressure on the system, whose most palpable manifestation was the impressive increase in the price of land, which quadrupled between 2002 and 2013. At the Amazon agricultural frontier, the price increased eightfold over the same period. In the state of São Paulo, the richest in the country, the median value of bare land of prime quality increased more than fivefold. As we can see in the graph below, after the long stagnation of the governments of Fernando Henrique Cardoso (1995–2002), there is an uninterrupted process of elevation throughout the Lula years, which is almost untouched by the crises of the period.

On the other hand, there is also an external pressure, due to the explosion of the bubble in the price of commodities, a central inducer of investments in the sector. As a result, previously well-established support from middle-class and dominant sectors linked to agribusiness, as well as from its representatives in Congress, the so-called ruralist group, has been undoing. Of course, it is not the only one, but one of the most important factors to understand the current political crisis in Brazil, which, as we can see, has an environmental element not negligible in its origin.

What we propose here, therefore, is to draw attention to a variable not so prominent in the analysis of the recent evolution of Brazilian society and economy: the dynamics of accumulation in the countryside and the interaction between profit, land rent and the struggle for environmental preservation as determinants of the capitalist trajectory. An appeal that is justified by the

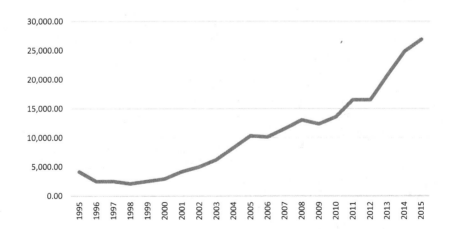

Figure 10.2 Price of land

São Paulo State, median R$/ha
Source: Anuários do Instituto de Estudos Agrícolas do Estado de São Paulo

growing weight of the agribusiness sector in the country, becoming the largest individual export segment in the country, accounting for about 45% of total Brazilian exports.

It would be simplistic, however, to see in this a mere process of primarization of the productive structure of the country. Agriculture, the sector generally more averse to the introduction of new technologies, has modernized rapidly in recent times in Brazil. It is, of course, a conservative modernization, whose dynamics of growth and transformation are led by the figure of powerful landowners (*latifundiários*). Large estates continue to be the dominant form in the archaic land structure prevailing in the country; moreover, a process of land concentration was on course in the last decade.

However, one cannot deny the modernizing character of the country's agricultural evolution. This can be seen, on the one hand, in the form of production, by the increasing use of chemical fertilizers, machines that automate productive stages, transgenic seeds and disseminated use of satellites. On the other hand, in the relations of production, which professionalize and approach rapidly the design of industrial relations, with process control concentrated on the figure of managers, and through the introduction of production control methods and division of labor typical of capitalist factories. As a result, Brazil led the increase in total productivity of agricultural factors among the largest economies on the planet, with an average growth of 4% between 2000 and 2015, according to the OECD.

The quantitative evolution in production ended up imposing a qualitative leap in the sector, increasing the intensity of the agricultural activity as a way to overcome both natural obstacles (poor soil fertility at the agricultural frontier, at least initially) and artificial obstacles, imposed either by the resistance of social and indigenous movements, or by the state, which sought to establish in the last ten years new policies of regulation of the relation man (capital)-nature. However, the rising land prices, as a result of the increased demand of landowners for a share of the surplus value of productive activities in the countryside (the so-called land rent), has put an unbeatable pressure on agribusiness in Brazil.

One can note, from the chart below, how the productivity of the agribusiness's most important crop in the state of São Paulo has been practically stagnant in the last fifteen years. The increase in the area produced, stimulated by the rise in soybean prices in the period and by environmental deregulation in the region, was not followed by large increases in the quantity produced. That is, the logic of production in the richest region of the country adopted an extensive dynamic, without significant incorporation of new production techniques. And, possibly, the rising in land rent has great responsibility in this phenomenon. Owners tend to take advantage of increasing portions of the surplus value, making it difficult to reinvest in technical improvements in the sector, forcing producers to devastate the environment in search of gains that compensate for the use of an increasingly valued soil.

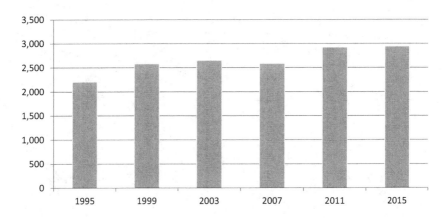

Figure 10.3 Productivity of soybeans crops
Estado de São Paulo, kg/ha
Source: Anuários do Instituto de Estudos Agrícolas do Estado de São Paulo

As Collins (2017) rightly puts it,

> Rising land values suck purchasing power and demand out of the economy, as the benefits of growth are concentrated in property owners with a low marginal propensity to consume, which in turn reduces spending and investment. In addition, most new credit creation by the banking system now flows in to real estate rather than productive activity. This crowds out productive investment, both by the banking system itself and non-bank investors who see the potential for much higher returns on relatively tax free real estate investment.

The intensification of production in the field, which produces social and environmental costs in terms of river pollution, increased deforestation of riverbanks and hilltops, augmented production of chemical residues and soil exhaustion, reinforces economic pressure through the increasing differential of productivity in the lands, source of the land rent mass in the economy. In a short period of time, organic intellectuals of the agribusiness sector began to adhere to the thesis of political rupture as a way out of stagnation due to the rapid increase in production costs and reduction of profit margins, in a context of high land rent, falling commodity prices and limitation of expansion capacity to new territories at the agricultural frontier.

Environmental policies during the 'Lula years'

Brazil is, at the same time, the lung and the barn of the world. The Amazon forest and other smaller biomes that are territorially significant because of their contribution to biodiversity (the country concentrates one of the largest contingents of existing species) are threatened by the greatest producers of meat, soy, corn and coffee on the planet. The barn strides over the lungs. Only recently protective measures started to be taken in order to mitigate the damage from deforestation and environmental pollution.

The truth is that the military dictatorship (1964–1985) delayed the environmental debate in the country, and promoted the internalization of productive activity, with the support of international capitals. The soybean crop, now a multibillion dollar chain in the country and widespread throughout the Amazon region, is an originally military project. With the democratization process in the early 1980s, a national ecological movement emerged. The movement is confused with the very origin of the Workers' Party, whose socialist ecological wing has been represented since the early years of its existence (Oliveira, 2008). Nationally and internationally renowned environmentalists such as the tapper Chico Mendes, the indigenous leader Marcos Terena and the economist Carlos Minc become members of the party. In the founding manifesto of the PT, in 1980, we can read that the social control of natural wealth was one of the central objectives of this party organization, in a clear progressive view to the environmental issue:

> The Workers' Party wants the people to decide what to do with the wealth produced and the country's natural resources. The natural riches, which until now have served only the interests of the great national and international capital, should be put at the service of the well-being of the collectivity. For this, decisions about the economy must be submitted to popular interests. But these interests will not prevail as long as political power does not express a real popular representation based on grassroots organizations, so that workers' decision-making power over the economy and other levels of society can be effective.
>
> (Partido dos Trabalhadores, 1980)

However, a more critical and in-depth position on the environmental issue with a clear agenda on the subject was rare in the party, with the exception of the positions of Buaiz (1988) and Minc (1991) in official publications. With all these limits, in the government program launched in 1989, when the PT was one step closer to winning the first direct elections for president after dictatorship, we can find a specific chapter dedicated to 'ecology and the environment'. It signaled at that moment for the need to place limits on the national productive system in order to guarantee the preservation of the environment. Among the measures recommended was an ecological agrarian reform, the control of the emission of pollutants, the demarcation of indigenous territories, the adoption of a specific development plan for the Amazon, the suspension of mechanized monoculture in the *Cerrado* biome, and limits to mining and to the use of agrochemicals (Partido dos Trabalhadores, 1989). A bold plan, defeated thanks to mass media manipulation of the electoral process, and that today seems far from the environmental practices of the party.

In fact, in order to govern the country, the party abandoned several of its 'radical' premises, adopting a more pragmatic stance, be it economical, productive, or environmental. Likewise, the environmental policies of the period governed by the center-left party stand out for promoting a new regulatory apparatus in the country. Although its results have been rightly criticized (Penido et al., 2014; Schmitt and Scardua, 2015; Lisboa, 2011), because it was based on an ambiguous concept of sustainability, sometimes permissive and flexible in relation to the protection of the ecological heritage, it had the merit of avoiding a much greater environmental devastation in the period. In the table below, we list the main policies and actions adopted and environmental laws enacted in the period governed by Lula and Dilma Rousseff.

Table 10.1 Environmental policies and bills adopted during the 'Lula years' (2003–2016)

Policy	Year/President	Description
Plano de Prevenção e Combate do Desmatamento na Amazônia (PPCDAM)/*Plan to Prevent and Fight Deforestation at the Amazon*	2003/LULA	Promotes land and territorial planning, monitoring and control, promotion of productive and sustainable activities, and infrastructure
O Plano de Desenvolvimento Sustentável da Amazônia (PAS)/*Sustainable Development Plan for the Amazon*	2003/LULA	Commitment between ministries, state governments and development agencies for the adoption of coordinated and environmentally sustainable policies
Nova Lei da Biossegurança/*New Biosecurity Bill*	2005/LULA	Liberalizes transgenic seeds, conditioned to the approval in a special State commission (formed by representatives of the government)
Programa Nacional de Formação de Educadoras(es) Ambientais (ProFEA)/*National Program of Training of Environmental Educators*	2006/LULA	Training of popular environmental educators, based on edicts for establishment of collectives in different institutions and social movements
Plano Estratégico Nacional de Áreas Protegidas (PNAP)/*National Strategic Plan for Protected Areas*	2006/LULA	The main aim of the plan is to develop conservation strategies to 25% of Brazilian territory under legal environmental protection

(*Continued*)

Table 10.1 (Continued)

Policy	Year/President	Description
Instituto Chico Mendes de Conservação da Biodiversidade (ICMBio)/*Chico Mendes Institute for the Biodiversity Conservation*	2007/LULA	National instituted devoted to the management of natural conservation units
Política Nacional de Mudanças Climáticas – PNMC/*Climate Change National Policy*	2009/LULA	Commitment to reduce greenhouse gas emissions until 2020
Política Nacional de Resíduos Sólidos/*National Policy for Solid Waste*	2010/LULA	Maps the areas where waste are deposited or handled and encourage sustainability and recycling
Plano de Ação para Prevenção e Controle do Desmatamento e das Queimadas no Cerrado/*Plan for Prevention and Control of Deforestation and Fires in the Cerrado*	2010/LULA	Recovery of degraded forest areas, and environmental management
Lei Complementar 140/*Complementary Bill n. 140*	2011/ROUSSEFF	Decentralizes environmental management and inspection for federative entities
Plano de Ação para Produção e Consumo Sustentáveis/*Plan for a Sustainable Production and Consumption*	2011/ROUSSEFF	Initiatives focused on cleaner production and sustainable consumption, such as government sustainable acquisitions, construction, and recycling
Marco da Biodiversidade/*Biodiversity Bill*	2015/ROUSSEFF	Regulates access to genetic heritage and compensation to the traditional communities involved

The ecological footprint of capital and the need to impose limits to the system

The recent Brazilian case is a frustrated example of a strategy of class reconciliation to regulate the plundering of nature by capital. Although one can celebrate the momentary reduction in the pace of deforestation in strategic biomes for the planetary ecological balance, the current government, post-2016 coup, signalizes to the dismantling of the regulatory apparatus that allowed this result. A minister of the illegitimate administration that took place in august 2016, soon after Dilma Rousseff's impeachment, has even said that indigenous people, instead of deserving increasing areas to guarantee their original rights to land and help protect the nature that surrounds them, shall from now on collaborate with the market system.

The neoliberal restoration under course in the country with Mr. Temer's government will undoubtedly use all its resources to reduce the protected forest area, both in environmental reserves and indigenous territories, as well as to de-structure peasant activities and sustainable agriculture. Clearly, the aim is to liberate new areas for the full advance of capital and speculation without the previously existing bonds which, although limited, have resulted in a major containment of their almost obsessive expansion.

The failure of the progressive strategy of the 'Lula years' opens a unique opportunity to reassess the human/capital-nature relationship model in Brazil. The world looks very closely at developments in the country in the environmental sphere. Assuming an increase in the rate of deforestation, the Amazon forest would be doomed to disappear in a few decades. The consequence of this would be devastating, and is already included in the models of climate science: a rapid increase in the temperature of the globe and, as a result, an acceleration in the imbalances that endanger the very survival of humanity.

The absence of a global regulatory body for environmental issues makes it difficult for countries to set stricter rules on nature protection beyond commitments already established, such as the Kyoto Protocol and at international climate conferences. The environment, despite growing awareness of its importance to the survival of human life in the planet, does not benefit from the same instances of regulation as global trade (WTO), health (WHO) or finance (IMF). At the same time, governments strategies to combat global warming are merely palliative, and do not seem to be sufficient to ensure an interruption in the scale of climate change observed by many indicators in recent years.

Practical measures like the ones Brazil experimented under the Workers' Party administration are obviously important; nevertheless, they seem doomed to show unsustainable limits if not accompanied by a radical reorientation of the very productive system. A productive system, as we saw, dominated by the interests of a very conservative rural elite, which are undetached from its dependence from international capitals and the speculative use of the land. Moreover, a qualitative deficiency of this system is that it uses a great portion of the territory to grow exporting crops, in spite of producing the real needs of the populations in terms of food and land. A metabolic – and social rift – that tends to increase unfortunately in the near future, unless we stop seriously to think about our role in this fragile planet.

Sustainable consumption or recycling policies will no more suffice as the risk of catastrophic climate change events grows higher everyday now. Besides, the trends of behavioral changes toward 'environmental friendly' consumption do not affect the actual root of the environmental problem at present: the emission of greenhouse gases by the large industry, deforestation, and agricultural and livestock production. That is why we need to consider a radical questioning of the capitalist system, before it is too late, especially in what concerns the nature of the property and the use of land and other means of production, as well as our relation to nature in society. This means not only a radical economic shift in the way we use to produce commodities, but also includes a cultural change in the way we deal with animals and their ecosystems.

Considered as something unimaginable a few decades ago, an indispensable source, alongside labor, of value and wealth, severely blessed in the course of annihilation due to incessant accumulation of capital, nature may soon become its greatest tormentor.

References

Buaiz, Vitor. A ecologia contra a barbárie. *Teoria e Debate*, n. 4, 1988.
Chattopadhyay, Kunal. The Rise and Fall of Environmentalism in the Early Soviet Union. *Climate & Capitalism*, November 3, 2014.
Collins, Josh Ryan. How Land Disappeared From Economic Theory. *Evonomics*, April 4, 2017. http://evonomics.com/josh-ryan-collins-land-economic-theory/
Engels, Friedrich. *Dialectique da la Nature*. Paris: Éditions Sociales, 1975.
Foster, Jonh Bellamy. *Marx' Ecology: Materialism and Nature*. New York, Monthly Review Press, 2000.
Foster, Jonh Bellamy. The Paradox of Wealth: Capitalism and Ecological Destruction. *Monthly Review*, v. 61, n. 6, 2009.
Foster, Jonh Bellamy, and Clark, Brett. Ecological Imperialism: The Curse of Capitalism. *Socialist Register*, v. 40, 2004.
Foster, Jonh Bellamy, Clark, Brett, and York, Richard. *The Ecological Rift: Capitalism's War on the Earth*. New York, Monthly Review Press, 2010.
Harris-White, Barbara. Ecology and the Environment. In FINE and SAAD-FILHO (eds.), *The Elgar Companion to Marxist Economics*. Northampton: Edward Elgar, 2012.
Lauderdale, Earl of. *An Inquiry Into the Nature and Origin of Public Wealth and Into the Means and Causes of Its Increase*. London: Longman, 1804.
Lisboa, Marjane V. Balanço da política ambiental do governo Lula: grandes e duradouros impactos. In M. Paula (org.), *Nunca antes na história desse país. . . ? Um balanço das políticas do governo Lula*. Rio de Janeiro: Heinrich Böll Stiftung, 2011.
Marx, Karl. *Le Capital*. Paris: Presses Universitaires de France, 1993.
Medeiros, João Leonardo, and Barreto, Eduardo Sá. Lukács e Marx contra o "ecologismo acrítico": por uma ética ambiental materialista. *Economia e Sociedade*, Campinas, v. 22, n. 2 (48), 2013.
Minc, Carlos. Ecologia. Verdes revolucionários. *Teoria e Debate*, n. 13, 1991.
Oliveira, Wilson J. F. Gênese e redefinições do militantismo ambientalista no Brasil. *Dados*, v. 51, n. 3, 2008.
Partido dos Trabalhadores. *Manifesto de Fundação*. 1980. http://www.pt.org.br/manifesto-de-fundacao-do-partido-dos-trabalhadores/
Partido dos Trabalhadores. *As bases do Plano de Ação de Governo*. 1989. http://www.enfpt.org.br/wp-content/uploads/2017/05/As-bases-do-Plano-de-Acao-de-Governo-PAG-1.pdf
Penido, Yvaga P., Kaplan, Leonardo, and Loureiro, Carlos F. Políticas públicas instituídas pelo Ministério do Meio Ambiente: análise da documentação e implementação do programa de formação de educadores/as ambientais (ProFEA). *Revista VITAS*, v. IV, n. 8, 2014.
Réclus, Élisée. Du Sentiment de la nature dans les sociétés modernes. *La Revue des deux Mondes*, n. 63, mai 15, 1866.
Schmitt, Jair e Scardua, Fernando P. A descentralização das competências ambientais e a fiscalização do desmatamento na Amazônia. *Revista de Administração Pública*, v. 49, n. 5, 2015.
Sodré, Nelson Werneck. *Fundamentos do Materialismo Histórico*. Rio de Janeiro: Civilização Brasileira, 1968.
Viola, Eduardo J. O movimento ecológico no Brasil (1974–1986): do ambientalismo à ecopolítica. *Revista Brasileira de Ciências Sociais*, v. 1, n. 3, 1984.

11 Higher education

Development of underdevelopment or a tool to overcome it?

Reginaldo Moraes

The establishment of a public education system in Brazil is a relatively recent phenomenon. In the early twentieth century, while attending high school had already become a realistic prospect for every American teenager, the poor included, provided they were white, in Brazil something similar to that is only produced in the 1970s. American higher education becomes overwhelmingly public and widespread in the aftermath of World War II. In Brazil, a first attempt at massification takes place in the late 1990s – and under the primacy of for-profit private schools.

There are two main factors driving the expansion of the Brazilian public school. One is persistent, slow, and somewhat silent: the urbanization and industrialization process. Yes, slow, but only from a given perspective, as actually urbanization in Brazil is ten times faster than in England and three times faster than in the United States. Still, it is a process that spans generations. The urbanization process also prompted a strong internal migration flow: the country 'flowed' to the southeast. Something similar happens with the manufacturing industry – with its peculiar characteristic of being under the hegemony of foreign company subsidiaries. This model also exhibits a key feature in the establishment of 'social scales': appalling income inequality.

The second factor driving the school system growth and profile was the State's visible hand. In the higher education segment, in particular, there are two landmarks. The first is the university reform carried out by the military dictatorship in 1969, under overt orientation of the US Agency for International Development (Usaid). The second landmark takes place in the second half of the 1990s with the neoliberal reforms dictated by multilateral agencies, also under hegemonic control of the United States.

In the 1970s, the reform led to the expansion of the system through a multiplication of isolated, private colleges that were induced to present themselves as 'nonprofit institutions' yet were actually run by businesspeople. The leap was crystal clear. In 1968, the higher education student body was a universe of slightly over 100,000 souls. And it was concentrated in public schools (75%). The private sector was made up entirely of nonprofit institutions, most of them confessional schools. In the mid 1980s, as the dictatorship crumbled, this figure exceeded 1.5 million – yet the public sector accounted for 35% of total enrollments. The private sector had changed: it was already peopled with education companies.

The second milestone, circa 1995, was a federal reform that induced schools to more clearly assume their legal status: either companies or nonprofit institutions. And it established standards and requirements for their various configurations and sizes: universities, university centers, isolated schools. More relevant than that reform, however, was the adoption of a little-noticed 'capital formation' policy for private schools. In 1995, the Ministry of Education negotiated with national development bank BNDES a highly generous funding scheme – which would recreate, in a much larger scale, this private sector. A huge network of schools and facilities was set up with these funds – with credit extended at generous, even negative, interest rates. Five years later the private sector offered twice the number of undergraduate places. What we see in this time series is not steady growth. It is a leap in nature from 1995 to 2000. The turning point can be clearly seen in Graph 11.1.

The way had been paved for a new industry – one rapidly heading toward consolidation and financialization. Thereafter, consecutive stimulus policies were demanded by the sector – and provided by the government. Policies designed to leverage this installed, and potentially, idle capacity. Tax breaks, student credit, scholarship programs. With the take-off propelled by the State, it was necessary to sustain cruise speed, with fuel that was also provided by the State.

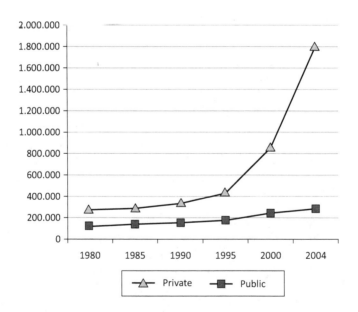

Graph 11.1 Undergraduate places offered

A simplified map of the system

A profile emerged from this combination of drivers – a slower urbanization and industrialization driver, and salient and more easily measurable one, federal government action. Total figures are very impressive: almost 300 public institutions and 2,000 private ones; 32,000 on-campus courses and another 1,200 distance learning courses; 400,000 faculty members; and over six million students attending on-campus courses and another 1.2 million enrolled in online education programs.

The profile of this complex can be built based on three more salient features. Let us see which.[1]

The sector is dominated by private supply

We have already mentioned the predominance of the private sector in the annual supply of college places. This flow of new entrants (Graph 11.2) is made clear in the 'inventory' of enrollments.

The student body has a high percentage of 'non-youths'

The system comprises a significant contingent of students who are above the 'adequate age bracket', i.e., over 24 years old (Graph 11.3). There are reasons for that being so, and these are not the same we find, for example, in European countries, where such trend is accounted for by the demographic aging of society. In Brazil, besides this factor, we should take into account a sort of 'unmet demand', or an accumulated stock of students not admitted at the right time.

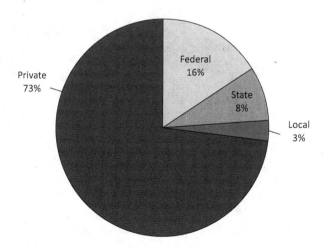

Graph 11.2 Undergraduate enrollments, Brazil, 2013

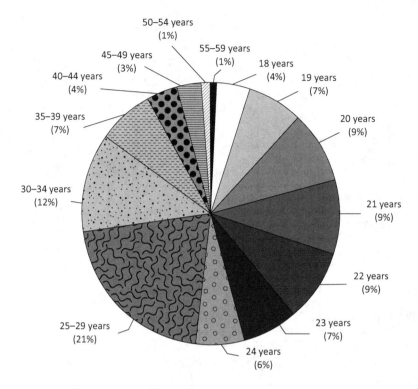

Graph 11.3 Undergraduate enrollments by age

A great number of students work and attend evening classes that are mostly offered by the private school system

This (older) profile of the student body is relevant for understanding student distribution and their unequal access to the various higher education subsectors. Not only is this student body older, but it is also composed of people who went back to school after having joined the labor market. These are working students in search of courses that may adjust to their working hours: night courses. And this is how we view the distribution between public schools, in general, more selective and prestigious, and private sector schools, in general lower quality and less prestigious. The private sector is not so much larger than the public system when we consider enrollments in daytime courses (Graph 11.4).

Yet the gap is striking when we look at the number of enrollments in night courses, that is, those attended by older students who are employed in the labor market (Graph 11.5).

Higher education   213

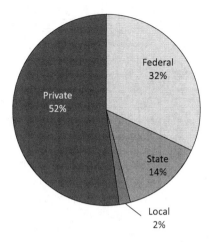

Graph 11.4 Undergraduate daytime enrollments

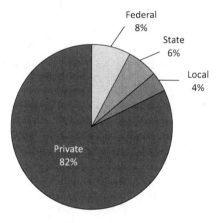

Graph 11.5 Undergraduate evening enrollments

The federal higher education system – universities and institutes – has grown dramatically over the last ten years. It nearly doubled in size and spread all across the nation, creating points of access not only in state capital cities, but also in smaller towns. Still, it is far from meeting the demand and for from striking a balance with the private schools as regards a particular audience. The Higher Education Census reveals that, in federal schools, 62.3% of the student body is aged 24 years and under. In the private schools, this percentage is 41.7%. In the 24–40 age bracket enrolled in federal universities the percentage is of 31.5%, whereas in private schools it is 42.4%; and the 40 year-plus students in federal universities account for 6.5% of total enrollments, against 10.3% in the private higher education system.

From outline to analysis to reform

Although comprised of several components, this profile is somewhat easy to be accounted for. The free public system is small and turns away a great number of students, whereas the private, and paid for, system takes them. Another explanatory element is the fact that public schools hesitate to offer night course places. In the beginning of 2000 in federal universities, less than 20% of enrollments were in night courses, a proportion that was exactly the opposite in private schools. Working students had more difficulty in getting through the *numerus clausus* of public schools: students from higher social strata, with greater cultural capital, and educated in more sophisticated secondary schools leaped ahead. What's more, working students, if they managed to enter the public school, faced the additional hurdle of timetables that conflicted with their breadwinning activities.

Over the past 20 years, the arrival of this host of students to higher education reflects a sort of race against backwardness, a recovery of ground, at every educational level. In 1990, more than 50% of the secondary students were above the 'adequate age bracket', i.e., were aged 18-plus. In the 2000s, this ratio drops to 30%. The 'old' wave reached the second tier, thus adding to higher education figures.

Thus, Brazilian higher education has a peculiar profile: a selective sector comprised of public schools and a 'mass' sector dominated by the for-profit private sector, which benefits from public funding allocation while simultaneously enjoying a poorly regulated environment. Strictly, the public segment is also divided, with the constitution of an even more select core group of 'research universities'. To use an image by Steven Brint, it is as if there were three clothing sectors, a high fashion sector, a ready-made sector, and a low-income sector.

The implications of such a model are very serious for the aspirations of a consistent, sustainable, and coherent development model.[2] A project like that calls for the adoption of programs designed to produce 'infrastructures of knowledge' in the fields of education and research. It is hard to imagine such a policy in the context of higher education with the profile we outlined. A similar policy does not seem to have been set in place ever before in the world, and nothing points to its likelihood of ever coming to exist. Even more worrying is to see that the private for-profit sector is the major provider of higher education credentials – diplomas and certificates – in segments like management, pedagogy, law, engineering, medicine, and nursing. What we have in this sector is, therefore, the management of businesses, of the laws, of technical innovation, as well as of strategic wellbeing policies. And all of that depends, above all, on education and capacity-building policies that are managed and shaped by increasingly more short-term profit-oriented agents.

Can the public sector reverse that? Yes, it can, but for that it must compete with the private sector and defeat it. First of all, it must understand from where the private sector draws its energies. It must examine which of these energies are drained from the public sector itself, with no or low offsetting mechanisms. Regulation of the private sector is something both urgent and difficult. About ten years ago, the Lula administration sent a bill for the purpose of reforming higher education to Congress. The bill was weak, but even so it introduced regulations the private sector deemed unacceptable. Hence, it was buried by a conservative, privatization-oriented delegation, as well as by the nihilist far-left. One of these weak regulations aimed at something strategic if the goal is to move forward in terms of public control: participation by faculty and students in the schools' decisionmaking bodies. The system continues with almost no regulation of that sort. As the organized teachers' and students' movements are almost exclusively focused on the public schools, political pressure on the sector depends on lawmakers and State agents. Well, this business segment also knows how to lobby and to fund electoral campaigns. Strengthened over the past 20 years, it has accumulated resources to do so.

But, besides regulating the private sector, the government must create alternatives in terms of the supply of school places that may address the needs of the students 'selected' by private institutions. And this means being more flexible in creating educational structures. It is pointless and unfeasible to construe this expansion on the basis of establishing Humboldtian universities in every village in the country. We need a network of diversified, combined, and interconnected 'points of access'. And these should be distributed in such a way that every student can reach one of them in no more than 30 minutes from their homes or jobs. These points cannot be cathedrals – they must be small parishes and chapels. And they have to develop methods and procedures that are suitable to this new audience.

Third, the international experience shows that we must take into account not only the broadening of access, but also of achievement and quality. Hence, in addition to compensatory permanence policies, the government must address the lack of coordination between higher education and the other two levels, the secondary and *fundamental* schools. Adjusting one side while simultaneously reforming the other. These levels' present quality bottlenecks must be addressed. In effect, many studies have shown that more than 80% of all occupations and job vacancies require, at most, knowledge hypothetically learned during the last years of *fundamental* school. What's more, about 90% would only require secondary education. In one word, operating the world of production and social services depends on a set of skills and a level of knowledge that may be deemed elementary. Reading and writing adequately; doing the four arithmetic operations and solving simple problems like percentages, rules of three, first-degree equations, elementary geometry; having basic notions of natural and human sciences (geography, history). Strictly speaking, today our higher education might (just might!) be close to that. Or, to put the problem in another way, the quality of our education is so precarious that our students only come to master these contents and skills when they get to college – if so! Therefore, increasing the number of years in school does not mean more knowledge, it means just that: more years in school. Moreover, there also seems to be an inflation of credentials – or of the requirement of credentials that are clearly above the needs of the occupation. Or the selling of such illusions. Brazilian society is marked by extreme economic inequality and social polarization (including prestige). The contest for a college credential must be viewed in that perspective. Pressure on the higher education supply, too.

The conundrums of education begin with the design of the relations between the various levels and types of schools in supply. And with the role each one plays – or should play.

Observed from this angle, a reform of the system would have to go much further the administrative, legal, and financial aspects. It should start with a basic question, what kind of education system (higher education included) do we need to have? What should we expect from it?

There are those who set out to analyze our problems and their solutions from a blank slate: by rebuilding the whole construction with a fully-integrated education system that is completely reformed from the mother's womb. This exercise is useful and necessary in order to rebuild the school of those already coming and of those who are going to come. But what should we do with those who are already here and had none of that? There are millions of them. Should we just ignore them? Is that acceptable from an ethical and political point of view? And is it possible – more so if we think that they are the ones who set the country's cogs in motion? What if we start erecting the new building with them?

A policy designed to reform education must be systemic – an integrated policy for the whole system, from the nursery school to the graduate program. And it must be a policy based on what is to be achieved yet taking into account what is available now – institutions and practices, people and capabilities. Many of the reform solutions will be temporary fixes, meant only for the transition. Their duration will be limited. Others will be more lasting. Without such modesty in planning and setting goals, it will be hard to nurture the indispensable ambition of which dreams are made of. Reform-driven projects must be ambitious yet, at the same time, cannot be decoupled from the elements found in the present reality. And they must not overlook the fact that those who prepare the delicacy of the future need to eat today.

The engineering of institutional innovation, of public policy innovation, must be deeply national, deeply rooted in the aspirations, behavior, and inclinations of the Brazilians. Yet, at the same time, it must be wise enough to learn from other societies and from other experiences.

Notes

1 The data I used to prepare the graphs for this chapter were taken from the 2013 Higher Education Census Summary, document which is available at the Inep website: http://portal.inep.gov.br/superior-censosuperior-sinopse (last accessed January 25, 2016).
2 We have learned from the masters of Brazilian developmentalism, as Celso Furtado, that a development with such contours must meet at least six criteria: durable and steady economic growth; reduction in the predatory use of natural and human resources; national integration and alleviation of regional and social inequalities; internalization of dynamic (economic and technological) factors; internalization of decisionmaking centers; incorporation of the masses in the economic, social, and political process.

12 The impact of conditional cash transfer programs in Brazil and their limits

Robério Paulino

Brazil has been experiencing in the past two years one of the most severe political crises of its history, after the polarized 2014 presidential elections, with the losing side not accepting the results of the election and obstructing the government's initiatives in the National Congress, which raised the tension, debilitated the government and resulted in the impeachment of president Dilma Roussef in 2016, even before she could complete half of her second term. This took place at the cost of contributing to aggravating the economic deacceleration experienced in the country, which now also combines with an acute political crisis, with accusations and revelations of several corruption scandals, involving the republican powers and almost all political parties.

One of the elements of current dispute and strongly discussed among the population in the past 15 years involves the relevance and justification or not of the cash transfer programs for millions of low-income families. The more conservative sectors of the population have been criticizing the implementation of these programs since the governments of president Fernando Henrique Cardoso (FHC), but raised the level of criticism during the governments of president Luís Inácio Lula da Silva (Lula) and Dilma Rousseff.

In the past 25 years, even in a scenario of adoption of a neoliberal economic orientation, several governmental programs aimed at fighting poverty and promoting social development were implemented in the country, whether as a result of the pressure for the universalization of new social rights inserted into the 1988 Constitution, partly as a result of the redemocratization process of the country, whether as a result of promises made in elections by the candidates or also of international commitments made by the country in connection with goals of multilateral organizations for the reduction of poverty, such as the UN's Millenium Development Goals, of which Brazil is a signatory party.

Within a macroeconomic scenario of tax austerity pursued by all governments in this period, in harmony with the World Bank's policies (Fiszbein et al, 2009), which has been restricting the universalization of rights, the option for fighting extreme poverty has been conducted through social policies focused on the most vulnerable groups of the population, through the conditional cash transfer programs, such as the Family Allowance Program [Programa Bolsa Família – PBF], currently in effect, and around which a major debate has been going on in the country, related to its relevance and its actual outcomes.

It should be stressed that the option for focused social policies for fighting extreme poverty is not exclusive of Brazil. They have been implemented in several Latin American countries, with special emphasis, because of its amplitude and relevance, on the programs implemented in Chile (Chile Solidário) and in Mexico (Oportunidades), which, along with the PBF, have become the object and parameters for the discussion about the fighting against poverty all over the world (Soares et al., 2007).

In Brazil, the social issue has always been considered a secondary issue. Similarly to the South of the United States, the formation of the country relied on the large estate, slavery and monoculture tripod. The country, while a colony of Portugal, was the largest importer of slaves of the Americas, having received, alone, almost 60% of the ten million African slaves that are estimated to have arrived alive at the continent, a number ten times higher than the number of African slaves that were taken to the 13 American colonies of England, which would later become the United States of America (Florentino, 2005).

The country was also one of the last to end slavery and, after the abolition, the Blacks here never received any piece of land, and there has never been any policy directed to their integration into the national economy. Unlike the United States of America, a country that based its initial wealth upon its rural basis of millions of small farmers, which helped it create a powerful internal market and later facilitated its industrialization, Brazil never conducted an effective distribution of its land, the main source of survival and income all over the world until the 19th century. This was one of the factors that led capitalism to develop so late in Brazil.

Until the end of the 19th century, the country remained essentially as a rural, exporter slave-based nation, which also delayed the dissemination of salary relationships, therefore without a relevant internal market, with its capitalist rural elite dependent upon the demand of external markets, especially the European ones, consequently with their backs to Brazil, with no concern whatsoever about the living conditions of its population. An elite of slaveholding mentality and estranged in relation to the living conditions of its own people.

The social issue in Brazil has always been considered a secondary issue and any protest was treated with extreme violence by the State. The construction of the social protection, through rights, services and public programs was very much postponed in Brazil, as a result of a late capitalism, with a fragile working class, until at least the 1950s. The primitive capitalist accumulation occurred as a result of four centuries of slavery, of a sad colonial past, which left painful scars in the social history of the country, marked to this day by a profound wealth gap.

Only after the 1930s, with the negative impact of the Great Depression on its exports, the country started to change its economic structure (Furtado, 2005). In the period from 1930 to 1970, Brazil starts to build a modern economy, of industrial and urban basis, leaving behind in part its rural past, based on the export of basic products, which characterized its economic history until then. With the emergence of a working class, the country starts to take its first steps towards the constitution of social policies (Draibe, 1993). During the governments of Getúlio Vargas, in the 1930s, it emerges the Consolidation of the Labor Laws [Consolidação das Leis do Trabalho – CLT], which regulated labor rights and duties. In the rationale of a State that pursued, above all, the development, focusing on the capital-labor relationships, few attention, therefore, was paid to the social rights and the citizenship (Draibe, 2003).

During the 20th century, slowly, however, social policies in Brazil moved from a more 'corporate' social protection system pattern, aimed exclusively at specific categories of workers, as it initially happened in some European countries (France, Germany), to use the classification made by Gosta Esping-Andersen (1990), to the establishment of more comprehensive social policies directed to other popular sectors, although limited, during the dictatorship period, later reaching universalization with the new social rights inserted into the 1988 Constitution, after the authoritarian period.

Before the 1980s, which witnessed many reforms, the shy Brazilian Protection System exhibited a strong centralization at federal level, both financial and political, in addition to an institutional fragmentation and strong clientelistic use of the social policies by the regional and local political groups, which ended up restricting the efficiency of such public policies as a means of income redistribution (Draibe, 1993). After that decade, it started an important process of unification of programs, followed by a decentralization of its management, through covenants and partnerships among the different spheres of the federation, which was accelerated in the following decades.

Even expanded in the last two decades of the 20th century, the new social rights, many of these inserted into the new 1988 Constitution, and the public services in Brazil, especially in the areas of education and health, remained, however, mostly precarious, because their implementation occurred at a moment when the country started to receive the tax containment and State reduction policies, of neoliberal nature, as recommended by the Washington Consensus. The Unified Health System [SUS], for instance, in its concept and universalized reach, is the largest public health system in the world, having conducted, for instance, in 2014 more than four billion procedures and 1.4 billion medical appointments. However, although it provides free medical care to millions of people every day, it remains very precarious because of budgetary restrictions.

In the US, at least until the 1980s – before that country starts to experience a de-industrialization and financialization process – social protection occurred through the companies, for those that remained employed, usually with long term jobs and relatively predictable life (Sennett, 1999) and, therefore, with guaranteed social assistance. Only a small percentage of people, something like one fifth of the population, needed the coverage of a public system, which ended up being slashed after the 1980s. In Brazil, we observe an inversion of this proportion. With more fragile companies, lower salaries and a much higher poverty level, the majority of the Brazilian population, around 80%, depends, for instance, upon the public health system, (Vianna and Machado, 2008). Only more recently it has been tried to introduce private social security and assistance systems. But only around one fifth of the Brazilian population can afford to pay private health and social security services. The vast majority of the population continues to be extremely dependent upon public education, health and social security services.

Therefore, public services and the cash transfer programs play such an essential role in a country with vast parts of the population facing prolonged poverty and marginalization.

During the Workers' Party (PT) governments, of presidents Lula and Dilma Roussef, many cash transfer programs were kept or established. The most important and far reaching ones were: Programa Bolsa Família [Family Grant], Minha Casa Minha Vida [My House My Life], Programa Universidade para Todos (Prouni) [University for Everyone Program] and Luz para Todos [Light for Everyone].

The Family Allowance Program started in 2003, uniting four previously existing social programs: Bolsa Escola [School Allowance], Bolsa Alimentação [Food Allowance], Vale Gás [Cooking Gas Ticket] and Cartão Alimentação [Food Card]. It's a program that reaches today more than 13.5 million families, with a decentralized management shared by the federal and state governments, and by the municipalities. We will analyze this program in detail further in this book, its objectives, results and controversies.

The My House, My Life Program exists since 2009 and sought to unify other programs in order to make it possible the construction of millions of homes for poor families, with a view to reducing the housing deficit in the country, estimated at around six million units at the start of the program. It is also a federal program, included in the Growth Acceleration Program (PAC), an anticyclic economic strategy, adopted in 2007, which sought to mitigate the effects of the global economic crisis started in 2007/2008 in the US. It is, likewise, implemented in a partnership between the States, municipalities, contractors and social movements. Since its release, in March 2009, until 2016, the program had already contracted 4.2 million homes, with 2.6 million having already been delivered, in spite of its deacceleration since then. Because the program involves a sector that hired millions of workers for the construction of the housing units, demands many materials from the national industry, and stimulates consumption, it has contributed to dynamize the economy in the period.

The Program Light for Everyone was established in 2003 with the goal of providing universal access to electricity to families that, still in the 21st century, hadn't had access to such achievement. The initial goal was to serve two million families, especially in the rural environment. The program needed to be extended until 2011 in order to complete all the hired connections, with the president Dilma Rousseff creating in that same year the so-called New Program Light for Everyone, extended until 2014, seeking to reach primarily families of the rural environment of the Northeastern, Center-Western and Northern regions of the country.

In the field of education, in 2004 it was created the ProUni, with the goal of granting scholarships, full or partial (of up to 50%), to students with good performance in the National High School Exam (ENEM). This program was included in the National Education Plan (PDE) and intended that until 2011, at least 30% of the young people aged between 18 and 24 could have access to higher education. The private universities that take part in the ProUni receive from the federal government, in return, a waiver of the payment of taxes, such as the Income Tax, Social Contribution on the Net Profit (CSLL), PIS and Cofins.

In spite of the criticism that they receive, there is no doubt that – if one does not take into account the horizontal cuts in other social policies, caused by the tax containment policies, or the non-accomplishment of more structural reforms that were part of the initial proposals of the Workers' Party – these programs represent an unprecedent effort in the country's history of focused transfer of cash to poor families. The programs of fighting against poverty run by governments that preceded Lula's government, whether during the military period or even in Fernando Henrique Cardoso's government, cannot be compared, whether in terms of the number of recipient families, whether in terms of the financial resources involved, to the programs implemented during Lula's government (Marques et al., 2006).

However, in spite of that, there is few consensus in the country in relation to these programs, especially the Family Allowance, the biggest of them, because of the monetary values involved and the beneficiaries affected. From the right, the criticism has a liberal nature, often based on prejudice, criticizing the very relevance of conducting cash transfer programs to poor people, which, according to these sectors, should seek to leave poverty through their own merit, pay for all the services, without what they call 'paternalism' of the State. From the left, the criticism has a more rational focus and the key argument is that the social policies aimed at fighting poverty should be universalized and not focused, that is, they need to be guaranteed rights, and not concessions of a government, in addition to debates about the conditionalities, the economic effects, among other criticism.

Because of the issue of space of this study, in order to refine the study and taking into account that the purpose of this text is mainly to discuss the impact of conditional cash transfer programs, we will conduct next a more thorough assessment of the Family Allowance Program. This choice can be justified because it is the largest program of fight against poverty in the country, whether because of the values involved or because of the number of beneficiaries. The Family Allowance is also one of the programs that has drawn the most attention of governments, multilateral agencies and researchers around the world so far as the reduction of poverty is concerned. The decision to conduct a more thorough analysis can also be explained because the conditionalities demanded from the families also lead us to discuss the quality of the other public services in the country, that is, it involves a discussion of the entire Brazilian social protection system.

In addition to conducting a more thorough analysis of the Family Allowance Program, this study is also aimed at presenting an overview of the controversies surrounding its relevance and results, ending with a more general assessment of the real impact of this program on the century-old structure of huge social inequality of the country, especially when one compares its results with the performance or not of other more structural social reforms, which are so strongly desired by social movements of the country, and which were defended by the Workers' Party itself.

The Family Allowance Program and its reach

The Family Allowance Program is today the widest conditional cash transfer program in the world. In March 2017, it reached 13.6 million families, something around 50 million people, transferring $2.4 billion BRL to the beneficiaries that month, according to the Ministry of Social Development (MDS). The program's annual budget predicted for 2017 is $29.8 billion BRL (MDS, 2017a).

As it has already been mentioned, the conditional cash transfer programs in Brazil did not start in Lula's government. What Lula actually did was to expand and consolidate the social assistance network that already existed during the Fernando Henrique Cardoso (FHC) government (Hall, 2006), unifying the cash transfer programs of the previous government, the Bolsa Escola [School Allowance], Bolsa Alimentação [Food Allowance], Cartão Alimentação [Food Card] and Auxílio Gás [Cooking Gas Assistance] (Law 10.836 of January 9th, 2004). The program also sought to unify the scattered actions of the federal, state and municipal governments into a single, national direct cash transfer program, through agreements and covenants.

The Family Allowance, however, was not implemented in the first year of Lula's government, in 2003. During the electoral campaign and even before his taking of office as president, Lula and his team had already defined the fighting against poverty as the focus of his social policy, having initially released, in a hastily manner, the Zero Hunger Program [Programa Fome Zero] with a view to generating impact. That program involved, among other objectives, transferring cash to families in situation of extreme poverty, provided that it would be used in the acquisition of food products as defined by the government. With the operational failure of that program, in early 2004, Lula's government created, within its first ministerial reform, the Ministry of Social Development and Fight against Hunger, centralizing all the social and conditional cash transfer programs in a single program, the Family Allowance.

The advocates of the FHC government seek to present the Family Allowance Program as a continuation of previous programs of the FHC's administration. However, the fact is that in Lula's administrations, those public policies were not only unified in a single program, the volume and the scope of federal resources spent in conditional cash transfer programs were considerably expanded (Silva et al., 2007). In addition, the expansion of the Family Allowance Program was conducted in an exceptionally fast pace, with the number of recipient families jumping from 3.6 million in 2003 to 11.1 million in 2006. By the end of 2004, the Family Allowance Program was already implemented in 5,533 municipalities (99.5% of the country's cities), reaching 6,571,842 families, with an annual budget of $5.3 billion BRL. In 2014, it achieved 56 million people, from 14 million families. The spending with the program, as a percentage of the Gross Domestic Product, jumped from under 0.05%, in 2003, to almost 0.5% in 2013, that is, it underwent a tenfold increase in ten years.

The program focuses on families in situation of poverty (monthly per capita income between $85.01 BRL and $170.00 BRL) and of extreme poverty (monthly per capita income of up to $85.00 BRL). In July 2017, the average value of the benefits was $178.44 BRL, with variations according to the number of members of the family, the age of each member and the family income declared to the Single Registry of Social Programs, kept by the Federal Government. In order to register in the Family Allowance in 2017, the family needs to provide evidence that it is in a situation of extreme poverty. The families whose average of the income of all of its members does not exceed $170.00 BRL are entitled to receive the benefit. In the event that the monthly income of the family continues to be lower than $85.00 BRL per person, the family may receive an additional assistance (MDS, 2017b).

The Program is based on three key foundations: cash transfer, conditionalities and the complementary programs. According Campello and Neri (2013), MDS (2011), with the cash transfer, one seeks to provide the families with immediate relief from poverty and the conditionalities would expand the access to basic social rights. In addition, the complementary programs are aimed at encouraging the development of the families in other spheres, so that the beneficiaries may overcome their situation of vulnerability.

The conditionality consists of, when registering in the program and receiving the benefits, these families must, in return, comply with commitments in the fields of health and education in relation to the children. More specifically, the conditions that the families must fulfill in order to access the program's benefits are: (a) to follow the vaccination schedule of the children, as established in the vaccination card, and to follow the growth and development of the children under the age of seven; (b) women aged between 14 and 44 are required to undergo medical monitoring and, if pregnant or breastfeeding, they are required to undergo prenatal follow-up, monitoring their health and that of their babies; (c) all children and adolescents aged between 6 and 15 must obligatorily be enrolled in school and keep a minimum school attendance percentage of 85% of the hourly load; (d) students aged between 16 and 17 are required to maintain a minimum school attendance of 75%; (e) the children and adolescents under 15 years of age, who are at risk or have been rescued from child labor by the Child Labor Eradication Program (PETI), must participate in the Services of Interaction and Strengthening of Ties and to maintain a minimum attendance percentage of 85% of the monthly hourly load of these services.

As the program's target audience is made up of families with very low per capita income, studies showed that the receiving of the Family Allowance in fact changed the basic life conditions of the beneficiaries, taking into account that a larger part of the financial resources received are channeled into the buying of food supplies. A study about the impact of the then Food Allowance program observed that, in the families with monthly per capita income lower than $90.00 BRL, at the time of the study, the trend was to channel 89 cents of each BRL of the benefit to the consumption of food (Ministério da Saúde, 2003).

In addition, in 2003, according to Sergei Soares and Natália Sátyro (2009), the scenario was of discoordination and 'chaos' among the different government spheres, in the management of those various previous programs, especially between the Federal Government and the municipal administrations.

In an attempt to solve the discoordination problems and the problems generated by the overlapping of those various public policies, still in the FHC's government, it was adopted an institutional innovation, which was the creation of the Single Registry of Social Programs (CAD Único). Created in the FHC's government, through the Decree n° 3.877, on July 24th, 2001, and later improved during Lula's governments, this Single Database is a valuable tool used by the public management in the different spheres, for the identification of families in situation of poverty in all municipalities of the country. Because of it, it became possible to store, with relative security, the registration data of the families in situation of vulnerability and, thus, improve the focus on poorer families (Valente, 2003)

In order to be admitted to this database, created by the Decree n° 3.877 of July 24th, 2001, families reply to a questionnaire in the city halls, involving information about the characteristics of the domicile, family members, schooling level and professional qualification of the members of the domicile, as well as data about family expenses. This database enables the federal government to perform a socioeconomic diagnosis of the families and forward them to the appropriate social programs. Some authors, such as Soares and Sátyro (op. cit.), consider the Single Registry as an actual permanent census of the Brazilian poor population, which has been continuously improved. In fact, this database has been intensely used by planners from all over the country and by Brazilian researchers and researchers from around the world.

In the dynamics of the decentralization started in the previous government, the relationships between the municipalities and the Federal Government (Union) started to become more evident already from 2005 onwards, when the federal government started to admit municipalities to the program through the signing of adherence agreements, thus outlining the attributions of each federal entity. The federal government is assigned the implementation and supervision of the Single Registry and the centralized administration of the program, through the national bank Caixa Econômica Federal (CEF), which pays the benefits to the families. The municipalities, with technical support and supervision of the federal states, must conduct the registration of the families, sending and monitoring the return of the data to the CEF, thus maintaining the Single Registry's database always updated, always in contact with the beneficiaries, to whom they must inform about their situation in the program.

Although the decentralization of the program is praised by several agents and authors, taking into consideration the major heterogeneity of an almost continental country like Brazil, the program's operation still continues quite centralized in the Federal Government, because the definition of the beneficiaries, of the thresholds for admission of the families to the program, of the available global budget, occurs exclusively at this government sphere. In 2017, for instance, there was a reduction in the number of recipient families, because of the federal budget cuts. By consulting data of the Ministry of Social Development (MDS) (2017a), one may observe that in March this year the payments were made to 13.6 million recipient families; whereas in July of this same year, the benefits would be paid to only 12.7 million of these (MDS, 2017b), a cut of 900,000 families.

The controversies surrounding the program

Many points of controversy and dispute took over Brazil during Lula's administration surrounding the outcome of the Family Allowance Program (PBF), in terms of its validity, of its effects on the reduction of inequality, of the correctness or not of the option to focus, among others. In the following pages, we seek to present some of these points of controversy and tension.

Focus or universalization

There has been in Brazil, since the option for focused programs in the FHC's administrations, a fierce discussion, in the more knowledgeable sectors of the population and among managers and researchers, which intensified during Lula's administration. In one hand, the defenders of the cash transfer programs focused on the poorer people, of a more liberal matrix, such as Cardoso (2004), arguing for the need of the rational use of scarce resources, of the tax sustainability. On the other hand, those who defended the expansion of the rights for everyone, even though not every one of those stood against the focused policies (Camargo, 2003).

This first point of controversy, perhaps the most intense, exists, therefore, since the inception of the Family Allowance Program and opposes the need for universal social policies – seen as permanent and as rights – and the focused policies, such as the cash transfer programs to the poorer people. Several critics argue that the focused policy attacks only one part of the origin of poverty, casting to a secondary role the need for more horizontal, wide and permanently inclusive public policies, which would be the universal policies (Kerstenetzky, 2009)

Other authors, such as Lavinas (1999), since the FHC's government, and Mattos and Ponczek (2008), also argued that the focus might lead to an estigmatization of the poor families before the population, in addition to a dependency of the beneficiaries, as these programs would be poorly articulated with more comprehensive social policies, of universal nature.

Discouragement to work

Among vast conservative sectors of the Brazilian population, always critical of the Workers' Party and of Lula's administration, this was perhaps the most widely used argument against the Family Allowance Program. Mixing arguments of morality and of liberal nature, such criticism stated that the PBF would encourage these families to stay idle, to 'vagrancy', as nobody should receive money from the Government without 'sweating blood', that is, everyone should leave poverty and improve their financial situation through their own effort, as the opportunities are equal to everyone, a conservative argument that has already been very well disputed by Krugman (2012).

Against such arguments, in a more rational view, and grounding her study in data of the 2006 PNAD [National Household Sample Survey], Kerstenetzky (2009), although critical of the option for the focus, proved quite the opposite, revealing that the participation of the adult beneficiaries of the program in the job market is higher than in the whole of the population. Whereas Medeiros et al. (2007a, 2007b) presented the challenge that it would then be necessary to indicate the level of transfers above which there might be an encouragement to idleness. Opposing the conservative arguments, these researchers showed that, although the PBF implied an average increase of 11% in the beneficiaries' income, the values obtained from the Family Allowance Program's benefits would not be enough to lead to a discouragement to work, which led them to conclude that such arguments would be based more on prejudice than on empirical evidence, thus pointing to the more misleading than scientific nature of the 'laziness cycle' that might be generated by the transfer of cash to the poorer individuals.

The program's conditionality requirements

The imposition of conditions to be fulfilled by the families in order to receive the benefits also generated quite a lot of controversy. There was an intense debate, particularly among researchers, about the fairness of these conditionalities. The developers and defenders of the program argued that the adoption of conditions, which encouraged the insertion of the families in the public education and health services, would lead to the disruption of the cycle of poverty throughout time (Estrella and Ribeiro, 2008; Ferreira et al., 2011; Oliveira et al., 2011). Whereas critics, such as Zimmermann (2006), Monnerat (2007) disputed the conditionalities, taking into account that, according to them, it should be considered that the access to the minimum food supplies is a right of everyone, ensured by the 1988 Constitution, which entailed that there should be no conditionalities for accessing the benefit. For some of these authors, to demand that the population comply with certain conditions in order to have access to the cash transfer programs means to deny the basic right of these families to receive their share of the socially produced wealth, which should be distributed by these programs and by other universal social policies with no strings attached (Silva et al., 2007; Marques and Mendes, 2006).

Monnerat et al (2007) agrees that such conditionalities may facilitate the access of parts of the population that otherwise would hardly manage to access such services. However, she disputed the capacity of the education and health services in the country, usually very precarious, to absorb in a satisfactorily manner the rise of demand caused by the program's compensation requirements. Silva (2007), even while acknowledging that the conditionalities are a structuring pillar of the cash transfer programs, goes on the same direction and argues that the basic social services in the fields of education, health and labor are insufficient, both in quantity and in quality, in order to meet the basic demands of the families included in these programs. Thus, according to him, it would be unfair to demand that they comply with those conditionalities, taking into account that the State itself, in its different spheres, cannot provide such services in an appropriate manner.

Other researchers, such as Estrella and Ribeiro (2008) also disputed the conditionalities, pointing out that the basic education was already universalized in the country and that, thus, the government should focus instead on improving the quality of the education and health services provided and not on its access. In addition, these authors also disputed the efficiency in the control of such compensation from the families. Seeking to investigate the impact of the conditionalities, Mourão et al, 2012) could not find significant differences in the school attendance of recipient and non-recipient students aged between 6 and 17.

In favor of the conditionalities, the results of a research conducted by Pires (2008, 2013), performed about the registration of the beginning of the PBF, revealed that, before admission to the program, there was a high percentage of children and young people that didn't study and also didn't work (45% of the young people above 18 years of age), which would provide evidence that the conditionalities would be somehow fulfilling the desired role. Melo and Duarte (2010) also investigated the correlation between the inclusion into the PBF and the school attendance of children and adolescents aged between 5 and 14 in the family agriculture, in four states of the Northeastern region of the country, where is located a large part of the program's beneficiaries. The results of the investigation revealed that the participation in the program did raise the school attendance of these children in an interval between 5.4% and 5.9%, depending on the federal state, with the conditionalities of the programs, however, being efficient in the case of the girls, but rather inefficient for boys, probably because there is a higher demand for their workforce in the rural setting.

Authors that dispute the effect of the conditionalities ponder, however, that there is always a positive correlation between family income and years of schooling of its members, both in the case of recipients and non-recipients, that schooling is always a factor of raising of income in any studied population (Tavares, 2010; Cacciamali et al., 2010).

Financial impact and multiplying effect of the program

Another important point of discussion involves the real effects of the program on the whole of the economy of the country, of the regions and of the municipalities. As discussed by Demo (2006) and Castro (2009), among the population, vast sectors disputed the social and economic justification of this spending.

Opposing those that doubted the fairness of the public spending in cash transfer programs, and particularly of the Family Allowance, several investigations sought to prove its positive, multiplying effect, on the economy. A research conducted in 2011 by the IPEA [Brazilian Institute of Applied Economic Research] concluded that 56% of the spending with the federal government's social programs ended up returning to the public coffers in the form of collected taxes, and, according to that study, the largest multiplying agent was the Family Allowance Program. According to the study, of each $1.00 BRL spent with the program, the GDP raised by $1.44 BRL, whereas the families' income raised by 2.25%, after this spending went through the entire circuit of multiplication of income in the local and national economies. The study came to the conclusion that the Family Allowance Program generates more gain for the national economy than its cost, with this multiplying effect being twice larger that that generated by the payment of the public debt's interests, taking into account that, unlike the latter, the most part of the PBF's spending with the families goes directly to the consumption chain (IPEA, 2011). In a new and meticulous study (Neri et al, 2013), an assessment showed that these effects are even bigger.

Even without opposing the programs and considering the PBF as a successful experience, some authors, like Ferreira et al. (2011), warned about the dangers that these investments in cash transfer programs could induce the municipal administrations of small municipalities to a lesser effort in generating their own tax revenues and in improving the quality of life of their population. The same discussion exists in Brazil about the role in terms of encouragement to accommodation that the Fund of Participation of the Municipalities – FPM, a federal constitutional transfer to federal states and municipalities, could play on the municipal administrations (Araújo and Siqueira, 2016).

In a study conducted about an assessment of one decade of the Family Allowance Program, Campello and Neri (2013) argued, however, that the cash transfers made to the families by the programs, in addition to helping them, greatly helped the economic and social development of the country. Sicsu (2017) argued that Lula's administrations should not be characterized just as an 'age of consumption', but rather that the measures aimed at the strengthening of the internal market had a very positive effect to raise the investment in the country.

Rosinke et al. (2011) remember that, in addition, the cash transfer programs help the country in times of crisis, mitigating its impact, serving as a tool to hold the level of consumption. Studying the effects of the Family Allowance Program on the economy of the municipalities, they concluded that this program sets in motion a significant portion of the local economies, with positive results. They also stressed that the families, with an increased monthly fixed income, began to have access to microcredit, and could now buy in the local market not only food but also household appliances, building materials and other products in installments, increasing the circulation of income in the regions and stimulating the commerce and the local development, conclusions which are similar to those reached by Marques (2005). The studies indicated that the lower the Human Development Index (IDH) and the available revenue of the municipality, the higher the impact of the cash transfers on the local economy. It should be stressed that in municipalities of the Northeastern region, there are cases where up to 45% of the population receive the PBF benefits, which alters considerably the flow of income in the municipal economy (Marques et al, 2006).

Results in the reduction of hunger and poverty

In spite of the controversy surrounding the Family Allowance Program, which is the result of the political polarization that Brazil has experienced in the past years, there is a consensus among the researchers that the PBF fulfilled one of its objectives, which was to promote an immediate reduction of poverty for millions of families, through direct cash transfer. Several well-grounded studies proved this outcome of the program. Indicators from official organizations also revealed such conclusion, such as those of the National Household Sample Survey (PNAD) and the communications, reports and other studies of the Institute of Applied Economic Research (IPEA).

These results were confirmed by several other studies, such as the research conducted by Dias (2008) and by IPEA (2011), which showed that, although the values of the PBF's benefits are very low, and thus not changing the actual life conditions of the families from a structural perspective, they represent a significant rise of their income, when one takes into consideration their situation of extreme poverty. This becomes even more relevant when one study (Duarte et al., 2009) showed that 88% of the assistance received by the families are used in the buying of food, with the children as the main beneficiaries.

Several studies attested the reduction of poverty and of inequality in the period of application of the PBF. Data about the reduction of poverty between 2003 and 2012 showed that the indexes of poverty and extreme poverty fell significantly. According to PNAD data, between 2003 and 2011, the proportion of the population with per capita household income below the highest poverty threshold fell from 24.4% to 10.2%. The reduction of the absolute poverty index may be observed in Graph 12.1.

Between 2003 and 2009, the growth of the real per capita income of the 10% poorest individuals was 69%, according to the PNADs. This rate of growth of the poorest individuals' income was 550% higher than that of the wealthy individuals, in an inverse dynamics to what happened in countries such as the United States and England, and even in the other BRICs countries (China, India, South Africa and Russia) (IPEA, 2012).

All the indicators pointed, therefore, to a reduction of the extreme poverty in the country during the application of the PBF. When we look at universal indicators, it may also be observed that Brazil was one of the countries who

Graph 12.1 Population with per capita household income below the highest poverty threshold. Millenium goals (%)

Source: Graph prepared with data from IPEA (2012, p. 10), from PNADs

contributed the most towards the fulfillment of the Millenium Development Goals (MDGs) established by the United Nations, especially in Goal A of the MDG 1, of reduction of extreme poverty. This can also be observed through the data of the 5th National Report of Follow-up of the Millenium Development Goals (IPEA, 2014), which point both to a substantial reduction in those indexes of extreme poverty and to a reduction of the Gini coefficient.

The world, too, has been reducing the extreme poverty rates in the past decades, as encouraged in MDG 1, which recommended reducing extreme poverty by half between 1999 and 2019. However, even having reduced this index from 47% to 22% in the period between 1990 and 2013 (before what was expected, then), there are still more than 1.2 billion people around the world in this situation, living with an income lower than US$1.25 a day. But when one takes into consideration the size of its population, Brazil was one of the countries that contributed the most to achieve goal A of the MDG 1, reducing extreme poverty not by half, but to less than one seventh of the 1990's level: from 25.5% to 3.5% in 2012 (IPEA, op. cit.). Soares et al. (2010) showed that the PBF was responsible for a significant part of this reduction in the extreme poverty in Brazil.

The poorer the family, the more significant are the benefits of the program. Soares et al (op. cit.) also concluded that the PBF had considerable effects for the reduction of the child malnutrition, to prevent new generations of children completely marginalized and with severe delay in development.

There were also other controversies surrounding the Family Allowance Program (PBF), such as the construction of self-sustained exit doors from the

232 Robério Paulino

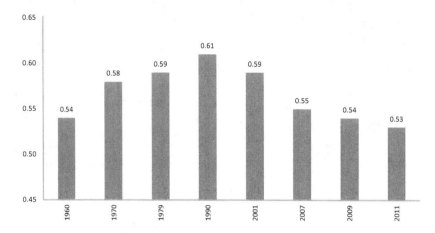

Graph 12.2 Evolution of inequality (Gini coefficient)

Source: Graph prepared with data tabulated by the Institute of Applied Economic Research [IPEA] (2012, p. 8), from the National Household Sample Surveys [PNADs]

program to the families (Sousa, 2009), the repressed demand of the program, among others, but we won't deal with them here because of the limit defined for the study.

The comparison of the advances with what was not achieved

Seeking a global assessment of the impacts of these programs, the question that we may formulate is then: after three and a half terms of Workers' Party governments, did the programs of direct and conditional cash transfer to the poorer families, substantially expanded already in the first Lula's administration, change from a structural perspective the historical matrix of inequality in the Brazilian society, attacking the more profound generating factors of the century-old social apartheid in the country?

The possible replies to this question depend, evidently, upon the ruler that one uses to measure the results of these programs, that is, upon the different viewpoints from which one may look at the question. If the ruler is only to provide the more marginalized sectors of the population with immediate relief from poverty, without attacking the more structural factors that reproduce it constantly in the country, then you'll get one reply. If the results achieved are discussed taking as parameter the non-achievement of these other structural changes, then the reply shall be different.

In spite of all the criticism from the country's conservative sectors, forever insensitive to the deep social inequality, as it has been showed by several studies and as we sought to do in this study, there is no doubt that there is nothing in the country's documented History, in the past six decades, that may be compared to the fast reduction of absolute poverty in Brazil from 2003 onwards, as we could observe from Graph 12.1. Between 2004, year when one could observe the first impacts of the Zero Hunger and of the Family Allowance (PBF) program, and 2011, it was eight consecutive years of fall in the absolute poverty index. Until June 2012, it was 11 consecutive years of fall in the Gini coefficient curve (IPEA, 2012). The impact of the conditional cash transfer programs, and, particularly, of the PBF, is indisputable in the reduction of extreme poverty in Brazil, alleviating the suffering of 50 million beneficiaries, one quarter of the Brazilian population, for which one may state that it is an absolutely successful program if the parameters are the very goals established by the program. PBF, in this context, is unparalleled in the world.

However, when you look from another perspective, we might make the following question: is that what one might expect from a left-wing government, of a party that emerged from the working classes, of which people expected more daring changes in favor of them? Second, are these gains of the poorer families definitive, have they been transformed into vested rights, taking them permanently away from poverty, or can they be annulled in a short period of time by the new governments and by the new political and economic conditions? Have the structural factors that re-feed poverty on a daily basis in the country been changed during Lula's and Dilma Roussef's governments? Has the essence of the neoliberal policy that has been applied in the past 27 years, which has been slashing social rights and reducing public spending, been changed with these programs in this period? Unfortunately, the answer to these questions is no.

The fact is that, even after 13 years of governments of the Workers' Party and its programs, Brazil continues to be a deeply unequal country, and the fundamental structure that daily re-feeds this inequality has not been changed.

As it has been said in the beginning of this study, Brazil never conducted a real Land Reform and the Workers' Party has also never committed to facing the large estate, one of the fundamental pillars of the Brazilian conservationism, which overthrew Dilma Roussef's constitutionally elected government. The Workers' Party even placed a representative of the large estate in its cabinet. In the 1950s, the main source of survival in Brazil continued to be the land. And perhaps the most important century-old factor for inequality in Brazil has been precisely the concentration of land and the exclusion of millions from it since the colonization.

Until recently, all over the world, a small farm or rural estate was the best social security and the food and housing security that a family could have. In it, a family could plant and raise animals for food, especially for the children: the adults could work and then live their old age relatively safe as to food and housing. Unfortunately, in Brazil, even after the Workers' Party governments, the land-ownership structure remains deeply concentrated and millions of people never had access to a piece of land. The shy distribution of lots that occurred in the period did not essentially change this century-old matrix.

It is true that the rural population has been diminishing all over the world and the country is increasingly urban. But its agricultural production focused on the export agribusiness keeps the best land away from the production of food, extracting perhaps from the poor families in the big cities, through the rise of prices, the same value or more than what is given to them through the cash transfer programs. One should take into account that the average income gain of the recipient families with the Family Allowance Program was 15%, as indicated in several studies. A simple rise of prices at this rate or at a higher rate can annul such gains of the families.

Another reform that could have been implemented but that the Workers' Party governments did not have the courage or the willingness to do was the reform of the Brazilian tax structure, very unfair, which concentrates income and wealth at each purchase and sale operation. Unlike even many other capitalist countries, where there is progressiveness in the incidence of taxes, in Brazil, the tax structure, like a Robin Hood in reverse, is extremely regressive, with the poor individuals paying proportionally much more taxes than the wealthy, taking into account that the taxes in the country are mainly levied on the products and the production and much less on the income and the capital gains. Therefore, what one gives with one hand through these cash transfer programs is taken away with the other. The Workers' Party governments did not dare institute a progressiveness of the taxes, as it occurs in many capitalist countries in the world, taxing the wealthy and facilitating for the poor, keeping unchanged a perverse tax structure, that causes poverty and inequality.

In addition, the federal tax revenue is largely transferred to the payment of the federal public debt, which consumed, annually, something around 45% of the Federal General Budget in the past years, transferring to the financial sector, through the high taxes levied on products, a large proportion of the income of the poor and medium class families. The Lula's and Dilma Rousseff's governments didn't change a thing in this concentrating mechanism of the public debt. On the contrary, they put a banker in the command of the economic policy.

The new government of Michel Temer has been raising taxes fast. It has done so on fuels and announces raises on the income tax, which may more than annul part of the gains from the social programs. Still in 2016, with the economic crisis encouraged by the political crisis experienced in the country, for the first time in 11 years, there was a reduction of the earnings of the Brazilian worker. According to data from Brazilian Institute of Geography and Statistics [IBGE, 2016], the average income that was $1,950.00 BRL in 2014, fell to $1,850.00 BRL in 2015, a 5% reduction in the workers' earnings in only one year, which shows how the gains obtained by the cash transfer programs may be removed in a few years.

The conclusion from a wide perspective that goes beyond the surface of the issue is that the conditional cash transfer programs of Lula's and Dilma Roussef's governments, although they were important for providing millions of families with relief from immediate poverty, they changed only the epidermical, but not the century-old matrix that generates a deep inequality in the country, which means that their gains may be reduced or even annulled in a short period of time by the more conservative governments that are now taking over the country, as these benefits have not been turned into permanent rights; they are governmental programs, thus temporary, in addition to being directed only to specific social sectors and not universal rights.

In fact, the programs of this modality never went far from the recommendations of the World Bank in the last three decades, of reducing the size of the State and its scope, of cutting spending and universal rights in a horizontal way, applying in a focused manner only compensatory programs to the poorer segments of the population. The effort made by the Workers' Party governments must not be disregarded at all, as we previously showed, but the party wasted a great opportunity of structurally changing the country, proving that it wasn't up to the challenge.

By betting in alliances with the conservative sectors of the agro-capitalist and financial elite in order to obtain governability in a patrimonialistic and rotten State, that is, in the institutional path, deaccelerating the social fights, the Workers' Party fell prey to the capital's trap, of having to apply the neoliberal program, although in a pace slower than the one desired by capital. The Brazilian big business, however, never accepted the expansion of new social rights in Brazil, obtained especially in the 1980s, while around the world governments eliminated them. Today, the Workers' Party see its role being discarded by this very same capital and by its representatives in the parliament, which imposed the impeachment of president Dilma, legally elected, while they conduct a real massacre against Lula.

The allies of yesterday are rapidly conducting a deep reversal of the few social rights obtained with such struggle of the Brazilian people and they shall also impose cuts in the cash transfer programs, if the popular reaction does not stop them. The survival of these conquests of the Brazilian people will ultimately depend upon the intensity of the social fights in the coming years.

References

Araújo, J. M., and Siqueira, R. B. Demanda por gastos públicos locais: evidências dos efeitos de ilusão fiscal no Brasil. *Revista Estudos Econômicos*, v. 46, n. 1. São Paulo, January/March 2016.

Banco Mundial. *Conditional Cash Transfers: Reducing Present and Future Poverty*. Washington, DC, 2009

Fiszbein, Ariel, Schady, Norbert, Ferreira, Francisco H. G., Grosh, Margaret, Keleher, Niall, Olinto, Pedro, and Skoufias, Emmanuel. 2009. Conditional Cash Transfers : Reducing Present and Future Poverty. World Bank Policy Research Report. Washington, DC: World Bank. https://openknowledge.worldbank.org/handle/10986/2597 License: CC BY 3.0 IGO.

Cacciamali, M. C., Tatei, F., and Batista, N. F. Impactos do Programa Bolsa Família federal sobre o trabalho infantil e a frequência escolar. *Revista de Economia Contemporânea*, v. 14, n. 2, 269–301, 2010.

Camargo, J. M. Gastos sociais: focalizar *versus* universalizar". *Ipea. Políticas Sociais – Acompanhamento e Análise*, n. 7, ago, pp. 117–121, 2003.

Campello, Tereza, and Neri, Marcelo C. (orgs). *O Programa Bolsa Família uma década de inclusão e cidadania*. Brasília: Ipea, 2013. Disponível em: www.ipea.gov.br/portal/images/stories/PDFs/livros/livros/livro_bolsafamilia_10anos.pdf. Access: em June 30, 2017.

Cardoso, R. Sustentabilidade, o desafio das políticas sociais no século 21. *São Paulo em Perspectiva*, vol. 18, n° 2, pp. 42–48, 2004.

Castro, Henrique Carlos de Oliveira de; Walter, Maria Inez Machado Telles; Santana, Cora Maria Bender de; Stephanou, Michelle Conceição. Percepções sobre o Programa Bolsa Família na sociedade brasileira. Revista Opinião Pública, Campinas, v. 15, n. 2, p. 333–355, November 2009. http://dx.doi.org/10.1590/S0104-62762009000200003. Access: February 20, 2017.

Demo, Pedro. *Pobreza política: a pobreza mais intensa da pobreza brasileira*. Campinas: Autores Associados, 2006.

Dias, M. N. A. *O Programa Bolsa Família no município de Bacabal - MA: avaliação de implementação com o foco nas condicionalidades*. Postgraduate Program in Public Policy, Master's degree in Public Policy (Master's degree dissertation), Universidade Federal do Piauí, Terezinha, 2008. http://acervodigital.mds.gov.br/xmlui/bitstream/handle/123456789/481/www.dominiopublico.gov.br-download-texto-cp070042.pdf?sequence=1. Access: July 27, 2017.

Draibe, S. *O Welfare State no Brasil*. Núcleo de Estudos de Políticas Públicas. UNICAMP. (Caderno de Pesquisa, n.08). Campinas, 1993.

Draibe, S. A política social no período FHC e o sistema de proteção social. *Tempo Social*. São Paulo, v. 15, n. 2, pp. 63–102, November 2003.

Duarte, G. B., Sampaio, B., and Sampaio, Y. Programa Bolsa Família: impacto das transferências sobre os gastos com alimentos em famílias rurais. *Revista de Economia e Sociologia Rural*, v. 47, n. 4, pp. 903–918, 2009.

Esping-Andersen, G. *The Three Worlds of the Welfare Capitalism*. Princeton, NJ: Princeton University Press, 1990.

Estrella, J., and Ribeiro, L. M. Qualidade da gestão das condicionalidades do Programa Bolsa Família: uma discussão sobre o índice de gestão descentralizada. *Revista de Administração Pública*, Rio de Janeiro, v. 42, n. 3, pp. 625–641, 2008.

Ferreira, M. A. M., Jimenez, B. S., and Holzer, M. The Contributions of Public Management in Improving Citizens' Quality of Life: An Analysis of Brazil's Conditional Cash Transfer Program. In *Public Management Research Conference*, 2011, Syracuse. Anais eletrônicos. Syracuse, 2011, pp. 1–35.

Florentino, M. G. (Org.). *Tráfico, cativeiro e liberdade: Rio de Janeiro, século XVII–XX*. Rio de Janeiro: Civilização Brasileira, 2005.

Furtado, C. *Formação Econômica do Brasil*. Rio de Janeiro: Companhia Editora Nacional. 32 Edição, 2005.

Hall, A. From Fome Zero to Bolsa Família: Social Policies and Poverty Alleviation Under Lula. *Journal of Latin American Studies*, n° 38, pp. 689–709, 2006.

IBGE. Ministério do Planejamento, Desenvolvimento e Gestão. Instituto Brasileiro de Geografia e Estatística - IBGE. Diretoria de Pesquisas. Coordenação de Trabalho e Rendimento. Pesquisa Nacional por Amostra de Domicílios. Síntese de indicadores 2015. Rio de Janeiro. 2016. https://biblioteca.ibge.gov.br/visualizacao/livros/liv98887.pdf. Access: February 20, 2017.

IPEA. Gastos com a Política Social: alavanca para o crescimento com distribuição de renda. *Comunicados do Ipea*, n° 75, Fevereiro de 2011. Disponível em: www.ipea.gov.br/portal/index.php?option=com_content&id=7110. Acess: July 20, 2017.

IPEA. A Década Inclusiva (2001–2011): Desigualdade, Pobreza e Políticas de Renda. *Comunicados do IPEA*, n° 155, 25 de setembro de 2012. www.ipea.gov.br/agencia/images/stories/PDFs/comunicado/120925_comunicadodoipea155_v5.pdf. Access: July 27, 2017.

IPEA. *Objetivos de Desenvolvimento do Milênio: Relatório Nacional de Acompanhamento*. Coordenação: Instituto de Pesquisa Econômica Aplicada e Secretaria de Planejamento e Investimentos Estratégicos; supervisão: Grupo Técnico para o acompanhamento dos ODM. – Brasília: Ipea: MP, SPI, 2014. www.ipea.gov.br/portal/images/stories/PDFs/140523_relatorioodm.pdf. Access: July 27, 2017.

Kerstenetzky, C. L. Redistribuição e desenvolvimento? A economia política do Programa Bolsa Família. *Dados, Revista de Ciências Sociais*, v. 52, n. 1, pp. 53–83, 2009.

Krugman, P. *Os conservadores e o mito da igualdade de oportunidades*. São Paulo: O Estado de São Paulo, January 2012, p. A8.

Lavinas, L. Renda mínima: práticas e viabilidade. *Novos Estudos Cebrap*, n. 53, pp. 65–84, p. 72, March 1999.

Marques, R. M., and Mendes, Á. The Social in Lula's Government:The Construction of a New Populism. *Revista Economia Política*, v. 26, n. 1, January/March 2006, São Paulo. Disponível em: www.scielo.br/scielo.php?script=sci_arttext&pid=S0101-31572006000100004. Access: em: July 23, 2017.

Marques, Rosa Maria. A importância do Bolsa Família nos municípios brasileiros [The importance of the Family Allowance in the Brazilian municipalities]. *Caderno de Estudos Desenvolvimento Social em Debate*, Brasília, MDS, n. 1, 2005.

MARQUES, R., MENDES, A.; LEITE, M. G. e JANSEN, M.R. O Bolsa Família e o BPC: cobertura e importância nos municípios. [The Family Allowance and the Continuous Benefit (BPC): Coverage and Importance in the Brazilian Municipalities: Research Report]. Secretaria de Avaliação e Gestão da Informação. Relatório de pesquisa. MDS, Brasília, 2006

Mattos, E., and Ponczek, V. O efeito do estigma sobre os beneficiários de programas de transferência de renda no Brasil [The Effect of the Stigma on the Beneficiaries of Cash Transfer Programs in Brazil]. *Working paper*, São Paulo, 2007. www.eesp.fgv.br/publicacao_detalhe.php?idPublicacao=481. Access: July 21, 2008.

MDS. *Bolsa Família vai repassar R$ 2,4 bilhões aos beneficiários no mês de março* [Family Allowance Will Transfer $2.4bn BRL to the Beneficiaries in March]. Brasília: Ministério de Desenvolvimento Social, março, 2017a. www.mds.gov.br/webarquivos/sala_de_imprensa/boletins/release/2017/marco/20032017_boletim_pagamento_marco.html. Access: July 25, 2017.

MDS. *Governo federal repassará R$ 2,3 bilhões aos beneficiários do Bolsa Família em julho* [The Federal Government will transfer $2.3bn BRL to the beneficiaries of the Family Allowance in July]. Brasília: Ministério de Desenvolvimento Social, julho, 2017b. http://mds.gov.br/area-de-imprensa/noticias/2017/julho/governo-federal-repassara-r-2-3-bilhoes-aos-beneficiarios-do-bolsa-familia-em-julho. Access: July 25, 2017.

Medeiros, Marcelo, Britto, Tatiana, and Soares, Fábio. Programas focalizados de transferência de renda: contribuições para o debate [Focused Cash Transfer Programs: Contributions to the Debate]. *Texto para discussão*, n. 1283, 2007a. Brasília, Ipea.

Medeiros, Marcelo, Britto, Tatiana, and Soares, Fábio. Transferência de Renda no Brasil [Cash Transfer in Brazil]. *Novos Estudos*, n. 79, p. 5–21, November 2007b.

Melo, Raul da Mota Silveira, and Duarte, Gisléia Benini. Impacto do Programa Bolsa Família sobre a frequência escolar: o caso da agricultura familiar no Nordeste do Brasil [Impact of the Family Allowance Program on the School Attendance: The Case of the Family Agriculture in the Northeast of Brazil]. *Rev. Econ. Sociol. Rural.*, v. 48, n. 3, pp. 635–657, 2010. www.scielo.br/scielo.php?pid=S0103-20032010000300007&script=sci_abstract. Access: July 20, 2017.

Ministério da Saúde. *Avaliação do Programa Bolsa Alimentação – Estudo 2: Análise de Impacto Preliminar* [Assessment of the Food Allowance Program – Study 2: Preliminary Impact Analysis]. Brasília: Ministério da Saúde, 2003.

Monnerat, Giselle Lavinas, Senna, Mônica de Castro Maia, Schottz, Vanessa, Magalhães, Rosana, and Burlandy, Luciene. Do direito incondicional à condicionalidade do direito: as contrapartidas do Programa Bolsa Família [From the Unconditional Right to the Conditionality of the Right: The Compensations of the Family Allowance Program]. *Ciência e saúde coletiva*, v. 12, n. 6, pp. 1453–1462, 2007. www.scielo.br/scielo.php?pid=S1413-81232007000600008&script=sci_abstract&tlng=pt. Access: July 18, 2017.

Mourão, L.; Macedo de Jesus, A.; Ferreira, M. C. Evaluation of the Brazilian Family Grant Program: a quasi-experimental study in the State of Rio de Janeiro. Psicologia: Reflexão e Crítica. vol.25 no.4. Porto Alegre, 2012. In: http://www.scielo.br/scielo.php?script=sci_arttext&pid=S0102-79722012000400011. Access: February 20, 2018.

Neri, Marcelo Côrtes, Vaz, Fabio Monteiro, Souza, Pedro Herculano Guimarães Ferreira De. Macroeconomic Effects of the Bolsa Família Program: A Comparative Analysis of Social Transfers. In Tereza Campello and Marcelo Cortês Neri (Editors), Bolsa Família Program: a decade of social inclusion in Brazil. Brasília: Ipea, 2014. *Disponível em: http://www.mds.gov.br/webarquivos/publicacao/bolsa_familia/Livros/Bolsa10anos_Sumex_Ing.pdf* Access: February 20, 2018

Oliveira, Fabiana de Cássia Carvalho;, Cotta, Rosângela Minardi Mitre, Sant'Ana, Luciana Ferreira da Rocha, Priore, Silvia Eloíza and Franceschini, Sylvia do Carmo Castro. Programa Bolsa Família e estado nutricional infantil: desafios estratégicos [Family Allowance Program and the Child Nutritional Status]. *Ciência & Saúde Coletiva*, v. 16, n. 7, Rio de Janeiro: July 2011. In: www.scielo.br/scielo.php?script=sci_arttext&pid=S1413-81232011000800030&lng=es&nrm=iso&tlng=pt. Access: July 26, 2017.

Pires, André. Bolsa Família e políticas públicas universalizantes: o caso de um município paulista. In: *Cadernos de Pesquisa. Tema em destaque, políticas e programas de educação no Brasil.* V.38. n. 134. São Paulo, Maio/Ago., 2008.

Pires, André. Afinal, para que servem as condicionalidades em educação do Programa Bolsa Família?. Ensaio: aval. pol. públ. Educ. Rio de Janeiro: 2013. Disponível em: http://www.scielo.br/scielo.php?pid=S0104-40362013000300007&script=sci_abstract&tlng=pt. Access. February 20, 2018.

Rosinke, João Germano; Heck, Cláudia Regina; Dalfovo, Wylmor Constantino Tives and Ruscheinsky, Aloisio. Efeitos sociais e econômicos para o desenvolvimento local através das contribuições do Programa Bolsa Família no município de Sinop-MT no período de 2004 a 2009 [Social and Economic Effects for the Local Development of the Contributions of the Family Allowance Program in the Municipality of Sinop-MT in the Period From 2004 to 2009]. *Revista Interações, Campo Grande*, v. 12, n. 1, p. 77–88, January/June, 2011.

Sennett, Richard. *A corrosão do caráter: as consequências pessoais do trabalho no novo capitalismo* [The Corrosion of the Character: The Personal Consequences of the Work in the New Capitalism]. Rio de Janeiro: Record, 1999, 204p.

Sicsu, J. *Governos Lula: a era do consumo?*[Lula's Governments: The Age of Consumption?]. Texto para Discussão 021, Instituto de Economia, Universidade Federal do Rio de Janeiro. Rio de Janeiro: 2017.

Silva, M. O., Yasbek, M. C., and di Giovanni, G. *A política social brasileira no século XXI: a prevalência dos programas de transferência de renda* [The Brazilian Social Policy in the 21st Century: The Prevalence of the Cash Transfer Programs]. 3 ed. São Paulo: Cortez, 2007.

Soares, F.V., Ribas, R. P., and Osório, R. G. Evaluating the Impact of Brazil's Bolsa Família: Cash Transfer Programs in Comparative Perspective. *Latin American Research Review*, v. 45, n. 2, pp. 173–190, 2010.

Soares, S., Osório, R. G., Soares, F. V., Medeiros, M., and Zepeda, E. *Programa de transferência condicionada de renda no Brasil, Chile e México: impactos sobre a desigualdade* [Conditional Cash Transfer Program in Brazil, Chile and Mexico: Impacts on Inequality]. Brasília, DF: IPEA, 2007.

Soares, S., and Sátyro, N. *O Programa Bolsa Família: desenho institucional, impactos e possibilidades futuras* [The Family Allowance Program: Institutional Outline, Impacts and Future Possibilities]. Brasília: IPEA, Texto para Discussão, 2009, n° 1424. www.ipea.gov.br/portal/index.php?option=com_content&view=article&id=4980&catid=272. Access: July 25, 2017.

Sousa, J. M. C. de. *A superação da pobreza através da distribuição justa das riquezas sociais: uma análise da consistência teórica do Programa Bolsa Família e das perspectivas dos beneficiários de saída auto-sustentada do programa* [The Overcoming of Poverty Through the Just Distribution of Social Wealth: An Analysis of the Theoretical Consistency of the Family Allowance Program and of the Perspectives of the Beneficiaries of a Self-Sustained Exit of the Program]. Dissertation (Master's degree in Public Administration) – Escola Brasileira de Administração Pública e de Empresas da Fundação Getúlio Vargas, Rio de Janeiro, 2009.

Tavares, P. A. Efeito do programa bolsa família sobre a oferta de trabalho das mães [Effect of the Family Allowance Program on the Supply of Employment of the Mothers]. *Revista Economia e Sociedade*, Campinas, v. 19, n. 3 (40), pp. 613–635, dez. 2010. www.scielo.br/pdf/ecos/v19n3/08.pdf. Access: July 23, 2017.

Valente, A. L. O Programa Nacional de Bolsa Escola e as ações afirmativas no campo educacional [The National School Allowance Program and the affirmative actions in the educational field]. *Revista Brasileira de Educação*, n. 24, set./out./nov./dez, pp. 165–182, 2003.

Viana, A. L. D., and Machado, C. V. Proteção social em saúde: um balanço dos 20 anos do SUS [Social Protection in Health: An Assessment of the 20 Years of the Unified Health System (SUS)]. *Physis: Revista de Saúde Coletiva*, v. 18, n. 4, pp. 645–684. Biblioteca Digital da Produção Intelectual – BDPI, Universidade de São Paulo. São Paulo: 2008. www.producao.usp.br/bitstream/handle/BDPI/9466/art_VIANA_Protecao_social_em_saude_um_balanco_dos_2008.pdf?sequence=1. Access: July 25, 2017.

Zimmermann, C. R. Os programas sociais sob a ótica dos direitos humanos: o caso do bolsa família no Governo Lula no Brasil. *Sur. Revista Internacional de Direitos Humanos*, [online] v. 3, n. 4, pp. 144–159, 2006. www.scielo.br/pdf/sur/v3n4/08.pdf. Access: July 25, 2017.

13 Conclusions

Pedro Chadarevian

Several are the labels used to define Brazil, always in the superlative. A giant of the tropics, the largest economy in the south of the globe, the fastest growing country in the 20th century. Why then does it remain strangely condemned to be the eternal 'country of the future', to resume the expression coined by Stephen Zweig in 1941? Brazil is certainly, many claim, a land of contrasts: alongside its advanced industrial complex, the great infrastructure works and the skyscrapers of its multitudinous metropolis live together tens of millions of families in conditions of great social vulnerability. But perhaps the one who best explains the fate of the Latin American colossus is Celso Furtado, for whom a development project in the tropics was doomed to an 'interrupted construction'.

The construction that Furtado refers to is a more just, democratic and egalitarian country. The logic of his collectivist discourse derives from Keynes, and his ideas definitely inspired the lefts in power in Brazil, from Goulart, the president deposed by the military coup in the 1960s, to Lula and Rousseff, the president deposed by the judicial plot, 50 years later.[1]

The diagnosis of this perspective on development is that the elite paradoxically resist the modernization of the country. Its fundamentally anti-national nature – the first to ally with foreign capital – subverts the working class to harsh conditions of exploitation, sharpening distributive conflict. Its project of power resulted in the huge gap between rich and poor in Brazil, which has deepened with the crises of the lost decades of 1980 (that of hyperinflation) and 1990 (that of neoliberalism). The dismantling of homes of poor families often left no other way than underemployment, informality, and even crime. The country holds the record number of homicides on the planet, more than 60,000 a year, a number of victims of a conflict of a particular type that surpasses that of real wars such as Syria. At the root of this conflict stands income inequality. Inequality that imposes a practically insurmountable gap between, on the one hand, a reduced elite with privileged access to quality (private) education and health, decent housing and the best security that money can buy, and, on the other hand, a mass of miserable dependents of a failed state that did not do much more than reproduce the conditions for the gap to remain.

Except for the 'Lula years'. In this short period of 13 years, the favorable conditions for establishing a redistributive process in the Brazilian economy were met. This was reflected in different aspects, such as the increasing share of wages in national income, or the greater access by poor families to consumer goods, credit, air travel, and higher education. In these booming years, the dignity and hope of a people once abandoned to their fate was rescued. The integration of these poorer strata into the formal economy seemed like a big deal.

All have benefited, although the income growth of the richest has been at a slower pace. The rise of the popular classes, however, provoked the rage of the wealthier classes who perceived this historical movement of social inclusion as a threat to their privileges. The angry reaction on the part of right-wing sectors that have resumed hegemony in the post-coup of 2016 is not an exclusivity of the Brazilian scenario, and occurs as a confrontation with the prominence of progressive governments and social movements in the period. Latin America was the scene in the recent period of a transformation in the composition of the State, with the opening for greater participation of workers and minorities. From Chávez to Morales, Mujica to Rousseff, Correa to the Kirchners, there are many nuances in nature and depths of the reforms undertaken that affected the regime of accumulation and social relations of production. The trait that unites them is the search for a socially fairer and a growth strategy economically less dependent on foreign capital. Or as Cristina Kirchner defined it, 'an economic model of social inclusion, economic growth and technological and productive development'.[2]

This true Latin American insurrection in the economic, political, and social narrative, which questions the status quo of the empire of great capital, is part, in turn, of the rather particular global reality of the beginning of the 21st century. The context manifests itself in its appearance as an age of intolerance, of 'skepticism with democracy',[3] given the rapid spread of conservative ideology in customs, morality and politics, while propagating liberal dogmas for the management of the economy. However, in observing it more closely, we note that, especially in Latin America, it is a concrete project of power that is not based on the national production of wealth, but rather on the productive dynamics of large multinational stateless corporations, and their local rentier allies. The 'intolerant' are a politically organized force against democratic values, which are embedded in the authoritarian neoliberal tradition, sometimes assuming openly fascist facets, such as the European neo-Nazis, the American white supremacists or the supporters of a new military intervention in Brazil. They are paradoxically against the growth of the state, while advocating increasing control over individual freedoms (expression, worship, teaching, and thought) and repression of minority rights (racial, sexual, political, and religious).

The prevailing sense of intolerance stems from the growing dissatisfaction of middle-class sectors with the advances of left-wing values around the planet. It's a new, multipolar world, in which the most dynamic economy is a communist one, where an Afro-American can govern the US, a trade unionist Brazil, and a woman Germany – and where even the pope is progressive. In this world reformist and collectivist ideals spread, with evident reflexes in the intensification of the class struggle, and in the growing prominence of the popular insurgency (such as the *occupy* and *indignados* movements, the Arab spring, 'Chavismo', new Peronism, 'Lulismo'). Only in a world governed by a pressure for the radicalization of democracy does the emergence of such a powerful reactionary force make sense.

This reaction is not exactly a novelty, it occurred at other significant moments in history, always as a movement that opposes social evolution – Maoism brought about Kai Shek in China, Latin American nationalism led to the military dictatorships, the European welfare state devised Thatcher's anti-unionism, Weimar ended up in Hitler, Danton stopped at Robespierre, Lula at Temer. . . . Fortunately, history also shows us that the general tendency of its movement is towards progress, although following a tortuous and contradictory path.

★ ★ ★

The great challenge of this book was to interpret a constantly changing reality in which on every new day, unexpected and sometimes unimaginable events came to the fore and changed the course of the country. In short, writing history the very moment it changes is beyond challenging, it is risky. All care is little to avoid that an interpretation does not expire after a few months.

For this reason, we chose to deal with a past that, despite the setbacks of the post-impeachment years of 2016, is still present in the material life and in the dream of Brazilians. A time in which it was sought, although in a deeply contradictory way, to rescue a popular national project for Brazil. A time some sought to sediment under the ashes of tyrannical authoritarianism and shameless neo liberalism, keeping the economy in recession under the applause of the stock market. . . . Only an illegitimate government could impose such regression. Never has this agenda been able to convince the Brazilian electorate. Dilma Rousseff's refusal to accept it was one of the reasons for her downfall, as Temer himself would confess in an interview months after the coup.

The collapse of the Brazilian economy would certainly have been much greater if the country had not accumulated historically high international reserves. Or if there were no social protection mechanisms such as 'bolsa família' (family allowances) and a high minimum wage for the country's historical average; if it were not for the force rescued from the state-owned companies like Petrobras and Eletrobrás, and from the large national companies that have internationalized.

By the time we finished drafting this work in October 2017, even with the PT deprived of power, we cannot say, however, that the 'Lula's era' was definitely over. The specter of Latin America's greatest popular leadership in the early 21st century is still around the Brazilian political scene. His legacy survives not only on the concrete possibility of a return of the party to power – with every condemnation he suffers, his popularity increases even more – but on the concrete evidence of the transformation his project has brought. This is what provokes the conspiratorial movement behind the scenes of Brasília, both in the offices of the public prosecutor, in the corridors of the National Congress or in the military barracks.

Here is a very well-established point throughout the pages of this book, the institutional shift to which we draw attention seems clear. And it has been particularly important in the five constituent elements of a growth regime: the state, money, the wage relation, capitalist competition, and external insertion. The growing role of the State was felt in the increase of the expenses destined to the expansion of the infrastructure, the incentives to the private initiative and the financing of education and social security. Monetary policy management underwent a subtle but striking alteration as the real interest rate was reduced, allowing a decrease of the domestic debt burden and a consequent stimulus to the economy. The wage relationship changes substantially as a result of full employment policy, leading to a rise in the worker's income over several years in a row. There is also a change in the competitive structure of the market, with the decisive participation of state-owned enterprises, as well as large national groups in accumulation. Finally, as a result of a diplomacy that places the country as a global player, the economy experiences a new form of external insertion, with the internationalization of national capitals, reduction of external debt and record accumulation of international reserves. In general, the combination of these institutional elements ushered in a new growth regime. Its main brand was a beneficial economic dynamism, both for capital that expands and diversifies as it has long been seen, as well as for labor, in view of its distributive effects.

Nonetheless, internal and external obstacles were put at the forefront of this development and led to a depletion of the model in 2015 and the subsequent crisis. Internally, maintaining a situation of full use of the means of production over a long period increased the cost of production and brought pressure on the rate of profit. The conflict for the control of the budget was aggravated, while the government, politically cornered, multiplied the benefits to the bourgeoisie. Adding to this is the reversal of the external scenario and the terms of trade, positive during much of this 'Lula's era'.

But, fundamentally, there is a wear and tear of coexistence that seemed at first impossible, an alliance of classes with conflicting interests: on the one hand, a distributive pressure on the part of social movements; on the other hand, a speculative, rentier pressure, favorable to the establishment of a regime of accumulation by spoliation.

One could question whether the government could not have deepened the model to actually put the country on a structural change route. We have seen, throughout the chapters, what path this would be: the establishment of a progressive tax structure; the fight against technological dependence and, therefore, the revision of the role of foreign capital in the country; the imposition of limits on financialization; an educational reform to bridge the gap between rich and poor; a political reform to control the manipulation of the big economic groups on the parties and the media; a reorientation of the productive system, to make it less dependent on the extraction of natural resources that threaten the rainforest and the climate.

However, to insist on this hypothesis without contextualizing the political crisis would be to incur a fatal error. In the last years of the 'Lula's era', the correlation of forces fell in favor of the more conservative factions of the ruling class. A phenomenon, by the way, global, as we have seen above. In Brazil, it took the form of an overwhelming political conspiracy. Sustained in a legal, cybernetic, and media war, the anti-socialist and moralist narrative gained ground rapidly in the country, especially in the richer regions of the South and Southeast. There was the birth of the extreme right-wing virtual movements that put thousands on the streets, against the corruption of the parties, for the impeachment and the return of the military. The traditional parties that opportunistically attempted to co-opt these movements did not succeed. On the contrary, in feeding them, the hate speech left the social media commentary bar to assume a central role in Brazilian politics. It is as if the lesson of the dark ages of the 20th century has not been properly understood: one pays with its own freedom by tolerating those who cry out for intolerance.

The clues pointed out here further illuminate the account that allows us to understand how development in Brazil always seems to be pregnant with its own collapse. At the end of yet another frustrated cycle of economic and social modernization, the sensible question to ask is: how do we avoid this trap?

Notes

1 Furtado, the most celebrated economist in Brazil, was secretary of state for planning under the Joao Goulart administration (1961–64), and advisor to the Workers' Party.
2 At the openning of the *Congreso de Economía Política para Argentina*, Teatro Roma, Buenos Aires, 05/10/2017.
3 A Judith Butler's original concept, from the title of a seminar organized by her in Brazil in 2017.

Index

accumulation regime 34–38, 51, 53–55, 71, 83, 241, 243
Agamben, G. 181–182
agribusiness 39, 58, 152, 181, 200, 202–203, 234–235
agroindustry *see* agribusiness
Argentina 8, 14, 21, 22, 33, 49–53, 55, 57, 59–63, 65, 67–69, 71, 73, 75–79, 90, 169, 170

banks: active role 124; asymmetric power 124; Central Bank 123–124, 128, 191, 234; and financial inclusion 116; National Bank for Economic and Social Development (BNDES) 139–140, 147, 155, 157, 210; private 115–117, 122, 134, 147, 152, 194; public 116, 120, 122, 124–125, 147, 151–152, 155, 225; retail 115–117, 122, 124, 126–127; United States 166
Bolsa Família (family allowances) 4, 12, 120, 218–219, 221–234, 242; conditionalities 224, 227; controversies 226–227; economic impacts 228–230
Boyer, R. 83, 110

capital 164–165, 168, 174, 198–200, 235, 241, 243; accumulation 56, 83, 86, 102, 131, 153, 162, 164, 172, 175, 188, 198, 219; alliance with 194; average return on 20; circuits of 162–168, 171, 175; cultural 214; domination/rule of 4, 134, 167; fictitious 102, 199; financial 136, 142, 166, 171; flight 60, 63–64, 164, 167, 172, 193; foreign 36, 44, 58, 68, 133, 152–154, 156, 166, 204, 207, 240–241, 243; globalized 134; goods 62, 120, 144; gross fixed capital formation 132, 135–136, 141–143, 145, 156; human 51; as an instrument of justice 13; intensity 17; intensive sectors 145; internationalization of 39, 154, 164, 242–243; market 41, 134, 153; national 36, 166, 170–171; -nature relation 196, 202, 206–208; outflows 67; productive 75, 77, 90, 98; productivity 69; profitability of 31; relation with labor 84, 90, 153, 220
Cardoso, F. 134–136, 155, 167–168, 171–173, 180, 201, 218, 222–223, 225–226
Central Bank *see* banks
Chile 17, 20–22, 170, 219
China 14, 17, 21, 22–23, 27, 31, 51–53, 67, 77, 90, 145, 166, 170, 181, 230, 242
Collor, F. 136, 167–169, 171, 180, 186, 190, 192–193
commodities 8, 23, 164–166, 171–172, 175, 183, 197, 208; boom 106, 201; declining prices 31, 42, 140, 154, 203; high prices 38; and money 54; volatility in prices 52
competitiveness 53, 60, 63, 67, 75, 110, 132, 150, 153, 165, 175
consumption 69, 109, 114, 119, 120, 152, 157, 207, 221, 229; *see also* demand
corruption 4, 10, 132, 146–147, 151–152, 157, 192–193, 218, 244
coup d'état 4, 8, 142, 148, 167, 175, 179, 180, 182, 186–187, 189, 206, 240–242
credit 36, 42, 69, 72, 75, 79, 114–118, 122, 126, 133, 138, 143, 147, 203, 210, 241; crunch 128; habits 124; micro- 229; policies 120, 127, 148, 151, 156
crisis 69, 229; of 1929 7, 219; 1970s 166, 196; 1980s 98, 191, 240; of 1998 60; of 2002 60; of 2008–2009 8, 9, 24, 28, 33, 37, 51, 69, 79, 115, 118–121, 123, 138, 143, 147, 149, 158, 165, 193, 221; account system 50, 61; Argentinean 63;

Asian 62, 167; balance of payments 67, 133; Brazilian crisis of 2015–2018 14, 21, 22, 30, 109, 132–133, 151, 175, 182, 189, 201, 218, 234, 242–244; credit 124; of domination 191; energetic 141; exchange anchor 57, 59, 68; governability 68; hydrological 146; hyperinflationary 57, 59; monetary 78; of the populist regime 189; public debt 57, 78, 154; realization 164; regime 78; Russian 167

currency 39, 42, 55, 66, 72, 164; appreciation 19–21, 23–24, 30, 68, 78–79, 150, 154; board 58–59, 78; crises 61, 79; depreciation 21, 23–24, 26–28, 56, 67; devaluation 23–24, 33, 39, 42, 44, 61, 63, 133, 154; injections 36; and monetary regime 36; overvaluation 49; political functionality 64; *see also* money

debt 120, 126, 243; default 64; domestic 71; external 57, 59–62, 77–78, 243; public 38, 50, 52–53, 57–58, 60–61, 63–64, 66, 69–72, 75–77, 79, 90, 134–135, 140, 157, 229, 234; securities 67

de-industrialization 17; early 21–24, 26–27, 30–31, 49, 51, 52, 58, 67, 98, 113, 220

demand 203; aggregate 83, 149, 158; domestic 75–76; effective 153; for labor 85; policy 77, 108; private sector 146–147; stimuli 90; structures 90

dependency 153, 166, 170, 172, 175, 243; theory 13

derivatives 72

development model 3, 8, 33, 49, 50, 51, 53–57, 59, 60, 64, 75–76, 114, 126, 152, 194, 214, 240–241; *see also* accumulation regime

Dutch disease 51–52, 67, 71

economic growth 4, 8, 14–16, 50, 51, 62–64, 72, 83, 90, 93, 98, 110, 127–128, 134, 147, 150, 153, 157, 165, 241; acceleration of 49, 60, 69; and Brazilian miracle 59, 60, 166, 191; driven by exports 15; driven by wages 58; fragility of 67; inability to promote 33; recovery in 28; sustainability of 82

education 12, 24, 52, 180, 221, 224, 227–228, 240, 243; basic 228; financial 114, 123–124, 128; higher 4, 209–217, 222, 241; public 9, 110, 131, 140, 150–151, 193, 220–222

employment, and globalization 19–20

England *see* United Kingdom
environment 12, 30, 138, 148, 196–207, 217, 244
exchange rate 52–53, 66; anchor 57, 59–61; competitive 59, 62, 64, 67; policy 69; regime 54–56, 62, 71, 167, 174; selective 133; speculative attack 68

financialization 24, 82, 87, 90–91, 98, 102, 106, 108–110, 113–114, 156, 166, 210, 220, 243
Fordism 53, 133, 154, 164, 191; post- 35, 154
foreign exchange reserves 6, 57, 69, 162, 167, 172, 174, 242–243
Furtado, C. 217, 240, 244

Gramsci, A. 179
growth *see* economic growth

Honduras 5, 43
Hong Kong 15, 31
hyperinflation *see* inflation

impeachment 3, 8, 10, 11, 43, 140, 142, 145–146, 152–153, 167, 180, 194, 218, 235, 242, 244; *see also* coup d'état
imperialism 171, 198–199; self- 191
import substitution 15, 49, 56, 64, 67, 165–167, 174–175
India 27, 145, 230
industrialization 7, 14, 57, 59, 187–188, 191, 202, 209, 210, 219; export-driven 166; truncated 15
inequalities: and affirmative action 4; causes 234; and corruption 132; economic 216; income 77, 82, 108, 113, 151, 172, 209, 230–232, 240; indicators 38; racial 194; social 88, 217, 222–223, 233; and tax reform 24, 30
inflation 14, 27, 42, 54, 57–59, 61, 64, 66–67, 69, 86, 102, 125, 140, 148, 155, 164; and indexation 78; losses to 85; stabilization plan 134; target 36, 44, 68, 75, 109, 135, 141, 151–152, 155
interest rate 61, 64, 67–69, 71, 74–75, 78–79, 90, 106, 117, 124–125, 133, 143, 146, 150, 152, 154, 157, 167, 174, 243
international reserves *see* foreign exchange reserves
international value chains 16, 31, 150, 171
investment 37, 50, 51, 53, 66, 72, 102, 106, 109, 146, 150, 152–153, 203, 229;

abroad 17; in Brazilian reals 68; costs 17; foreign direct 31, 60, 171–172, 175; foreign portfolio 172–173; in human capital 51; in infrastructure projects 132, 138, 143–144, 146, 151, 153; in manufacturing 21; private 42, 131, 136, 147–149, 153; public 36, 131–135, 138–140, 142, 147, 151, 153, 155

June 2013 demonstrations 9, 193
Justicialist Party 57–58, 78

Kirchner, C. 241
Kirchner, N. 78, 241

labor costs 52–53, 64, 77, 102, 109, 150
land 43, 183, 189, 198–200, 207, 233–234; law 183; prices 201–203; reform 205, 212, 219, 233; rent 201–203; structure of propriety 183, 188, 202, 206, 233
Lula, L. 3, 4, 6, 8, 9, 13, 33, 60, 93, 109, 132–133, 136, 139–142, 145, 147, 149–153, 156–158, 162–163, 167–169, 171–173, 175, 179, 180–181, 192–194, 200, 205–207, 215, 218, 221–223, 225–226, 229, 232–235, 240–242, 244

Marx, K. 163, 196–198
Marxism 51
Ménem, C. 57, 78
Mexico 16, 17, 20, 21, 22, 23, 24, 31, 77, 169, 219
military 243–244; regime 59, 79, 166–167, 180, 187–191, 204, 209, 220, 241–242; use of surplus 165
money 49–51, 54–57, 163, 166, 172, 243; centrality of 53; credit 72; economic functionality 67; functional forms 56, 76; new denomination of 60; public function of 63; symbolic functionality 50, 57, 63

neoliberalism 4, 8, 33, 51–53, 56, 60, 63, 106, 114, 133–134, 136, 142, 152, 154, 162, 164–165, 167–172, 174–175, 180, 207, 209, 218, 233, 235, 241–242; crisis 38, 42, 240; *see also* Washington Consensus

oligarchies 8, 12, 58, 167, 182–183, 185–190, 194
Operation Car Wash 5, 9, 10, 147

Paraguay 5, 43
Perón, J. D. 57, 78

Peronism 58, 242
Petrobras 4, 5, 132, 135, 139–142, 144–147, 152, 155–157, 187, 242
Portugal 181, 183–184, 188, 190, 219
post-Keynesianism 51, 61, 124, 133
poverty 82, 220–227, 231; fight against 68, 152, 180, 218–219, 222–223; reduction 75, 88, 120, 149, 230–234; and tax structure 234
primarization 14, 170, 202
privatization 4, 33, 36, 58, 60, 62, 108, 134–135, 139, 153–155, 171, 174, 215
productivity 31, 86, 90, 95, 109, 131, 153, 157, 164; of agricultural factors 202; capital 69; chains 15; gap 15; growth 23, 53, 60, 66, 84–86, 110; labor 20, 22, 28, 69, 102, 163; multinational firms 19; service sector 17
profits 61–62, 64, 66–67, 69, 72, 90, 102, 106–107, 109, 110, 125, 152, 163–164, 167, 172, 174, 189, 201, 203, 234, 243; financial 110; repatriation of 60; share 93

regulation: French school of 3, 13, 34, 37, 39, 43, 54, 82–83, 110, 164; mode of 62, 68, 71
Rousseff, D. 3, 5, 7, 9, 10, 11, 13, 43–44, 102, 109, 132, 136, 140, 142, 144–147, 149, 150–153, 167, 180–181, 186, 194, 205–206, 218, 221, 233–235, 240–242
Russia 27, 145, 167, 170, 197–198, 230

slavery 180–185, 188, 191, 219
South Korea 15, 21, 22, 31, 90
state 60, 78, 86, 90, 106, 113, 123, 133–134, 141, 144, 151–153, 165, 175, 180–188, 190–191, 202, 205, 209–211, 213, 215, 219, 220, 222, 235, 240–241, 243; fiscal crisis 61; -owned enterprises 131–136, 142, 151–156, 164, 171, 174, 242–243; role in the economy 134–135, 163
strikes 125, 189, 192

technology 52, 108, 164, 198, 202, 214, 217; national 144, 150, 152–153, 156, 172, 175, 241; revolution 16–19
Temer, M. 7, 145, 180, 207, 234, 242
Théret, B. 50, 54
trade: balance 25–28, 50–52, 59–60, 62, 68, 71, 79, 158, 167–168; and competition 22; and diplomacy 169; free 20, 49, 168; international 14, 20, 30

trade union 58, 66, 84, 108, 134, 189, 191, 193, 242; -ist 63
Trump, D. 14, 31

unemployment 6, 64, 69, 88, 98, 106, 109, 113, 119, 128, 143, 148, 157, 240
United Kingdom 90, 170, 183, 185, 209, 219, 230
United States 21, 24, 31, 77, 90, 134–135, 145, 157, 165–170, 183, 193, 209, 219, 220–221, 230, 241

Vargas, G. 186–188, 220

wages 53–54, 57, 61, 75–77, 110, 172, 174; declining 59, 64, 86, 234; determination 86; elasticity to economic growth 97; low 52, 79; policy 68–69, 71, 120, 151–152, 158, 242–243; and productivity 84, 113; rising 64, 66–67, 69, 106; share 90, 93, 95, 102–103, 108, 148–149, 241; *see also* labor costs
Washington Consensus 49, 57, 134, 165, 167, 220
Workers' Party (Partido dos Trabalhadores/PT) 6, 7, 8, 9, 10, 42, 43, 60, 138, 185, 190–191, 194, 200, 204–205, 207, 221–223, 226, 232–235, 242